Handel und Internationales Marketing
Retailing and International Marketing

Die Schriftenreihe fördert die Themengebiete Handel und Internationales Marketing. Diese charakterisieren – jedes für sich, aber auch in inhaltlicher Kombination – die Forschungsschwerpunkte der Herausgeber. Beide Themengebiete werden grundsätzlich breit aufgefasst; die Reihe bietet sowohl Dissertationen und Habilitationen als auch Tagungs- und Sammelbänden mit unterschiedlicher inhaltlicher und methodischer Ausrichtung ein Forum. Die inhaltliche Breite ist sowohl im Sinne eines konsumentenorientierten Marketings wie auch einer marktorientierten Unternehmensführung zu verstehen. Neben den Arbeiten, die von den Herausgebern für die Schriftenreihe vorgeschlagen werden, steht die Reihe auch externen wissenschaftlichen Arbeiten offen. Diese können bei den Herausgebern eingereicht und nach einer positiven Begutachtung publiziert werden.

The book series focuses on the fields of Retailing and International Marketing. These two areas represent the research fields of the editors—each of them as a single research area, but also in combination. Both of these research areas are widely understood. Consequently, the series provides a platform for the publication of doctoral theses and habilitations, conference proceedings and edited books, as well as related methodological issues that encompass the focus of the series. The series is broad in the sense that it covers academic works in the area of consumer-oriented marketing as well as the area of marketoriented management. In addition to academic works recommended by the editors, the book series also welcomes other academic contributions. These may be submitted to the editors and will be published in the book series after a positive assessment.

Marius Müller

Strategic Management of International E-Commerce Firms

A Multilevel Analysis of Geographic Scope, Foreign Direct Investments, and International Performance

Springer Gabler

Marius Müller
Fachbereich IV, Universität Trier
Universität Trier
Trier, Germany

Vom Fachbereich IV der Universität Trier zur Verleihung des akademischen Grades Doktor der Wirtschafts- und Sozialwissenschaften (Dr. rer. pol.) genehmigte Dissertation von Marius Müller
Trier, 2025
Betreuer: Univ.-Prof. Dr. Prof. h.c. Bernhard Swoboda
1. Berichterstatter: Univ.-Prof. Dr. Prof. h.c. Bernhard Swoboda
2. Berichterstatter: Univ.-Prof. Dr. Rolf Weiber
Datum der Disputation: 03.06.2025

ISSN 2626-3327 ISSN 2626-3335 (electronic)
Handel und Internationales Marketing Retailing and International Marketing
ISBN 978-3-658-49679-1 ISBN 978-3-658-49680-7 (eBook)
https://doi.org/10.1007/978-3-658-49680-7

This Springer Gabler imprint is published by the registered company Springer Fachmedien Wiesbaden GmbH, part of Springer Nature.
The registered company address is: Abraham-Lincoln-Str. 46, 65189 Wiesbaden, Germany

Foreword

Since the 2010s, digital firms have internationalized their businesses dynamically. Many of the world's prominent e-commerce firms (ECFs) derive a significant proportion of their sales from foreign operations, while their business and success still require local adaptation. However, in the literature less than a dozen quantitative studies on ECFs or i-businesses exist, only one addressing performance effects of ECFs' international decisions. Thus, the dissertation of Dr. Marius Müller significantly contributes to an important research area with distinct studies:

- "ECFs' *Geographic Scope. Roles of Intangible Resources and Country-Specific Moderators":* ECFs are known to internationalize with a greater scope than offline firms but it is important to analyze how their geographic scope depends on intangible resources acquired over time and whether their exploitation is affected by country-specific boundaries. Dr. Müller proposes a theory-based framework to analyze the effects of ECFs' intangible resources on geographic scope. Importantly, he applies multilevel modeling with cross-level interactions to provide insights into the role of country-specific moderators, i.e., rule of law, degree of country development, and logistics performance, based on data of 2,632 market entries over 24 years. Some ECFs have a wider geographic scope than others due to their use of specific intangible resources. However, these relationships change depending on the moderators, which explain country-specific variances differently.

- *"Determinants of Wholly Owned Foreign Direct Investments in ECFs: A Hierarchical Country- and Firm-Level Analysis":* Despite their global virtual presence, leading and dynamically expanding ECFs establish a physical presence in select countries to implement full local operations and management. This study proposes a framework for the specific, business model-related firm- and host-country antecedents of ECFs' wholly owned foreign direct investments based on data of 1,726 operation modes chosen from 2010–2020 and multilevel modeling. The results reveal that ECFs choose direct investments primarily based on their host country online experience, but business model-related country-level antecedents also explain the decision differently. The findings contribute to the emerging research on digital firms' internationalization and have implications for managers, for manufacturers using ECFs for their own expansion, and for politicians.

- The study *"Effects of International ECFs' Depth versus Breadth of Control on Foreign Sales Performance and the Role of Market Size and Growth as Context Factors"* addresses ECFs that may opt for high international control in terms of depth (i.e., by choosing fully controlled operation modes to enable local offers and management) or breadth (i.e., through a subsidiary network to scale their business model and supply chain). Dr. Müller explores respective effects on foreign sales performance and the role of local e-commerce market size and growth as context factors by referring to data on 1,144 control decisions over time. The results show that ECFs improve foreign sales performance best in terms of both the depth and breadth of international control but face trade-offs because both decisions affect performance differently and because market growth positively and negatively moderates the effects. This allows direct implications for firms expanding digitally abroad but possibly struggling with sales performance.

With his work, Dr. Marius Müller makes a significant contribution to international research. All studies are published in good journals and the first and second study won "Best Paper Awards" at the annual conferences of the American Marketing Association and the European International Business Academy. I am very happy with this twenty-third dissertation at my chair for Marketing & Retailing at Trier University. In addition to his very good research and teaching, Dr. Müller was involved in book projects, has organized all financial issues as well as examinations and has supported our high potential program with various excursions. I thank Dr. Müller for a long time of working together, since his initial bachelor's and further master's studies and later on (almost ten years). He is a great expert in e-commerce, retailing, and consumer goods distribution. Furthermore, he is a very honourable, hard-working, and kind-minded person. I wish Dr. Müller very warmly all the best for his career as well as his private life in the future.

Professor Dr. Prof. h.c. Bernhard Swoboda

Trier, May 2025

Acknowledgements

This dissertation was written during my time as a research assistant at the Chair of Marketing and Retailing at Trier University. As I approach the final stages of this challenging yet rewarding journey, I would like to take this opportunity to express my heartfelt gratitude to everyone who has supported me along the way.

First and foremost, I would like to express my profound gratitude to my supervisor, Prof. Dr. Prof. h.c. Bernhard Swoboda. I am indebted to him not only for the opportunity to pursue my doctorate, but also for his steadfast guidance and invaluable advice, which has been a constant support since my undergraduate studies. His trust in my abilities and his constructive feedback on all my academic papers, including this dissertation, have been a tremendous asset. I particularly appreciate his analytical and structured approach to solving all kinds of issues, which has always served as a model for me. Furthermore, I am grateful for the many opportunities he has given me to present my research at national and international conferences, including remarkable cities such as Miami, Seoul, and Lisbon. These experiences not only allowed me to engage in enriching exchanges with leading experts but also enabled me to witness the global resonance and significance of my work firsthand.

I would also like to express my sincere gratitude to my second examiner, Prof. Dr. Rolf Weiber (Trier University), for his thoughtful evaluation of my work, and to Prof. Dr. Lutz Richter (Trier University), who kindly agreed to chair my defense.

Furthermore, I would like to express my gratitude to my colleagues, Dr. Nils Fränzel, Nele Jacobs, Angelina Klink, Adrian Schütz and Dr. Lukas Zimmer. Together, we have navigated many ups and downs over the years, while they have encouraged me in times of uncertainty and enriched my everyday routine with countless memorable and fun moments. I especially cherished and will miss our morning ritual of sharing a coffee, as well as the occasional ice cream breaks on hot summer days. These simple pleasures became a daily source of motivation and camaraderie, lifting our spirits and strengthening our resolve, even in the face of the most challenging times.

I would also like to thank our dedicated secretaries, Ursula Fassbender and Gerti Weiß-Meerkamp. Their constant ear and dedicated administrative support have made my time here both easier and more enjoyable. I am also very grateful to our research assistants, who supported me throughout this period, especially during data collection.

Above all, I would like to express my deepest gratitude to my family and friends. Your unwavering support, encouragement, and understanding have motivated me to keep going even during difficult times. I am especially indebted to my parents, whose unwavering devotion and unconditional love have been an inexhaustible source of strength and confidence throughout my life and this doctoral journey – a support truly beyond measure. I am also grateful for the gentle comfort of my two feline companions, whose quiet presence brought solace and calm in moments when I needed it most.

Last but not least, I thank my partner for her tireless support, patience, and understanding, even during challenging times despite her own commitments, and for her belief in me, even when I struggled to do so myself. Without her, this journey would have been much more difficult, and for that I am truly grateful.

Marius Müller

Trier, May 2025

Summary

International e-commerce firms (ECFs) selling physical products to consumers via their own online shops or marketplaces have transformed global commerce. As digital firms, they take advantage of lower market entry barriers, allowing them to expand rapidly online without a need for physical presence. However, success abroad requires balancing both virtual and physical operations amidst dynamic, country-specific contexts that affect ECFs' business model and internationalization. Whether and how they leverage unique online resources and capabilities for their international decisions and how these contribute to their foreign performance remains largely unknown. Moreover, the role of important host country factors such as regulatory and specific infrastructural or market contexts in these decisions is unclear. Therefore, this doctoral thesis adopts a multi-theoretical approach to analyze the antecedents of ECFs' geographic scope, wholly owned foreign direct investments (FDI), and the effects of international control on their foreign performance. Importantly, diverse host country contexts that shape these decisions are considered by incorporating hierarchical multilevel modeling.

Study 1 explores how ECFs' intangible resources affect their geographic scope and how host countries' rule of law (ROL), degree of development, and logistics performance moderate the effects. Using expansion data of 263 ECFs in Europe from 1994–2018, the study shows positive effects of international online experience, website traffic, and social media use on geographic scope. The effects of international online experience and social media are amplified by all moderators.

Study 2 examines how ECFs' previously unknown online experiences and specific host country factors affect their wholly owned FDI over time. Using hierarchical data of the 241 leading ECFs from 2010–2020, it reveals that international and, more strongly, host country online experience drives their propensity to choose FDI in a country. Importantly, host countries' logistics performance, internet user population, and ROL also positively and jointly affect ECFs' FDI.

Study 3 analyzes how ECFs' depth and breadth of international control affect their foreign sales performance over time and how local e-commerce market size and growth moderate these effects. Based on hierarchical data of 184 leading ECFs in Europe from 2015–2020, it shows positive effects of both depth and breadth of control on foreign performance, the former having a stronger impact. Market growth, but not size, moderates these effects both positively and negatively.

In summary, this doctoral thesis reveals key antecedents of ECFs' virtual and physical presence decisions as well as effects of international control on foreign performance. Importantly, the critical role of host country factors in these decisions is stressed. The thesis thus provides valuable theoretical and practical implications, suggesting promising avenues for future research in this growing field.

Content

Figures

Tables

Abbreviations

AIC .... Akaike Information Criterion

b .... Unstandardized Coefficient

B2B .... Business-to-Business

B2C .... Business-to-Consumer

BIC .... Bayesian Information Criterion

bn .... Billion

C2C .... Consumer-to-Consumer

CAGR .... Compound Annual Growth Rate

CBEC .... Cross-Border Electronic Commerce

CD .... Country Development

CEO .... Chief Executive Officer

CLC .... Country-Level Control

CLV .... Country-Level Variable

CRM .... Customer Relationship Management

ECF .... Electronic Commerce Firm

e.g. .... Exempli Gratia/For Example

et al. .... Et Alia/And Others

etc. .... Et Cetera/And So On

EU .... European Union

Exp(B) .... Exponential Function/Odds Ratio

FDI .... Foreign Direct Investment

GCR .... Global Competitiveness Report

GDP .... Gross Domestic Product

GNI .... Gross National Income

H .... Hypothesis

IB .... International Business

i.e. .... Id Est/That Is

IL .... Individual-Level Variable

ILC ....Individual-Level Control

INT ....Internet Use

INV ....International New Venture

IT...................Information Technology

ITA ....International Trade Administration

IV ....Instrumental Variable

JV...................Joint Venture

log ....Logarithm

LP ....Logistics Performance

Max ....Maximum

MNE..............Multinational Enterprise

N ....Sample Size

ns ....Not Significant

p....................*p*-Value

p. ....Page

PLS ....Partial Least Squares

pp. ....Pages

R&D ....Research and Development

RBV ....Resource-based View

ROL ....Rule of Law

SD ....Standard Deviation

SEM ....Structural Equation Modeling

SMEs ....Small and Medium-Sized Enterprises

TMT ....Top Management Team

tn ....Trillion

UK ....United Kingdom

UNCTAD ....United Nations Conference on Trade and Development

USA ....United States of America

USD ....US Dollar

VHB ....Verband der Hochschullehrer*innen für Betriebswirtschaft e.V.

VIF ....Variance Inflation Factor

vs. ....Versus

WGI...............World Governance Indicators

WOS ....Wholly Owned Subsidiary

%...................Percent

A. Introduction

1. Focus and Relevance

Driven by globalization and digitalization, electronic commerce has fundamentally transformed the global business landscape (Yang et al. 2025). Global e-commerce is projected to generate USD 5.5 tn in revenue by 2027 at a steady 14.4% compound annual growth rate (CAGR; ITA 2024). This continued growth has driven the rise of *international e-commerce firms (ECFs)*, which sell physical products through their own online shops or marketplaces to consumers (Li et al. 2025; Swoboda and Sinning 2022). Unlike traditional manufacturing or service firms, ECFs benefit from reduced market entry barriers, enabling rapid virtual expansion without the need for a physical presence (Coviello, Kano and Liesch 2017; Schu and Morschett 2017). The internationalization process largely occurs "in space" rather than "in place" (Monaghan, Tippmann and Coviello 2020), although ECFs still rely on cross-border delivery unlike purely digital i-business firms. Thereby, ECFs face dynamic, country-specific contexts that affect their specific business model and internationalization (e.g., Eduardsen et al. 2023).

Over the past decade, leading ECFs such as Amazon, JD.com, or the Alibaba Group have capitalized on online internationalization with different strategies. While some export-focused ECFs serve foreign markets via generic dot-com domains (e.g., AliExpress.com), others, like Amazon, set up country-specific websites, indicating clear market entries. Since 1998, Amazon (2025) entered 21 markets with local domains, language, and currency, adapting to different country contexts. This makes Amazon the leading ECF worldwide in terms of e-commerce net sales (i.e., goods sold by ECFs directly). Meanwhile, pure online marketplaces such as Alibaba dominate gross merchandise value (i.e., the total volume of goods sold via a platform). However, manufacturers like Apple and commerce firms like Walmart also rank among the leading ECFs, striving to keep pace with the growing online competition (ECDB 2024a, see Table A—1).

Rank 2024	Company	Home Country	Founded	E-Commerce Net Sales (Billion USD)[1]	Revenue (Billion USD)[2]	Gross Merchandise Value (Billion USD)[3]
1	Amazon	United States	1994	231.87	574.79	729.30
2	JD.com	China	1998	122.99	153.11	501.30
3	Walmart	United States	1962	100.10	648.13	187.25
4	Apple	United States	1976	47.20	383.29	-
5	Alibaba Group	China	1999	28.21	132.86	1,097.16
6	The Home Depot	United States	1978	23.80	152.67	-
7	Coupang	South Korea	2010	21.22	24.38	49.67
8	Target	United States	1902	19.36	107.41	21.33
9	Vipshop	China	2008	15.45	27.16	27.16
10	Costco	United States	1983	13.97	242.29	-

Note: [1] Total income of goods directly sold by an ECF; [2] Everything that generates revenue for an ECF; [3] Total volume of goods sold by an ECF and marketplace sellers.

Table A—1: Leading E-Commerce Firms Worldwide by E-Commerce Net Sales

Source: Annual Reports; ECDB 2024a.

M. Müller, *Strategic Management of International E-Commerce Firms*,
Handel und Internationales Marketing Retailing and International Marketing,
https://doi.org/10.1007/978-3-658-49680-7_1

Digitalization of services and real-time integration of consumer data has enabled ECFs to develop unique online resources and capabilities supporting their internationalization (e.g., Cahen et al. 2025; Weiber and Mohr 2020, pp. 1101-1104). New consumer-related digital resources such as ECFs' social media may become more important than traditional experience-related ones (e.g., Knösel, Cheng and Shiu 2025). However, managing additional country-specific online shops can pose significant challenges. The latter requires technological server infrastructure and secure payment systems, as well as compliance with local regulations (e.g., Meyer et al. 2023). Accordingly, ECFs must carefully assess the expansion of their virtual presence abroad in terms of *geographic scope* (e.g., Kotha, Rindova and Rothaermel 2001). This involves identifying intangible resources that can be leveraged to expand their virtual presence and understanding how country-specific contexts affect the transfer of these resources to foreign markets (e.g., Liu, Zhang-Zhang and Ghauri 2020; Tolstoy et al. 2021). Addressing this issue, this doctoral thesis examines the antecedents of ECFs' geographic scope, defined as the number of foreign markets served with country-specific online shops (e.g., Schu, Morschett and Swoboda 2016).

Research on the antecedents of geographic scope and related constructs like international diversification has predominantly focused on manufacturing and service firms (e.g., Kirca et al. 2012a; see Section A.2.2.). Among many firm-level antecedents, scholars have especially highlighted the role of firms' intangible resources and capabilities. Thereby, international knowledge and experience stand out as major resources facilitating firms' further geographic expansion (e.g., Beleska-Spasova, Glaister and Stride 2012; Delgado-Gómez, Ramírez-Alesón and Espitia-Escuer 2004; Kirca et al. 2011). In contrast, for commerce firms, only one study has considered antecedents of their specific geographic scope decisions (Batsakis and Mohr 2017). Moreover, very few scholars have examined the role of external moderating factors such as host country risks or the degree of development (e.g., Jiménez 2010; Mansion and Bausch 2020). However, for digital firms, only Kotha, Rindova and Rothaermel (2001) have linked website traffic and reputation as specific intangible resources to geographic scope online. Consequently, insights into the role of ECFs' specific intangible resources and country-specific contexts that facilitate their transfer abroad are needed (e.g., Tolstoy et al. 2021).

Although ECFs primarily internationalize virtually, a selective physical presence can offer strategic local advantages (e.g., Brouthers et al. 2022). Since the business model relies on selling physical goods, quick and free delivery as well as locally adapted offers and services are crucial for competing in foreign markets (e.g., Hua and Wu 2024). However, ECFs require local warehouses or subsidiaries to manage adaptations effectively. Thus, ECFs must decide on different governance structures abroad, i.e., *entry modes* when initially entering a foreign market, and *operation modes* for their ongoing operations in foreign markets over time (e.g., Yang et al. 2025). Amazon's global presence exemplifies typical operation mode strategies of ECFs. Whereas a dot-com domain enables global exports initially, selected markets are subsequently entered via country-specific domains. The latter allow for a local online presence, while logistics are still outsourced. Over time, Amazon (2025) introduces additional wholly owned subsidiaries (WOS) in these markets (e.g., fulfillment centers) to introduce local offers, services, and management under full control (MWPVL 2025; see Figure A—1). In this dissertation, such mode decisions are referred to as *wholly owned foreign direct investments (FDI)*, defined as long-term investments in physical assets abroad with full ownership and control (e.g., Stallkamp, Chen and Li 2023).

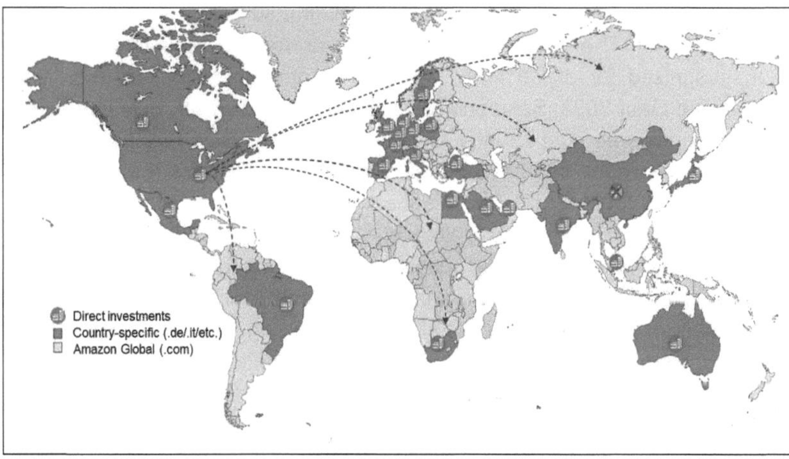

Figure A—1: Global Presence of Amazon
Source: Own Creation based on Amazon 2025; MWPVL 2025.

The traditional internationalization process, as outlined by Johanson and Vahlne (1977), is defined by path-dependent learning in international markets and a gradual increase in resource commitment. However, some key assumptions of this process have changed for modern firms in the digital era (Vahlne and Johanson 2017; Yang et al. 2025). While learning is still path-dependent, ECFs' focus has shifted from merely recognizing international opportunities to actively exploiting them (e.g., Swoboda and Sinning 2022). To be able to exploit local opportunities, ECFs must leverage unique learning capabilities and take advantage of specific country factors that support their business model abroad (e.g., Benmamoun et al. 2019). Surprisingly, the decision-making process that guides ECFs to opt for FDI in certain countries while maintaining a virtual presence in others is not well understood (e.g., Brouthers et al. 2022). Practically, experience from an online presence and infrastructural barriers such as logistics and internet infrastructure or regulations appear critical (e.g., in Zalando's European expansion, Zalando 2024). Consequently, this doctoral thesis investigates the specific firm- and country-level factors that jointly affect the likelihood of ECFs opting for FDI in foreign markets.

Antecedents of manufacturing or service firms' operation mode choice and FDI have been studied extensively in the literature (see Section A.2.3.). Studies on service firms, including commerce, have highlighted important antecedents of FDI such as institutional distance (e.g., Picot-Coupey, Burt and Cliquet 2014), different types of international experience (Evans, Mavondo and Bridson 2008; Pla-Barber, Villar and León-Darder 2014), and firm size (e.g., Ekeledo and Sivakumar 2004a). The critical role of distances or specific capabilities has also been recognized for digital firms' and ECFs' internationalization (e.g., Lee, Pattnaik and Gaur 2023; Schu and Morschett 2017). However, only three studies have considered host country factors in ECFs' decision-making, including the rule of law (ROL), internet use, and market attractiveness (Luo, Zhao and Du 2005; Rothaermel, Kotha and Steensma 2006; Schu and Morschett 2017). Concerning FDI decisions, only Stallkamp, Chen and Li (2023) have studied and confirmed the role of institutional distances for born digital firms' choice of FDI. In conclusion, research on ECFs' specific firm- and country-level antecedents of operation mode choice or FDI is still largely missing, despite a renewed debate in the literature (Brouthers et al. 2022; Hennart 2022).

Regardless of whether ECFs operate virtually or physically abroad, many increasingly depend on foreign sales as domestic markets slowly begin to saturate (e.g., Shein with a 51% foreign sales share, Apple.com with 45%, Amazon with 27%, ECDB 2024c; Tolstoy, Hånell and Özbek 2023). Whereas ECFs such as JD.com and Zalando seem to favor high international control via FDI, others, such as ASOS and Trendyol, primarily maintain a virtual global presence and exports. Despite these different strategies, all have achieved success abroad, leaving it unclear whether a physical presence is essential for foreign performance of ECFs (Swoboda and Sinning 2022). Moreover, ECFs face different local e-commerce market contexts, which vary considerably in terms of size and growth (e.g., Janjevic and Winkenbach 2020). For instance, the currently two fastest-growing e-commerce markets, India and Brazil, are growing at a high CAGR of over 14%, though India's market size of USD 121 bn is three times as large as Brazil's at USD 41 bn. Although domestic ECFs still dominate most of these growth markets, foreign players like Amazon have already taken the lead in some, such as Mexico and Italy (ECDB 2024b; ITA 2024; see Table A—2).

Rank 2024	Country	Continent	Top Online Store	Market Revenue in 2024 (Billion USD)	Compound Annual Growth Rate
1	India	Asia	ajio.com	120.76	+ 14.11%
2	Brazil	South America	magazineluiza.com	40.61	+ 14.07%
3	Argentina	South America	mercadolibre.com.ag	11.39	+ 13.63%
4	Turkey	Europe, Asia	trendyol.com	44.25	+ 13.57%
5	Mexico	North America	amazon.com.mx	42.24	+ 12.93%
6	Russia	Europe, Asia	wildberries.ru	86.60	+ 12.78%
7	China	Asia	jd.com	1,945.43	+ 12.17%
8	South Africa	Africa	takealot.com	4.64	+ 11.89%
9	Italy	Europe	amazon.it	38.59	+ 11.59%
10	United States	North America	amazon.com	1,036.48	+ 11.22%

Table A—2: Fastest Growing E-Commerce Markets Worldwide

Source: ECDB 2024b; ITA 2024.

For digital firms, the value of physical control in internationalization is increasingly debated due to their focus and reliance on digital capabilities, online networks, and global scaling opportunities (e.g., Mithani 2023; Tolstoy, Hånell and Özbek 2023). However, some traditional control mechanisms may still be critical to the business model of digital firms such as ECFs. In fact, relying fully on a virtual presence for foreign sales performance poses the risk of falling into a "virtuality trap" for ECFs (e.g., Sinkovics, Sinkovics and Jean 2013). Only high *international control* enables ECFs to introduce local offers and management or scale their business model and supply chain across countries through a subsidiary network (e.g., Batsakis et al. 2023). At the same time, ECFs may face trade-offs between local and central decision-making to increase their foreign sales performance (Evans, Mavondo and Bridson 2008; Swoboda and Elsner 2013). Moreover, these approaches may be affected by the local demand and growth opportunities in specific e-commerce markets, leading to further unknown trade-offs (Dong, He and Blut 2024; Schu and Morschett 2017). This thesis therefore aims to extend our knowledge and determine how ECFs may leverage higher control internationally to increase their foreign sales performance.

Scholars have studied the effects of control in terms of *depth* (i.e., local control via FDI) and *breadth* (i.e., control across countries via a WOS network) on performance separately (see Section A.2.4.); however, mostly for manufacturing firms (e.g., Giachetti, Manzi and Colapinto 2019; Kirca et al. 2011, Kirca et al. 2012b; Wan et al. 2023). Conversely, few studies that have examined these decisions within the context of international commerce firms have yielded inconsistent results (e.g., for high depth of control within markets, Evans, Mavondo and Bridson 2008; Gielens and Dekimpe 2001; for high breadth of control across markets, Chan, Finnegan and Sternquist 2011; Dimitrova, Kim and Smith 2019). With regard to ECFs, the literature on international performance outcomes is scant, with the majority of studies focusing on the effects of specific capabilities (Goldman et al. 2021; Tolstoy, Hånell and Özbek 2023; Tolstoy, Nordman and

Vu 2022). Only one study has considered specific host country market contexts in this regard (Eduardsen et al. 2023). Notably, only Swoboda and Sinning (2022) have examined performance outcomes of ECFs' international decisions, i.e., internationalization rhythm and speed. Surprisingly, the effects of ECFs' international control decisions on their foreign performance and the role of e-commerce specific market contexts remain unexplored (e.g., Meyer et al. 2023).

In summary, due to their specific hybrid business model, ECFs as digital firms are confronted with specific business challenges and host country environments as they expand virtually and physically. As a result, these firms must address critical decisions regarding: (1) their geographic scope across different country contexts, (2) managing wholly owned FDI, and (3) determining the degree of international control for successful internationalization. Gaining insights into these critical decisions is essential for ECFs to succeed in highly competitive global markets. This thesis thus aims to contribute to our limited knowledge by answering the following research questions:

(1) Whether and how (strongly) do intangible resources affect the geographic scope of ECFs and how do host country factors, i.e., ROL, country development, and logistics performance, moderate these effects?
(2) Whether and how (strongly) do specific firm- and host country-level factors drive ECFs' choice of wholly owned FDI?
(3) Whether and how (strongly) does ECFs' international control in terms of depth versus breadth drive their foreign sales performance and how do host countries' e-commerce market size and growth moderate these effects?

In this doctoral thesis, three different studies, outlined in Chapters B, C, and D, were conducted to answer these research questions. An extensive literature review on each topic, as presented in Section A.2., served as the basis for these studies and for identifying the specific research gaps.

2. Literature Review and Research Gaps

2.1. Overview

The following comprehensive literature review serves as a structured synthesis of the three major research streams that form the basis of this dissertation and its underlying studies. To ensure a high quality of literature, academic journals and studies were systematically assessed using the *VHB Rating 2024* journal ranking. Leading journals in the field of international business (IB) or related fields (e.g., logistics/distribution management) that have been awarded an "A" or "B" ranking according to the German Academic Association for Business Research (VHB 2024) were given preference. Owing to the specific subject matter, journals with a "C" ranking were also considered in selected cases. In Section A.2.2., the literature regarding antecedents of geographic scope is presented. Section A.2.2.1. first refers to studies on manufacturing and service firms broadly, while A.2.2.2. covers studies on commerce and online firms. Applying the same logic, A.2.3. first presents the literature on antecedents of manufacturing and service firms' operation mode choice and FDI (see A.2.3.1.), followed by the literature on commerce and online firms (see A.2.3.2.). Finally, Section A.2.4. relates to the third stream of research on the effects of international control decisions and ECFs' internationalization on performance. Again, research into the effects of international control is presented for manufacturing and service firms first in Section A.2.4.1. and subsequently for commerce firms in Section A.2.4.2. Due to a lack of research on online firms' performance, additional studies on the performance outcomes of further international capabilities or decisions of ECFs are considered in Section A.2.4.3. instead.

2.2. Literature on Antecedents of Geographic Scope

2.2.1. Manufacturing and Service Firms' Geographic Scope

As research on international decisions of online firms is still limited, the following literature review first considers the relevant literature in the offline context before outlining research gaps in the online context. Several studies have explicitly addressed antecedents of firms' geographic scope, while others have studied it as a part of related conceptualizations (e.g., international or geographic diversification; see Figure A—2). The most important antecedents at the firm and country level are addressed below in terms of thematic focus and theoretical context.

At the *firm level*, most studies have identified antecedents of manufacturers' geographic scope from the *resource-based view (RBV)*. In a fundamental study, Delios and Beamish (1999) are among the first to show a positive effect of technological resources on geographic scope. In contrast, marketing resources only have a positive effect in the case of high product diversification. Building on this, Delgado-Gómez, Ramírez-Alesón and Espitia-Escuer (2004) suggest that the availability of intangible resources such as experience has a positive effect on firms' geographic scope, especially for diversified firms. In a meta-analysis, Kirca et al. (2011) provide evidence for overall positive effects of firm-specific resources, such as research and development (R&D), advertising intensity, and international experience on increased multinationality, i.e., geographic scope. Ruzo et al. (2011) take a different approach, focusing on available scale resources (i.e., firms size) and structural resources (i.e., firms' export department), which have a positive effect on increased scope. Lin (2014) further add that firms' high organizational slack (i.e., excess resources) has a positive effect on geographic scope besides a rapid pace and irregular rhythm of internationalization. Gallego and Casillas (2014) further demonstrate how early exporters start exporting to a greater number of countries than firms that export at later stages. Thereby, profitability as a financial resource positively moderates this relationship. For related conceptualizations, Wiersema and Bowen (2008) argue in a similar context that industry globalization has a positive effect on international diversification and thus geographic scope. This is moderated by the extent of foreign competition and product diversification. Sambharya and Lee (2014) focus on firms' early innovation capabilities, showing a positive effect on firms' international diversification, including geographic scope.

Some scholars have focused on *knowledge from international experience* as one of the most important intangible resources for expansion. Beleska-Spasova, Glaister and Stride (2012) discuss positive effects of management experience, export knowledge, and export expertise on geographic scope, which then positively affects export performance. Love, Roper and Zhou (2016) further suggest that small and medium-sized enterprises' (SMEs) international experience, early internationalization, and prior management experience have a positive effect on geographic scope and export intensity. Navarro-García (2016) additionally considers factors such as export commitment and firm experiential resources, which all have a positive effect on the geographic scope of entrepreneurial firms.

Others have addressed specific *human resources.* Hitt et al. (2006), for example, stress positive effects of both human and relational capital on the internationalization of service firms. Moreover, there is an inverted U-shaped relationship between internationalization and performance, which is positively moderated by human capital but not relational capital. Mansion and Bausch (2020) also support these results, showing that human and relational capital have a positive effect on export propensity, intensity, and scope. However, these effects depend on the institutional environment such as degree of country development.

Further studies have stressed the important influence of the *top management team (TMT)* or the *chief executive officer (CEO).* According to George, Wiklund and Zahra (2005), internal ownership by the CEO or TMT has a negative effect on both the scale and geographic scope of SMEs' internationalization. In contrast, external ownership by institutional actors or venture capitalists has a positive effect on the scale of internationalization but a negative effect on their scope. Kirca et al. (2012a) specify these insights in a meta-analysis, revealing positive effects of CEO international experience on higher geographic scope, while their tenure shows no effect. Furthermore, the size, international experience, and education of the TMT have a positive effect on geographic scope.

In a similar vein, some studies have considered *family ownership* to be an antecedent. Lin (2012), for example, shows that family ownership in Taiwanese firms has a positive effect on the pace of internationalization, but a negative effect on the international scope and rhythm of internationalization. For a related conceptualizations, Bauweraerts et al. (2019) indicate a negative effect of the presence of a family CEO on export scope. However, for high levels of board service (e.g., advising management), the effect of a family CEO's presence becomes more positive, indicating that associated benefits of a service-oriented board may offset family CEO aversion regarding increasing scope.

Additionally, studies have examined conceptualizations related to geographic scope decisions from an *entrepreneurial perspective*. Drawing on the perspective of born-global firms, Kuivalainen, Sundqvist and Servais (2007) show that competitive aggressiveness as one dimension of entrepreneurial orientation has a positive effect on the degree of born-globalness, including firms' geographic scope of operations. Conversely, firms' risk-taking tendency has a negative effect on firms' degree of born-globalness. Felzensztein et al. (2015) further demonstrate that a high number of formal and informal networks increases the likelihood of entrepreneurs realizing a higher geographic scope. High levels of entrepreneurial innovation and proactiveness also have a positive effect on the likelihood of exporting, but not across all regions analyzed.

Regarding antecedents at the *country level*, relatively few studies exist. Jiménez (2010), for example, consider the effects of political risks. They suggest that a higher level of diversity in host country political risk is associated with an increased geographic scope. Moreover, firms' liquidity, the number of employees, and unrelated diversification also have a positive effect. Kirca et al. (2012a) further report positive effects of economic conditions in the home market and host country potential on increased geographic scope. For a related conceptualization, Jean, Kim and Cavusgil (2020) indicate that foreign market competition, institutional voids, and foreign market uncertainty have a positive effect on digital platform risk, which in turn has a negative effect on internationalization scope. This effect is positively moderated by firms' entrepreneurial orientation.

Author(s) and year	Research question	Theory/ framework	Sample and method	Core findings
Geographic Scope				
Beleska-Spasova, Glaister and Stride (2012)	How do important resources and capabilities drive export strategies in terms of spread, intensity, and performance?	- Resource-based view	- N=356, primary - Exporting firms/UK - SEM	- Management, export knowledge, and export expertise have a positive effect on export scope, which in turn has a positive effect on export performance. - Managerial knowledge, planning, and technology capabilities have a positive direct effect on export performance. - The possession of advanced technology has a positive effect on firms' export performance but not their scope.

Figure A—2 to be continued.

Figure A—2 continued.

Delgado-Gómez, Ramírez-Alesón and Espitia-Escuer (2004)	How does the availability of intangible resources affect international diversification in terms of concentration and scope?	- Resource-based view	- N=96, secondary - Public non-financial firms/ Spain - Binomial logit model	- The availability of intangible resources (e.g., experience) has a positive effect on firms' international diversification. - Diversified (vs. less diversified) firms typically accumulate more intangible resources, which leads to additional market investments and increasing geographic scope. - Firms with high levels of intangible resources more likely invest in markets where they have already established a presence to increase their international concentration.
Delios and Beamish (1999)	What are the antecedents and consequences of geographic scope decisions, especially performance?	- None	- N=399, primary - MNEs/Japan - Regression analysis	- Technological assets have a positive effect on firms' geographic scope, whereas marketing assets only have a positive effect in the case of high product diversification. - Even when the competing effect of proprietary assets is considered, geographic scope has a positive effect on firms' financial profitability.
Gallego and Casillas (2014)	How do export firms initiate internationalization activities and how do early exporters differ from others?	- Institutional theory - INV theory	- N=192, secondary - SMEs/Spain - Negative binomial regression	- Early exporters begin exporting to a greater number of countries than firms that export at later stages. - Early exporters prefer institutionally close countries to their country of origin in comparison to late exporters. - Profitability has a positive moderating effect on the relationship between age at entry and export scope.
George, Wiklund and Zahra (2005)	How does the ownership structure of SMEs affect their scale and scope of internationalization?	- Agency theory - Eclectic paradigm	- N=889, primary - SMEs/Sweden - Negative binomial regression	- Internal ownership (i.e., CEO/TMT) has a negative effect on both scale and scope of SMEs' internationalization. - External ownership (i.e., institutional/venture capitalist) has a positive effect on the scale of internationalization and a negative effect on geographic scope.
Hitt et al. (2006)	How do service firms' human and relational capital resources affect internationalization?	- Resource-based view	- N=72, secondary - Law firms/USA - Regression analysis	- Both human and relational capital have a positive impact on the internationalization of service firms. - There is an inverted U-shape relationship between service firms' internationalization and performance. - The link between internationalization and performance is positively moderated by human but not relational capital.
Jiménez (2010)	How does political and institutional risk affect the scope of MNEs' internationalization?	- Internationalization process theory	- N=166, primary - MNEs/Spain - Negative binomial regression	- MNEs are affected by institutional risk but only partially follow a traditional, gradual internationalization pattern. - MNEs with a greater geographic scope have a tendency to invest in more politically risky markets. - Firms' liquidity, number of employees, and unrelated diversification have a positive effect on geographic scope. - A higher level of diversity in host country political risk has a positive effect on firms' geographic scope.
Kirca et al. (2011)	How do firm-specific assets affect firm performance through multinationality?	- Internationalization theories - Resource-based view	- N=111, secondary - MNEs/Worldwide - Meta-analysis	- Firm-specific assets (i.e., R&D intensity and advertising intensity) as well as international experience have a positive effect on firms' multinationality. - Multinationality mediates the effects between firm-specific assets and firms' increasing financial performance, which is further moderated by R&D intensity.
Kirca et al. (2012a)	How do individual- and group-level drivers affect firm multinationality?	- Interaction paradigm - Upper echelons theory	- N=145, secondary - MNEs/Worldwide - Meta-analysis - Multilevel path analyses	- CEOs' international experience has a positive effect on firms' multinationality, while their tenure does not. - The size, international experience, and education of the TMT have a positive effect on firms' multinationality. - Industry competition, favorable economic conditions in the home market, and host country potential have a positive effect on multinationality.
Lin (2012)	How does family ownership affect the internationalization process in terms of pace, scope, and rhythm?	- None	- N=772, secondary - Public firms/ Taiwan - Fixed-effects regression	- Family ownership in Taiwanese firms has a positive effect on their pace of internationalization. - Family ownership in Taiwanese firms has a negative effect on their geographic internationalization scope and rhythm of internationalization.
Lin (2014)	How do organizational slack resources and performance aspirations affect the pace, scope, and rhythm of internationalization?	- Behavioral theory	- N=772, secondary - Public firms/ Taiwan - Fixed-effects regression	- Organizational slack in Taiwanese firms (i.e., available resources in excess) positively affects the speed, scope, and rhythm of firms' internationalization. - Performance falling below aspirations has a positive effect on firms' rapid pace, wide scope, and irregular rhythm in their internationalization processes.
Love, Roper and Zhou (2016)	Which factors determine SMEs' export performance and geographic scope of exports?	- Organizational learning theory - Internationalization process theory	- N=1,900, secondary - SMEs/UK - Ordered probit models	- SMEs' international experience, early internationalization and management team's prior experience have a positive effect on geographic scope and export intensity. - Firm age has a negative and website use has a positive effect on SMEs' extent of international activities. - "New to firm" and "new to industry" product innovations have a positive effect on geographic scope; the former more with country scope, the latter with regional scope.
Mansion and Bausch (2020)	How do intangible and knowledge-based assets affect export behavior of SMEs?	- None	- N=167, secondary - SMEs/Worldwide - Meta-analysis - Multivariate path analyses	- Intangible assets (i.e., human/relational capital) have a positive effect on export propensity, intensity, and scope. - Thereby innovation has a mediating role in the case of export propensity and intensity but not export scope. - Marketing intensity has a positive effect on the export propensity, intensity, and geographic scope. - The effects of intangible assets further depend on the institutional environment such as country development.

Figure A—2 to be continued.

Figure A—2 continued.

Navarro-García (2016)	Which drivers determine the speed, degree, and scope of firms' exporting activity?	- Resource-based view - Contingency approach	- N=212, primary - Exporting firms/Spain - SEM	- Export entrepreneurship is a construct that consists of speed, degree, and scope of firms' exporting activity. - Internal factors such as export commitment and firm experiential and structural resources have a positive effect on export entrepreneurship and are the dominant drivers. - In addition, external contingency factors making up the firm environment such as competitive intensity and distances between different export markets have a positive effect on export entrepreneurship.
Ruzo et al. (2011)	How do exporting firms' available resources affect their international marketing strategy?	- Resource-based view	- N=150, primary - Exporting firms/Spain - Multinomial logit analysis	- Export firms' available resources are important antecedents of their chosen export strategy (e.g., geographic scope) and performance. - Available scale resources (i.e., group of firms) and structural resources (i.e., export department) have a positive effect on firms' choice of internationalization strategy. - The internationalization strategy chosen does not have an effect on firms' export performance.
Related Conceptualizations				
Bauweraerts et al. (2019)	How does the presence of a family CEO in SMEs affect their international export scope?	- Socioemotional wealth perspective	- N=248, primary - Family SMEs/Belgium - Tobit regressions	- The presence of a family CEO has a negative effect on firms' international export scope. - For high levels of board service (e.g., advising the management), the effect of a family CEO's presence on export scope is more positive. - The associated benefits of a service-oriented board may offset family CEO aversion in terms of increasing scope.
Felzensztein et al. (2015)	How do networks and entrepreneurship orientation of SMEs affect their internationalization scope?	- None	- N=110, primary - SMEs/Chile - Logistic regression	- A higher number of both formal and informal networks increases the propensity of entrepreneurs to realize a higher geographic scope. - High levels of entrepreneurial innovation and proactiveness lead to a greater propensity of exporting, however not across all regions analyzed.
Jean, Kim and Cavusgil (2020)	What are drivers and outcomes of digital platform risk for INVs?	- Transaction cost theory	- N=273, primary - INVs/China - PLS regression	- Product specificity, foreign market competition, domestic institution voids, and foreign market uncertainty have a significant effect on digital platform risk, which has a negative effect on INVs' internationalization scope. - The degree of INVs' entrepreneurial orientation has a positive moderating effect on this relationship.
Kuivalainen, Sundqvist and Servais (2007)	How does entrepreneurial orientation affect the scale and scope of firms' born-globalness and consequently their performance?	- Born-global theory	- N=185, primary - Exporting firms/Finland - Regression analysis	- Competitive aggressiveness has a positive effect on the degree of born-globalness, which includes firms' international scope of operations. - There are significant differences in export performance (e.g., sales performance, profit performance, and sales) between true born-global and born-international firms.
Sambharya and Lee (2014)	How do innovative capabilities affect international diversification?	- Dynamic capability view - Evolutionary theory	- N=210, secondary - International MNEs/Europe, Japan, USA - Binomial regression	- MNEs' initial innovative capabilities have a positive effect on future international diversification (including scope). - International diversification has a positive effect on R&D intensity, patents, and technological capabilities. - MNEs may use their existing competencies to internationalize and over time renew such capabilities to adapt to dynamically evolving market requirements.
Wiersema and Bowen (2008)	How do industry globalization, foreign competition, and product diversification affect the degree and scope of firms' international diversification?	- Resource-based view - Transaction cost theory	- N=14,784, secondary - Exporting firms/USA - Panel tobit model	- Industry globalization has a positive effect on the degree and scope of international diversification. - The extent of foreign competition and product diversification moderate this relationship, whereas intense foreign competition has a positive effect on diversification. - There seems to be a trade-off between firms' product diversification and geographic diversification as international diversification appears to be impeded, when firms are already highly product diversified.

Note: BG=Born-Global; CEO=Chief Executive Officer; INV=International New Venture; MNE=Multinational Enterprise; PLS=Partial Least Squares; R&D=Research and Development; SEM=Structural Equation Modeling; SMEs=Small and Medium-Sized Enterprises; TMT=Top Management Team.

Figure A—2: Studies on Manufacturing and Service Firms' Geographic Scope as Dependent Variable

Source: Own Creation

2.2.2. *Commerce and Online Firms' Geographic Scope*

Only two studies have examined the antecedents of international commerce or online firms' geographic scope or related conceptualizations such as geographic diversification that include the former variable (see Figure A—3).

In the context of commerce firms, Batsakis and Mohr (2017) draw on transaction cost theoretical rationales, indicating a negative effect of product diversification on geographic diversification in terms of scope and internationalization speed. However, the effects are positively moderated by firms' international experience.

Concerning online firms, Kotha, Rindova and Rothaermel (2001) are the only scholars who have studied antecedents of online firms' propensity to internationalize, i.e., the geographic scope of their virtual presence. From a resource-based perspective, the authors identify specific intangible resources to be relevant in a digital age, i.e., firms' reputation and website traffic, which have a positive effect on online firms' geographic scope. Moreover, firms' competitive and cooperative activities have a positive effect on their increased online expansion.

Author(s) and year	Research question	Theory/ framework	Sample and method	Core findings
Commerce Firms				
Batsakis and Mohr (2017)	How does product diversification affect the internationalization scope and speed of international retailers?	- Transaction cost theory	- N=12, secondary - Retailers/South America - Random effects cross-sectional tobit panel	- Product diversification has a negative effect on the geographic diversification (scope) and internationalization speed of emerging market retailers. - International experience has a positive moderating effect on the relationship between retailers' product diversification and their geographic diversification in terms of internationalization scope and speed.
Online Firms				
Kotha, Rindova and Rothaermel (2001)	How do firm-level factors affect the propensity of pure internet firms to internationalize their web presence in terms of scope?	- Resource-based view - Dynamic strategic perspective	- N=81, secondary - Internet firms/USA - Regression analysis	- Two types of intangible assets, i.e., reputation and website traffic affect the propensity to internationalize. - Competitive and cooperative activity have a positive effect on internet firms' propensity to internationalize, whereby cooperative activity has a stronger effect. - Positive interaction effects between reputation and competitive and cooperative activity exist, such that reputation reinforces the effects of competitive and cooperative activity and the relation to internationalization propensity.

Figure A—3: Studies on Commerce and Online Firms' Geographic Scope as Dependent Variable

Source: Own Creation

2.3. *Literature on Antecedents of Operation Mode Choice and Foreign Direct Investments*

2.3.1. *Manufacturing and Service Firms' Operation Mode Choice and Foreign Direct Investments*

The IB literature in the context of manufacturing firms has examined both the antecedents of operation mode choices in general, as well as specifically focusing on binary FDI decisions (see Figure A—4). Thereby, scholars have identified numerous different factors from various theoretical perspectives at the firm and country level that influence firms' operation mode and FDI decisions.

At the *firm level*, one stream of literature has examined *characteristics of the TMT* or the *CEO* mostly drawing on a cognition or upper echelons perspective. Kishore, Agrawal and Rao (2004) suggest that strategic intent and task complexity affect operation mode choice in large firms. However, these effects depend on the respective growth stage of the e-commerce market. Jiang, Ananthram and Li (2018) suggest that senior managers with a more global mindset tend to choose operation modes with lower levels of ownership, which is, however, moderated by managers' decision-making style and prior international experience. Tasheva and Nielsen (2022) further consider the global dynamic managerial capabilities of the TMT, which has a positive effect on firms' different operation modes and indirectly firm performance. Regarding effects on FDI, Herrmann and Datta (2002) initially show a positive link between CEOs' functional background, international experience, and tenure on the choice of wholly owned FDI. Nielsen and Nielsen (2011) highlight the role of TMTs' international experience and diversity. TMTs' international experience has a positive effect on the likelihood of wholly owned FDI, while national diversity has a negative effect. Laufs, Bembom and Schwens (2016) find that the CEO's tenure has a strong effect on FDI mode choice of SMEs. However, this effect depends on CEOs' geographic experience and the level of political risks in the host country. Adomako et al. (2021) analyze psychological attributes of CEOs and find that CEOs' optimism has a positive effect on FDI modes. This relationship is moderated by the perceived ROL.

Some studies have explicitly analyzed *entrepreneurial characteristics* for operation mode choice. Ripollés, Blesa and Monferrer (2012) suggest that entrepreneurial orientation and early entry have a positive effect on international market orientation of international new ventures (INV), which has a positive effect on INVs' resource commitment and use of high control operation modes. Xue et al. (2021) report that entrepreneurs with an implicit achievement motive will choose operation modes with higher commitment only when they experience low levels of overseas operation complexity. Ipsmiller, Dikova and Brouthers (2022) stress the importance of SMEs' entrepreneurial orientation for choosing active online export as an operation mode instead of a default (dot-com) website for internationalization. Regarding FDI decisions, Kalinic and Brouthers (2022) show that entrepreneurial orientation has a positive effect on the probability of choosing non-FDI modes, while this effect is moderated by institutional distance.

Others have considered *family ownership* as an antecedent of FDI. Yamanoi and Asaba (2018) reveal that family ownership has a positive effect on the likelihood of wholly owned FDI being chosen, which is moderated by the level of corruption in a host country. Del Bosco and Bettinelli (2020) further show that cultural and institutional distance have a positive effect on the choice of wholly owned FDI of family firms, while geographic distance has a negative effect.

Scholars rooted in economics have stressed bounded rational decision-making and *transaction cost factors* as important antecedents. Chen and Hu (2002) find that Chinese firms choose high commitment modes, for example, when these investments involve marketing skills, a long-planned duration, or proprietary products. Regarding FDI, an early meta-analysis by Zhao, Luo and Suh (2004) shows that transaction-cost determinants of asset specificity, county risk, and advertising intensity are important antecedents of firms' FDI choice. Brouthers, Brouthers and Werner (2008) add that firms perceiving high demand uncertainty prefer shared control modes, while firms with strategic flexibility through international experience prefer wholly owned FDI. Brouthers (2013) specify that firms perceiving high levels of transaction costs prefer wholly owned FDI over joint ventures (JVs), concluding that operation mode choices of EU firms could best be explained by an extended transaction cost model and measures.

In contrast, other scholars have viewed operation mode choice under the lens of different *organizational resources* and *capabilities*, Blesa and Ripolles (2008) show that marketing capabilities have a positive effect on firms' higher commitment in terms of choosing FDI modes. Xie (2017) note that firm age has an inverted U-shaped relationship with firms operation mode choice for high commitment. Paniagua, Korzynski and Mas-Tur (2017) find that firms' use of online social network capabilities has a positive effect on FDI in terms of foreign capital expenditure and the number of cross-border affiliates. For FDI choice, Ekeledo and Sivakumar (2004a) draw on the RBV, showing that proprietary technology, experience, specialized asset, firm size, organizational culture, or positive reputation increase the likelihood of wholly owned FDI being chosen. Wei et al. (2014) further report positive effects of technology capability, firms size, and export experience on the likelihood of Chines firms' FDI. He, Brouthers and Filatotchev (2013) additionally discuss the positive effects of strong market orientation capabilities of Chinese firms, which depend on institutional distance.

Notably, a major stream in literature has specifically focused on firms' *learning capabilities* and international experience from an *internationalization process perspective*. For operation mode choice, Schwens et al. (2018b), note that SMEs with high host country and FDI experience tend to choose high commitment operation modes. In a meta-analysis, Tang and Gudergan (2018) demonstrate that international experience has a positive effect on operation mode choice across industries, while host country experience is most important. Regarding FDI decisions, an early study by Chung and Enderwick (2001) finds that experience with specific countries has an effect on the likelihood of FDI vs. export. Dikova and Van Witteloostuijn (2007) suggest that parent firms' technological intensity, international strategy, and experience determine mode choice. Both Pinho (2007) and Pehrsson (2008) support this, highlighting the role of market specific knowledge for wholly owned FDI. Dow and Larimo (2009) extend the experience concept by showing positive effects of international experience from similar countries on FDI in a host country, while dissimilar experience has no effect. Czinkota et al. (2009)

discuss the positive effects of international experience alongside product differentiation in the specific case of service firms. Schwens, Eiche and Kabst (2011) further show that the effect of international experience on SMEs' operation mode choice is contingent on the institutional context of the host country. Pla-Barber, Villar and León-Darder (2014) study both prior host country experience and prior FDI experience of service firms. The results appear somewhat contradictory, as the former has a positive effect on FDI choice of service firms, whereas the latter has a negative effect. Both are negatively moderated by cultural distance. In this context, Klier et al. (2017) also stress the moderating effect of cultural distance on the effects of different experience-based resources in mode choice. Amankwah-Amoah et al. (2022) indicate that foreign market knowledge indirectly drives firms' international performance through FDI. Wan et al. (2023) synthesize these findings in a recent meta-analysis, confirming the overall positive effects of international experience on wholly owned FDI, especially for host country experience.

The largest stream of research deals with *institutional distances* between firms' home and different host countries. Two early meta-analyses yield contradictory results. Tihanyi, Griffith and Russell (2005) find no support for general effects of cultural distance on operation mode choice, only for US multinational enterprises (MNEs). Magnusson et al. (2008) show negative effects of cultural distance on operation mode choice and moderating effects of time, MNE origin, and cultural distance measures. Hernández and Nieto (2015) show positive effects of regulative institutional distance on operation mode choice of European SMEs. Trąpczyński, Halaszovich and Piaskowska (2020) support these insights for formal institutional distance more broadly. Wu and Deng (2020) further discuss Chinese SMEs' institutional escapism, i.e., tendency to escape to host countries with institutions different from the home country with low commitment modes. Kostova et al. (2020) find overall negative effects of institutional distance on operation mode choice in a more recent meta-analysis. For FDI decisions, Dow and Ferencikova (2010) extend the concept of institutional distance and test multiple measures of psychic distance. Overall, FDI is preferred as psychic distance is low. However, different measures yield inconclusive results. Ang, Benischke and Doh (2015) report positive effects in case of acquisition choices, while the negative effect of informal institutional distance on FDI choice is also supported by Del Giudice et al. (2017). Batsakis and Singh (2019) are the first to consider added instead of regular distances. They show positive effects of both high and low added geographical and institutional distance on the choice of wholly owned FDI. Lo, Chiao and Yu (2016) further show different effects of socio-cultural, macroeconomic, and industrial policy distance dimensions on FDI. Challenging the role of distance, Harzing and Pudelko (2016) find support for a stronger role of host country contextual differences instead of distances. Focusing on individual dimensions of institutional distance, Moalla and Mayrhofer (2020) show that administrative and economic distance are critical for FDI, whereas cultural and geographic distance are less. However, two meta-analyses on antecedents of FDI suggest that the effects of distance remain inconclusive and context-specific. Beugelsdijk et al. (2018) find no support for the effect of cultural distance on MNEs' wholly owned FDI choice. In contrast, Zhang et al. (2023) report an overall negative effect of institutional distance on FDI but only for informal distance when tested separately.

At the *country level*, several scholars have in particular studied various *host country factors*. Efrat and Shoham (2013) reveal positive effects of the economic stability and the size of a host market on high commitment operation modes. Uncertainty avoidance has a negative effect in contrast. Regarding FDI decisions, Cui and Jiang (2009) discuss the importance of host market industry competition and market growth for Chinese firms' likelihood of choosing wholly owned FDI. While firms prefer FDI in the face of severe competition, they prefer JVs in case of high market growth. In a meta-analysis, Morschett, Schramm-Klein and Swoboda (2010) test the overall effects of several external antecedents of firms' wholly owned FDI. Power distance of the firm's home country has a positive effect on the propensity to establish wholly owned FDI. In contrast, country risk, legal restrictions, market growth, and market size have a negative effect on this choice. Another meta-analysis by Bailey (2018) finds positive effects of political stability, democracy, and ROL on the attractiveness of FDI and negative effects of corruption, tax rates, and culture. Specifically addressing negative effects of host country political constraints, Cuervo-Cazurra et al. (2023) discuss the moderating effects of the home country's political context.

Scholars have moreover identified factors related to *risk and uncertainty* as critical antecedents. From an institutional perspective, Tang and Buckley (2020) show that host country risk has a negative effect on operation mode choice in a meta-analysis of 64 studies. Institutional constraints on policymakers and risk-taking tendencies in the home country further positively moderate this relationship. Ipsmiller, Brouthers and Dikova (2021) draw on real option theory and explain negative effects of perceived demand uncertainty on Austrian SMEs' operation mode choice. Similarly, Li and Xiong (2022) find that when uncertainty of the industry environment is low, regardless of the institutional environment, Chinese firms tend to use cooperative modes. Regarding FDI decisions, Tsang (2005) draw similar conclusions. The level of risk in the host country has a negative effect on firms' likelihood of choosing wholly owned FDI in a country. Sánchez Peinado and Pla Barber (2006) find the same in the context of service firms' FDI decisions where the effects are moderated by various investment risks. Slangen and Van Tulder (2009) focus on host country governance quality as an indicator of uncertainty, concluding that firms prefer wholly owned FDI in countries with high governance quality, which reduces external uncertainty.

Author(s) and year	Research question	Theory/ framework	Sample and method	Core findings
Operation Mode Choice				
Chen and Hu (2002)	What are determinants of entry mode choice and consequences for performance?	- Transaction cost theory	- N=470, secondary - Foreign investment enterprises/China - Multinomial logit model	- WOS are more likely than contractual modes and equity JVs when the investments relate to certain marketing skills and a long-planned duration. - WOS are more likely than equity JVs when MNEs expand into markets with high regional growth, high industrial growth, or investing in smaller foreign operations. - WOS are more likely than contractual JVs when the investments relate to proprietary products or cultural distance is large between home and host countries.
Efrat and Shoham (2013)	How does the interaction between country and market factors and BGs' strategic orientation affect the choice of low vs. high commitment modes?	- None	- N=104, primary - High-tech born-globals/Israel - Regression analysis	- A host market's level of economic stability has a positive effect on the level of entry mode commitment. - Uncertainty avoidance in a country has a negative effect on the level of entry mode commitment. - The host market's size has a positive effect on the level of entry mode commitment. - Born-global firms' strategic orientation moderates the country effects, favoring high commitment entry modes.
Hernández and Nieto (2015)	How does institutional regulative distance affect the entry mode choice of European firms?	- Institutional theory - Transaction cost theory	- N=3,703, secondary - SMEs/Europe - Multilevel logit model	- Firms entering countries with lower levels of regulatory development than that of the origin choose modes that require a lower resource commitment. - Firms entering countries with higher levels of regulatory development than that of the origin choose higher resource commitment modes.
Ipsmiller, Brouthers and Dikova (2021)	How does demand uncertainty affect the export channel selection as real options of SMEs?	- Real option theory	- N=180, primary - SMEs/Austria - Multinomial logistic regression	- The choice of an export channel based not only on transaction cost factors but also considering real option factors tends to generate higher value. - SMEs that perceive higher levels of demand uncertainty tend to use export channels or shared option channels rather than complex channels such as WOS. - There is a negative moderating effect of strategic flexibility for shared option export channels.
Ipsmiller, Dikova and Brouthers (2022)	What drives SMEs' choice between customized (i.e., country-specific) vs. general virtual presence modes (standardized websites)?	- None	- N=176, primary - Exporting SMEs/Austria - Binomial logistic regression	- Entrepreneurial orientation has a positive effect on active online internationalization (i.e., country-specific websites) vs. default internationalization (general websites). - Competitive pre-emption (threats) has no significant moderating effect on the above relationship but a positive direct effect on active online internationalization. - The diversity of export experience across countries has a positive effect on active online internationalization.
Jiang, Ananthram and Li (2018)	How does senior managers' global mindset affect their entry mode choice?	- Cognition perspective	- N=345, primary - MNEs/China - Hierarchical regressions	- Senior managers with a stronger global mindset tend to prefer and choose a lower-level ownership entry mode for their foreign subsidiaries. - The tendency is stronger in cases where senior managers have a 'thinking' decision-making style vs. a 'feeling' decision-making style but weaker when senior managers have more experience in their positions.
Kishore, Agrawal and Rao (2004)	How does the e-commerce market growth and maturity stage affect the sourcing (entry) mode choice of large firms?	- None	- N=141, secondary - MNEs/USA - Content analysis - Logit regression	- Hybrid modes are preferred over hierarchical modes when the strategic intent of an e-commerce project is more business-focused during the growth phase. - Strategic intent does not have an effect on mode choices during the technology/market maturity phase. - When task complexity is high during the growth phase, hierarchical governance is preferred in terms of modes. - Both hierarchical and hybrid governance modes are preferred over market-related modes to manage task complexity, as technologies and their markets reach maturity.
Kostova et al. (2020)	How does institutional distance affect the internationalization of MNEs?	- Institutional theory	- N=137, secondary - MNEs/Worldwide - Meta-analysis	- In the literature there are three schools of thought on institutional distance, i.e., organizational institutionalism, institutional economics, and comparative institutionalism. - Institutional distance has a negative on entry mode choice, regardless of how entry mode is operationalized (i.e., dummy, continuous, or categorical). - Institutional distance has an overall negative effect on firm performance outcomes.
Li and Xiong (2022)	How does environmental uncertainty affect entry mode choice and what is the moderating role of technological heterogeneity?	- None	- N=54, secondary - Listed firms/ China - Logistic regression	- When the uncertainty of the industry environment is low, regardless of how uncertain the institutional environment is, most firms tend to choose a cooperative strategy. - A high degree of institutional environment uncertainty leads to firms choosing a new plant when the industry environment indicators become more turbulent. - Technological capability weakens the influence of environmental uncertainty on entry mode choice.
Magnusson et al. (2008)	How do cultural differences affect entry strategy and performance?	- None	- N=38, secondary - MNEs/Worldwide - Meta-analysis	- Cultural differences only have a small effect on both firm performance and the choice of entry mode strategy. - When MNE origin, time effects, and cultural difference measurements are accounted for as moderators, the relationships between entry mode and firm performance move in opposite directions.

Figure A—4 to be continued.

Figure A—4 continued.

Paniagua, Korzynski and Mas-Tur (2017)	How does the use of online social networks affect MNEs' FDI decisions?	- Internalization theory - Capability-based view	- N=4,563, secondary - MNEs/Worldwide - Fixed-effect panel	- The activity of a firm's online social networks has a positive effect on FDI, foreign capital expenditure, and the number of cross-border affiliates. - Capabilities enhanced by social media (e.g., customer reach or reputation) have a higher effect on B2C firms. - Institutional quality has no moderating effect on the relationship between online social network use and FDI.
Ripollés, Blesa and Monferrer (2012)	How does international market orientation affect the entry mode choice of INVs?	- None	- N=135, primary - INVs/Spain - SEM	- Entrepreneurial orientation and early entry have a positive effect on international market orientation in INVs. - The development of international market-oriented behaviors has a positive effect on INVs' resource commitment and thus their use of high control entry modes. - An early international entry affects INVs' capability to absorb foreign market knowledge.
Schwens et al. (2018b)	How does experiential learning about operation modes and markets affect future mode choices?	- Internationalization process theory	- N=179, primary - SMEs/Germany - Ordinal logistic regression	- An SME's degree of operation mode experience in terms of exporting and WOS has a positive effect on the SME's propensity to choose the same mode again. - SMEs with a combination of greater mode-specific and target market/region-specific experience are more likely to opt for a high commitment mode in the future.
Tang and Buckley (2020)	How does host country risk affect foreign ownership strategy and what is the moderating role of home country institutions?	- Internalization theory - Institution-based view	- N=64, secondary - MNEs/Worldwide - Meta-analysis	- Host country risk has a negative effect on firms' choice of an ownership strategy with full control. - Institutional constraints on policymakers and risk-taking tendencies in the home country positively moderate the relationship of host country risk and ownership strategy. - The combined effect of these two institutional factors has a negative moderating effect on the relationship.
Tang and Gudergan (2018)	How do firm-, industry-, and country-specific moderators affect the international experience – ownership strategy relationship?	- Dynamic capability view	- N=102, secondary - MNEs/Worldwide - Meta-analysis	- Sources of international experience, firm size, and level of economic development of the potential foreign market moderate the effect of international experience on ownership strategy when entering a foreign market. - The effect of international experience on ownership strategy does not depend on different industry contexts. - Country-specific experience exerts the strongest contingency effect on the relationship between international experience and ownership strategy.
Tasheva and Nielsen (2022)	How does global dynamic managerial capability affect MNEs' orchestration of global assets including entry modes?	- Dynamic capability view - Upper echelons theory	- N=165, secondary - Listed companies/Switzerland - Latent growth modeling	- Top management teams increase their global dynamic managerial capabilities over time. - Global dynamic managerial capability has a positive effect on the (re)configuration of firms' assets and resources across different geographic regions and different foreign entry modes. - The configurations of firms' global assets regarding different geographic regions and different foreign entry modes mediate the relationship between global dynamic managerial capability and subsequent firm performance.
Tihanyi, Griffith and Russell (2005)	How does cultural distance affect entry mode choice, international diversification, and MNE performance?	- None	- N=55, secondary - MNEs/Worldwide - Meta-analysis	- There are no significant relationships between cultural distance and entry mode choice, international diversification, and MNE performance. - Cultural distance has a strong negative effect on entry mode choice for US-based MNEs. - The relationship between cultural distance and international diversification is negative for high-tech industries but positive for other industries.
Trąpczyński, Halaszovich and Piaskowska (2020)	How do decision makers perceive institutional differences across countries and how do they affect ownership level decisions?	- Institution-based view - Upper echelons theory	- N=100, primary - Firms with FDI/Poland - Ordered probit models	- The direction of perceived formal institutional distance is important for different ownership levels in foreign affiliates. - The direction of distance moderates the negative effect of formal institutional distance on ownership levels of subsidiaries. - When the relative quality of formal institutions is lower than in the home country, the negative effect of informal institutional distance perceptions on ownership level of a foreign subsidiary is stronger.
Wu and Deng (2020)	How does institutional escapism affect entry mode choice of emerging market SMEs?	- Institution-based view	- N=319, primary - SMEs/China - Ordered logit regression	- SMEs tend to escape to a host country with institutions that are different from their home country and opt for an entry mode with low levels of commitment. - The decision on location and entry mode does not depend on the degree of economic development of a host country. - The escape orientation and arbitrage logic are not necessarily independent or separate as they are seen in the literature.
Xie (2017)	How does firm age affect the entry mode choices of emerging economy firms?	- Organizational ecology - Institutional theory	- N=388, secondary - Listed firms/China - Fractional probit regression	- Firm age has an inverted U-shaped relationship with the choice of high equity modes. - A high degree of marketization reinforces the inverted U-shaped relationship with high equity modes. - A high degree of marketization can decrease firms' chosen ownership at the low age stage as it increases their resource disadvantage and promotes their learning through intensified competition.

Figure A—4 to be continued.

Figure A—4 continued.

Xue et al. (2021)	How do entrepreneurs' unconscious motives affect their international commitment in terms of mode?	- Achievement motivation theory - Cognition theory	- N=115, primary - Entrepreneurs/China - Ordered multinomial analysis	- An entrepreneur with a strong implicit and explicit achievement motive more likely decides to make an early international commitment. - An entrepreneur that has an implicit achievement motive makes greater early commitment only when he experiences lower levels of overseas operation complexity. - Competitive intensity has a moderating effect and thus changes the direction of the relationship between achievement motives and the choice for early international commitment.
Binary Mode Choice in the Context of FDI				
Adomako et al. (2021)	How do psychological attributes of executives affect firms' entry mode choice and how does rule of law moderate this?	- Institutional theory	- N=227, primary - SMEs/Ghana - Binary logistic regression	- CEOs' level of optimism has a positive effect on the preference for equity entry modes. - A host country's perceived level of rule of law moderates the relationship between CEOs' optimism and preference for choosing specific foreign entry modes. - CEOs more likely opt for riskier modes in foreign markets when a host country has strong institutions.
Amankwah-Amoah et al. (2022)	How does equity mode choice mediate the relationship between foreign market knowledge and firms' international performance?	- Knowledge-based view - Upper echelons theory	- N=205, primary - SMEs/Ghana - Path analysis	- Foreign market knowledge has a positive effect on SMEs' preference for equity entry mode choice. - Financial slack has a positive moderating effect on the relationship between foreign market knowledge and the preference for equity entry mode choice. - Foreign market equity entry mode choice mediates the effect of foreign market knowledge on the firms' international performance.
Ang, Benischke and Doh (2015)	How do institutional differences influence the choice of using acquisitions as an entry mode?	- Neo institutional theory	- N=673, secondary - MNEs/Emerging markets - Hierarchical logistic regression	- The number of acquisitions of local and foreign firms in the same host country and industry has a positive effect on the subsequent adoption of acquisitions. - Cultural, regulatory, and normative distance have a positive effect on the choice of acquisitions, while geographic distance has a negative effect. - Regulatory distance positively moderates this relationship, while normative distance does not.
Bailey (2018)	How do institutional factors affect FDI attractiveness?	- Institutional theory	- N=97, secondary - MNEs/World wide - Meta-analysis	- Political stability, democracy, and rule of law have a positive effect on the attractiveness of FDI in a country. Corruption, tax rates, and cultural distance have a negative effect on the attractiveness of FDI in a country. - Environmental effects such as level of development, region of destination, and competitive industry environment moderate these relationships in different ways.
Batsakis and Singh (2019)	How does added distance affect the entry mode choice of MNEs and how is this link moderated by experience?	Transaction cost theory - Internalization theory	- N=134, secondary - MNEs/UK - Logistic regression	- In markets with high and low geographical and institutional distance to the home market, firms have a preference for market entry through WOS (vs. JV). - In markets with a medium distance, MNEs have a preference for using JVs as an entry mode. - Firms' international experience has a positive moderating effect on the described (U-shaped) relationship.
Beugelsdijk et al. (2018)	How does cultural distance affect key decisions of internationalization?	- Various internationalization theories	- N=156, secondary - MNEs/Worldwide - Meta-analysis	- Firms enter culturally distant locations less likely, however, they prefer greenfield investments and WOS through transfer of management practices if they do. - Cultural distance does not affect firms' capital investment and whether they enter through a JV or WOS. - Cultural distance has a negative effect on subsidiary performance but not on MNEs' overall performance.
Blesa and Ripolles (2008)	How do marketing capabilities affect firms' international performance via international commitment?	- Transaction cost theory - Dynamic strategy view	- N=581, primary - International firms/Spain, Belgium - SEM	- Marketing capabilities have a positive effect on international performance through higher commitment. - High direct investment entry modes have a positive effect on international economic performance. - The mediating effect of international entry mode on performance is affected by country effects, as Belgian firms exert a positive and Spanish firms a negative effect.
Brouthers (2013)	How do institutional, cultural, and transaction cost factors affect entry mode choice and performance?	- Transaction cost theory	- N=213, primary - MNEs/EU - Logistic regression	- Firms that perceive higher levels of transaction costs prefer to opt for wholly owned entry modes. - Firms that enter markets characterized by high legal restrictions and high levels of investment risk prefer to opt for JV entry modes. - Firms have higher mode performance when they adopt the entry mode predicted by the extended transaction cost model, when they enter markets with higher levels of market potential, and when they use wholly owned entry modes.
Brouthers, Brouthers and Werner (2008)	How do real option and transaction cost variables explain the relationship between mode choices and performance?	- Transaction cost theory - Real option theory	- N=160, primary - MNEs/Greece, Netherlands - Logistic regression	- When there is high demand uncertainty, firms prefer modes reducing downside risks while at the same time providing a proprietary channel for market knowledge. - Firms that perceive high demand uncertainty in a country prefer JVs over alternative non-option modes. - Firms prefer to use non-option entry modes when they possess strategic flexibility based on their international experience.

Figure A—4 to be continued.

Figure A—4 continued.

Chung and Enderwick (2001)	How do firms choose between exporting vs. FDI as a market entry mode?	- None	- N=124, primary - MNEs/New Zealand - Logistic regression	- Product type (services vs. other) and immigrant effects (Taiwanese owned or controlled vs. other) have a positive effect on the choice of FDI vs. exporting. - Firms' experience with Japan has a negative effect on the choice of FDI vs. exporting as an entry mode. - International business experience with other Chinese business countries, market size, and before or after-sales service do not have a significant effect.
Cuervo-Cazurra et al. (2023)	How do host country political factors affect the internationalization process and entry mode selection?	- None	- N=224, secondar - MNEs/Worldwide - Meta-analysis	- Host country political constraints have a negative effect on firm internationalization and FDI choice. - Home country's political constraints moderate the relationship between host country politics and internationalization. - Political risk in the home country moderates the relationship between host country politics and internationalization. - The weaker a home country's level of regulatory quality, the weaker the negative relationship between host country politics and firm internationalization becomes.
Cui and Jiang (2009)	How do Chinese firms choose between WOS and JVs as a market entry mode?	- Strategic behavior approach	- N=138, primary - Firms with outward FDI/China - Logistic regression	- Chinese firms prefer WOS when they adopt a global strategy, face severe host industry competition, and focus on asset seeking purposes in their FDI. - Chinese firms prefer JVs when firms invest in high growth markets to gain first or early-mover advantages. - Chinese firms choose a FDI entry mode in order to improve the effectiveness of asset acquisition, knowledge and learning as well as global strategy execution.
Czinkota et al. (2009)	What factors determine the entry mode choice of service firms?	- Eclectic paradigm	- N=110, primary - Business schools/USA - Logistic regression	- The size of a business school does not affect the likelihood of choosing an equity-based mode of entry. - Multinational experience and product differentiation have a positive effect on the likelihood of choosing an equity mode of entry. - Higher perceived market potential and greater contractual risk have a positive effect on the likelihood of entering a foreign market via an equity mode, whereas the investment risk does not.
Del Bosco and Bettinelli (2020)	How do family firms choose foreign ownership modes?	- Socio-Emotional Wealth Perspective	- N=701, primary - Family firms/ Italy - Logistic regression	- Cultural and institutional distance have a positive effect on the choice of full ownership modes of family firms. - Geographic distance has a negative effect on the choice of full ownership modes of family firms. - Family control moderates the relationship between distance and foreign ownership mode in the case of cultural and institutional distance, but not geographic distance.
Del Giudice et al. (2017)	How do cognitive dimensions influence SMEs' collaborative entry mode choice?	- None	- N=345, primary - SMEs/Italy - SEM	- High informal institutional distance has a positive effect on non-equity based (partnership, alliances) cooperative entry modes over equity-based modes (JV, acquisition). - Positive time trends, perception about a host country's partner size/resources, and perception of high power of a host country partner have a positive effect on equity-based (vs. non-equity based) collaborative entry modes.
Dikova and Van Witteloostuijn (2007)	What are drivers of entry and establishment mode choices in transition economies and how is it affected by the institutional environment?	- Williamson's new institutional economics	- N=160, primary - MNEs/Eastern Europe - Logistic regression	- Parent firms' technological intensity, international strategy, and experience affect both MNEs' establishment and mode choice (i.e., full vs. shared ownership). - Host country institutional advancement moderates the effect of both technological intensity and international strategy on the establishment and entry mode choice. - The combination of home country variables and investment restriction explains more than nine times as much variance as cultural distance.
Dow and Ferencikova (2010)	How does psychic distance affect market selection, entry mode choice, and performance?	- None	- N=87, secondary - FDI ventures/ Slovakia - Logistic regression	- The scales developed by Dow and Karunaratna are stronger predictors of market selection and FDI performance than the traditional Kogut and Singh index of psychic distance, however, not for entry mode choice. - As the results regarding entry mode choice are ambiguous, transaction cost approaches may not be adequate as a theoretical explanation.
Dow and Larimo (2009)	How do different factors of psychic distance and international experience influence market entry strategy?	- Uppsala model	- N=247, secondary - Manufacturers/ Scandinavia - Logistic regression	- Differences in religion, degree of democracy, and industrial development have a negative impact on a market entry strategy with high degree of control (WOS vs. JV). - International experience in similar countries has a positive effect on entry with a controlled WOS (vs. JV), however, this effect is diminished by psychic distance.
Ekeledo and Sivakumar (2004a)	To which extent do determinants of entry mode choice of manufacturing firms apply to service firms?	- Resource-based view	- N=130, primary - Service and manufacturing firms/USA - Binary logistic regression	- Proprietary technology, experience, specialized assets, firm size, organizational culture, or positive reputation increase firms' likelihood of choosing full control modes. - Tacit know-how does not have a significant effect on firms' choice of entry mode. - When the proprietary content of product, process, or managerial technology is high, a larger percentage of service firms (vs. manufacturing firms), tends to prefer full ownership modes.

Figure A—4 to be continued.

Figure A—4 continued.

Harzing and Pudelko (2016)	How does (cultural) distance affect the entry mode choice of MNEs and what is the role of host country differences?	- None	- N=817, primary - MNEs/World-wide - Logistic regression	- Controlling for home and host country context effects, the explanatory power of distance is highly limited. - Uncertainty avoidance and long-term orientation have a positive and access to capital a negative effect on greenfield investments (vs. acquisitions). - Investment restrictions and risk of political instability have a positive effect and economic development a negative effect on greenfield investments (vs. acquisitions).
He, Brouthers and Filatotchev (2013)	How is export performance improved through aligning export channel with market orientation and how is it affected by institutional distance?	- Resource-based view - Institutional theory	- N=195, primary - Exporting firms' CEOs/China - Logistic regression	- Companies with strong (vs. weak) market-orientation capabilities use hierarchical (vs. hybrid) export channels. - This relationship is moderated by the institutional distance between China and the export market. - The alignment of export channel choice with firm-level market orientation capabilities and institutional distance leads to better export performance.
Herrmann and Datta (2002)	What influence do demographic characteristics and international experience have on the choice of foreign market entry modes?	- Upper echelons theory	- N=126, primary - MNEs/World-wide - Logistic regression	- CEOs who have been in the position for a longer time tend to enter the market with a fully controlled mode. - The functional background (i.e., cognitive attitude and type of knowledge) and the international experience of the CEOs have a positive effect on a market entry with a fully controlled mode. - High performing firms exert a greater coalignment between CEO characteristics and choice of entry modes.
Kalinic and Brouthers (2022)	How does entrepreneurial orientation affect export channel selection and consequently performance of SMEs?	- Transaction cost theory - Institutional theory	- N=265, primary - SMEs/Netherlands, Italy - Logistic regression	- Entrepreneurial orientation is an important driver of export channel choice, in addition to transaction costs. - Export channel choice mediates the relation between entrepreneurial orientation and export performance. - Institutional distance moderates the relationship between entrepreneurial orientation and channel choice.
Klier et al. (2017)	How do different firm resources affect the establishment mode choice and how are they moderated by cultural distance?	- Resource-based view	- N=31, secondary - MNEs/World-wide - Meta-analysis	- Knowledge-based resources have a positive effect on the propensity of greenfield investments (vs. acquisitions). - Experience-based resources (i.e., general, host country, acquisition or greenfield experience) lead to a higher propensity of acquisitions (vs. greenfield investments). - Cultural distance has a positive effect on knowledge-intensive firms' preference for greenfield investments.
Laufs, Bembom and Schwens (2016)	How do CEO characteristics of SMEs affect equity entry mode choice and how is this moderated by geographic experience and political risk?	- Upper echelons theory	- [illegible] - SMEs/Germany - Binary logistic regression	- CEOs' age has no direct effect on the firm's mode of entry when contextual factors are not [illegible] - CEOs' tenure has a strong effect on SMEs' foreign market entry mode choice when geographic experience and the host-country's political risk are considered. - High levels of political risk in the foreign market have a negative effect on choosing equity-based entry modes in the case of older CEOs and those with longer tenure.
Lo, Chiao and Yu (2016)	How do different networks and factors of institutional environment influence the market entry strategy of SMEs?	- Network and institutional environment perspectives	- N=851, secondary - SMEs/Taiwan - Logistic regression	- Internal networks, perceived macroeconomic differences in the foreign market, and following customers into their market have a positive effect on market entry decisions in favor of WOS. - Firms prefer JVs when supplier relationships are strong and socio-cultural differences are high. - When SMEs' perceive differences in macro-economic and industrial-policy environments, they prefer WOS.
Moalla and Mayrhofer (2020)	What are relevant dimensions of distance that affect mode choice of French companies?	- None	- N=203, secondary - MNEs/France - Logistic regression	- Cultural, administrative, geographic, and economic distances all have an influence on the entry mode choice. - Considered simultaneously, administrative and economic distance have a strong effect on entry mode choice, whereas cultural and geographic distance have a weaker effect on the entry mode decision. - Host countries' government effectiveness is an important contextual factor that affects entry mode choice.
Morschett, Schramm-Klein and Swoboda (2010)	Which external factors affect the choice of market entry strategy?	- Various internationalization theories	- N=72, secondary - MNEs/World-wide - Meta-analysis	- Power distance of the firm's home country has a positive effect on the propensity to establish a WOS. - Country risk, legal restrictions, market growth, and market size have a negative effect on propensity of WOS. - The relationship between host country income level and entry mode depends, to some degree, on industry type. - For service firms there is a negative relationship between income level and WOS, whereas for manufacturing firms there is a positive relationship.
Nielsen and Nielsen (2011)	How does the international experience and diversity of origin of top manager teams influence controlled market entry choices?	- Upper echelons theory	- N=165, secondary - Listed firms/Sweden - Multilevel Bernoulli analysis	- Top management teams' international experience has a negative effect on the likelihood of shared ownership modes being chosen (vs. controlled WOS). - The nationality diversity of top management teams has a positive effect on the likelihood of a market entry mode with shared control being chosen (vs. controlled WOS).
Pehrsson (2008)	What influence do business relationships and international experience have on the choice of foreign entry modes?	- None	- N=173, primary - Manufacturing firms/Sweden - Logistic regression	- Product/market commonality and intangible resource commonality have a positive impact on the market entry decision with a fully controlled subsidiary. - The importance of foreign markets in generating international knowledge moderates the relationship of external drivers on firms' entry mode decisions.

Figure A—4 to be continued.

Figure A—4 continued.

Pinho (2007)	What are drivers and inhibitors of SMEs' entry mode decision?	- Eclectic paradigm	- N=87, primary - SMEs/Portugal - Logistic regression	- High international experience and ability to innovate have a positive effect on the likelihood of equity mode choice. - Greater market sales/growth potential has a positive effect on the likelihood of equity mode choice. - Higher market-specific knowledge has a positive effect on the likelihood of equity mode choice.
Pla-Barber, Villar and León-Darder (2014)	How do host country and mode experience affect the FDI choice of service firms?	- Knowledge-based view	- N=81, secondary - Hotel chains/ Spain - Logistic regression	- Host country experience has a positive effect on service firms' propensity of choosing FDI modes. - FDI mode experience has a negative effect on service firms' propensity of choosing FDI modes. - Cultural distance has a negative moderating effect on both relationships.
Sánchez Peinado and Pla Barber (2006)	What are drivers of service firms' FDI decisions?	- Transaction cost theory - Organizational capability theory	- N=113, primary - Service firms/ Spain - Logistic regression	- Firms' strategic motivations related to the following of clients or competitors and to asset exploitation have a positive effect on the likelihood of FDI modes being chosen. - Host country risk and cultural distance have a negative effect on the likelihood of FDI modes being chosen. - Specific characteristics of services moderate the relationships of these investment risk variables and entry modes.
Schwens, Eiche and Kabst (2011)	How do informal and formal institutional distance affect entry mode strategies of SMEs as contextual moderators?	- Institutional theory	- N=227, primary - SMEs/Germany - Binary logistic regression	- International experience, know-how, and strategic importance have a positive effect on equity mode choice. - The effect of international experience, proprietary know-how, and strategic importance on SME mode choice depends on the institutional context of the host country. - Informal distance and formal institutional risk positively moderate the know-how and entry mode relationship.
Slangen and Van Tulder (2009)	How does governance quality as an indicator of external uncertainty of foreign markets affect MNEs' choice for JVs?	- None	- N=150, primary - MNEs/Netherlands - Logistic regression	- MNEs prefer to enter countries with high governance quality through WOS and with low governance through JVs. - Governance quality of foreign countries is a better proxy of external uncertainty than the mostly measured cultural distance and political risk level. - Cultural distance has no effect, while political risk has the weakest effect of all elements of governance quality.
Tsang (2005)	What are determinants of Vietnamese firms' choice of entry mode?	- None	- N=2,416, secondary - MNEs/Vietnam - Logistic regression	- Investment duration and amount and advertising intensity have a positive effect on the likelihood of a WOS vs. JV. - Competitive intensity has a positive effect on the likelihood of choosing a WOS over a COOP mode. - The host country's level of risk has a positive effect on the choice of a JV or COOP mode vs. WOS. - Cultural distance has a positive effect on the likelihood of choosing a WOS over a JV or COOP mode.
Wan et al. (2023)	What are the antecedents and outcomes of entry mode choice?	- None	- N=230, secondary - MNEs/Worldwide - Meta-analysis	- Cultural distance, host country experience, international experience, R&D and advertising intensity, parent size, and unrelated entry all have an effect on ownership mode choice (i.e., WOS or not). - Choosing WOS has a positive effect on performance. - Host market size and host country and international experience have a positive effect on WOS choice.
Wei et al. (2014)	What are the determinants of exporting firms' choice for FDI?	- Productivity heterogeneity theory - Strategic tripod framework	- N=225, primary - Exporting firms/China - Logit and tobit models	- Technology-based capability and export experience have a positive effect on the propensity of FDI. - Firm size and being born-global have a positive effect on the choice for FDI, while age has no effect. - Entry barriers, regulatory uncertainty, and reduction of government interference have a negative effect on FDI choice, whereas protection of IPR has a positive effect.
Yamanoi and Asaba (2018)	How does family ownership affect investment mode choice and how does corruption in host countries moderate this?	- Socioemotional wealth perspective	- N=770, secondary - Listed firms/ Japan - Multinomial logit model	- Firms with greater degrees of family ownership more likely engage in greenfield investment and full equity ownership (vs. partial ownership). - These relationships are moderated by host country levels of corruption such that they are stronger in countries with higher levels of corruption.
Zhang et al. (2023)	How does institutional distance affect the choice of equity-based entry modes and what are moderators for this relationship?	- Institutional theory - Transaction cost theory	- N=219, secondary - MNEs/Worldwide - Meta-analysis	- Institutional distance has a negative effect on the level of entry mode commitment. - Formal institutional distance has a negative effect on equity-based entry mode, while informal institutional distance has a nonsignificant negative effect. - Contextual factors, measurement factors, and theoretical orientation have a moderating effect on the relationship.
Zhao, Luo and Suh (2004)	How do transaction cost determinants affect entry mode choice?	- Transaction cost theory	- N=38, secondary - MNEs/Worldwide - Meta-analysis	- The combined overall effects of transaction cost-based determinants are consistent with the predictions of transaction cost economics. - The findings of existing studies are moderated to varying degrees by both study-setting factors (e.g., location, country of origin, industry type) and statistical artifacts.

Note: B2C=Business-to-Consumer; CEO=Chief Executive Officer; COOP=Cooperative; FDI=Foreign Direct Investment; INV=International New Venture; IPR=Intellectual Property Rights; JV=Joint Venture; MNE=Multinational Enterprise; R&D=Research and Development; SEM=Structural Equation Modeling; SMEs=Small and Medium-Sized Enterprises; WOS=Wholly Owned Subsidiary.

Figure A—4: Selected Studies on Manufacturing and Service Firms' Operation Mode Choice and Foreign Direct Investments as Dependent Variable

Source: Own Creation

2.3.2. Commerce and Online Firms' Operation Mode Choice and Foreign Direct Investments

In contrast to the literature on manufacturing and service firms, studies on the operation mode choice of international commerce and online firms are scarce (see Figure A—5). To gain a comprehensive overview of the literature to date, selected conceptual studies and case study analyses are also considered here.

Only three empirical studies have examined antecedents in the specific context of commerce firms. Evans, Mavondo and Bridson (2008) find a negative effect of psychic distance on operation mode choice, while international experience has a positive effect. Drawing on the Uppsala internationalization process model, network theory, and the born-global literature, Picot-Coupey, Burt and Cliquet (2014) identify the perceived market attractiveness as well as strategic and ownership conditions as the critical antecedents of commerce firms' operation mode choice. Swoboda, Elsner and Olejnik (2015) specifically focus on preferred entry modes of commerce firms, which have a positive effect on subsequent mode choice (e.g., FDI). This effect is reinforced by international experience and expansion speed. Notably, Huang and Sternquist (2007) conceptually draw on institutional theory and propose that commerce firms' mode choice is related to the host country's ROL following an inverted U-shape. Likewise, home country policy and institutional distance are argued to be influential.

In the case of online firms, empirical insights into the specific antecedents of operation mode or FDI decisions are almost nonexistent. Conceptually, Ekeledo and Sivakumar (2004b) were the first to identify specific characteristics of service firms' mode choices in the context of e-commerce. The authors propose that the degree of firms' ability to digitalize services determines their operation mode choice. However, several internal and external factors (e.g., regulations, tariffs, and internet infrastructure) may affect this relationship. A decade later, Watson et al. (2018) discuss new digital and relational market entry strategies of online firms and ECFs. The authors argue that hybrid (i.e., digital and relational) strategies are suitable for ECFs with a strong online brand and customer relationships. Specifically, local legal, logistical, market, and cultural factors are argued to be critical contexts for ECFs' operation mode choices. More recently, Brouthers et al. (2022) have suggested that IB research has to consider "non-traditional" operation modes to understand digital firms' specific mode decisions. They argue that digitalization has led to new distinct types of market entry that allow for exploring and exploiting local resources differently. Pertaining to online firms and ECFs, they characterize "virtual presence" as a new and distinct operation mode not requiring physical entry anymore. Moreover, "managed ecosystems" relate to digital platform businesses and their unique network capabilities or digital infrastructure replacing the need for traditional FDI, for example. Responding to this, Hennart (2022) fundamentally disagrees, arguing that the new modes presented are essentially not new and can sufficiently be explained by transaction cost theory and traditional mode literature.

Based on a case study of eBay, Mahnke and Venzin (2003) found that digital information good providers tend to enter foreign markets through entry modes allowing the control of branding, advertising, and gaining access to customers. Thereby, online firms critically rely on specific e-commerce host country factors such as internet and telecommunication infrastructure for operation mode decisions. Wentrup (2016) suggest that online service firms focus on gaining first mover advantages. Thereby, they prefer controlled entry modes and consider online-oriented host country parameters such as internet penetration but still follow a gradual internationalization pattern. Cahen and Borini (2020) further highlight the importance of specific digital competencies (e.g., cross-cultural programming skills, global virtual networks) as critical capabilities for operation mode choice of digital firms. Based on their case study analysis of digital firms in Brazil, they propose that online international expansion has a positive effect on non-equity outward investments. Moreover, this association is moderated by the international orientation of the entrepreneur.

Empirically, only Stallkamp, Chen and Li (2023) have examined the specific FDI decisions of born digital firms. They find that cultural and geographic distance have positive effects on born digitals' FDI, but this link is moderated by the business model type (i.e., business-to-business (B2B) vs. business-to-consumer (B2C)). However, no study has specifically addressed ECFs' mode decisions or FDI so far, which are likely different due to their hybrid business models.

Author(s) and year	Research question	Theory/ framework	Sample and method	Core findings
Commerce Firms				
Evans, Mavondo and Bridson (2008)	How is psychic distance related to firm performance and which role do international experience and centralization play?	- Concept of psychic distance	- N=102, primary - International retailers/Worldwide - SEM	- Psychic distance has a positive effect on retailers' financial performance and strategic effectiveness. - The relationship between psychic distance and financial performance is mediated by entry strategy and adaptation. - International experience and centralization of decision-making do not affect psychic distance, but mode choice.
Huang and Sternquist (2007)	How do institutions affect the foreign market entry decisions of retailers?	- Institutional theory	- Conceptual	- Proposition: "The entry mode in terms of the level of resource commitment has an inverted U-shaped relationship with the strength of rule of law in the host country." - Proposition: "When government policies in the home country are less favorable, retailers will favor entry modes that involve relatively high resource commitments." - Proposition: "When the cultural distance between the host and the home countries is small, retailers will favor high-control modes of entry."
Picot-Coupey, Burt and Cliquet (2014)	What are the antecedents of retailers' expansion mode choice?	- Internationalization process theory - Network theory - Born-global theory	- N=43, primary - Fashion retailers/France - PLS SEM	- The international marketing plan, the perceived attractiveness of the foreign market, and strategic and ownership conditions are the major determinants of firms' expansion mode choice. - In contrast to the view of incremental international market development, fashion retailers likely open company-owned stores right from the entry stage. - Retailers may perceive both a high attractiveness and a large psychic distance, which leads to the choice of a resource-intensive mode in the overall assessment.

Figure A—5 to be continued.

Figure A—5 continued.

Swoboda, Elsner and Olejnik (2015)	How do past mode choices influence entry mode decisions?	- Institutional theory - Knowledge-based view	- N=30, secondary - Grocery retailers/Worldwide - Logistic regression	- A greater frequency of adopting a certain entry mode has a positive effect on choosing this entry mode again. - Political distance has a negative moderating effect on the relationship between a preferred mode and subsequent mode choices. - International experience and internationalization speed have a positive moderating effect on the relationship.
Online Firms				
Brouthers et al. (2022)	Which non-traditional entry modes can be defined that are unique to the digital context?	- Framework of non-traditional entry modes	- Conceptual	- Virtual presence modes relate to foreign entries in which no physical entry is undertaken for customer/user acquisition, although the firm appears to be in the country. - Managed ecosystems relate to foreign entries of multi-sided platforms, in which platforms leverage their firm-specific digital infrastructure and promote localization. - Capital access modes relate to foreign market entries for seeking and gaining access to new financial resources. - Innovation outposts relate to foreign entries for exploring resources in countries by gaining an insider status.
Cahen and Borini (2020)	Which capabilities enable digital firms' international online expansion and which equity mode is preferred?	- Resource-based view	- N=8, primary/secondary - Digital firms/Brazil - Multiple case study method	- International digital competence, i.e., cross-cultural programming skills, global virtual networks, cross-border digital monetizing adaptability, and business model reconfiguration, have a positive effect on the online expansion of digital firms. - Online international expansion has a positive effect on non-equity outward investments. - This relationship is moderated by the international orientation of the entrepreneur.
Ekeledo and Sivakumar (2004b)	How does e-commerce affect the market entry mode strategies of service firms?	- Resource-based view	- Conceptual	- Internationally traded services can be divided into two types of firms using e-commerce based on a firm's digitalization ability, i.e., full- and partial-digital services. - The digitalization ability benefits of a service determines the entry-mode choice of these firms. - Several internal and external factors such as cultural differences, regulations, tariff and non-tariff barriers, and internet infrastructure moderate the relationship between digitalization ability and entry mode choice.
Hennart (2022)	How much is new in Brouthers et al.'s new foreign entry modes and do they challenge transaction cost theory?	- Transaction cost theory	- Conceptual	- The four modes proposed by Brouthers et al. have already been explained by transaction cost theory. - The term "exploration" is inappropriate to describe most resource and strategic asset acquisition FDI. - Significant variation in embeddedness exists within some of the identified novel entry modes, which challenges the explanatory power of the framework. - The presence of intermediaries disrupts the proposed direct relationship between the need for embeddedness and the choice of entry mode.
Mahnke and Venzin (2003)	How does the internationalization process of digital information good providers look like?	- Internalization theory	- N=1, secondary - eBay - Exploratory case study analysis	- Digital information good providers aim to enter foreign markets through entry modes allowing for control of branding and advertising, gaining access to customers, and benefiting from economies of scale (i.e., network effects). - They prefer foreign markets with high internet penetration and strong telecommunication infrastructure. - They prefer to penetrate markets more rapidly than physical good providers because of lower costs of learning.
Stallkamp, Chen and Li (2023)	How does cultural and geographic distance affect the FDI choice of born digital firms?	- None	- N=129, secondary - Born digitals/USA - Conditional logit model	- Cultural and geographic distance have a positive effect on born digital firms' choice of FDI (vs. other modes). - The positive effect of distance is moderated by the business model type (i.e., B2B vs. B2C firms). - Acquisitions are related to cultural distance, whereas geographic distance is more related to greenfield FDI.
Watson et al. (2018)	How does the changing global business environment affect international market entry strategy?	- None	- Conceptual	- Digital strategies benefit ECFs with high brand strength and a product range that is easy to digitize. - Hybrid strategies benefit ECFs with a strong online brand presence and strong customer relationships. - Market entry strategies are affected by local legal, logistical, market, and cultural factors in digital environments. - Online retailing and relationship marketing combine digital and relational approaches that support expansion.
Wentrup (2016)	How do online service providers internationalize in terms of speed, geography, and mode of entry?	- Various internationalization theories	- N=19, primary/secondary - Service providers/Sweden - Case study analysis	- Online service providers typically aim for a rapid early pace of internationalization and a fast time-to-market to gain first-mover advantages. - Online service providers prefer controlled entry modes. - Online service providers choose foreign markets depending on online parameters like internet penetration.

Note: B2B=Business-to-Business; B2C=Business-to-Consumer; FDI=Foreign Direct Investment; PLS=Partial Least Squares; SEM=Structural Equation Modeling.

Figure A—5: Studies on Commerce and Online Firms' Operation Mode Choice and Foreign Direct Investments as Dependent Variable

Source: Own Creation

2.4. *Literature on Effects of International Control Decisions and E-Commerce Firms' Internationalization on Performance*

2.4.1. *Manufacturing and Service Firms' International Control Decisions*

International business research has analyzed various performance outcomes of manufacturing or service firms' international control decisions. On the one hand, scholars have studied the effects of firms' *depth of control*, conceptualized as operation modes, on performance. On the other hand, studies have examined the effects of firms' *breadth of control* across countries, conceptualized as firms' scope of subsidiary network, on performance. However, both decisions have only been studied separately so far and yield mixed findings (see Figure A—6).

Regarding the *depth of control*, most studies have focused on *overall firm performance* outcomes. Rasheed (2005) suggest a negative relationship between depth of control and international revenue growth when domestic markets are growing. In contrast, they find a positive effect when foreign market risks are high. An initial meta-analysis by Tihanyi, Griffith and Russell (2005) does not find a significant effect of depth of control on the performance of MNEs. In a replication of this study, Magnusson et al. (2008) are able to show a significant but weak relationship between cultural distance and performance via depth of control. These are moderated in opposite directions when MNE origin, time effects, and cultural distance measures are varied. Drawing on transaction cost theory, Brouthers and Nakos (2004) demonstrate how higher depth of control leads to better performance of SMEs. Brouthers, Brouthers and Werner (2008) additionally show that that control decisions explained by real option and transaction cost theory lead to better perceived performance. Kim and Gray (2008) provide similar results, indicating better non-financial performance but no significant differences for financial performance. Brouthers (2013) substantiate these findings further for a sample of EU firms. Chang, Chung and Moon (2013) also support these predictions, adding that high depth of control leads to better performance in industries characterized by high levels of intangible resources. Holtbrügge and Berning (2018) refer to a revisited internationalization process model, noting that Chinese firms perform better in Germany with high depth of control. Firms' home government support further moderates this relationship. A decade later, Zhao, Ma and Yang (2017) provide a further meta-analysis, showing that a high depth of control has an overall positive effect on firm performance. Substantiating these findings, Giachetti, Manzi and Colapinto (2019) also report overall positive effects of higher depth of control on firm performance. Thereby, the relationship is stronger for firms entering developing (vs. developed) countries. Finally, Wan et al. (2023) conclude that choosing high control within countries not only results in better firm performance but also higher firm survival in a recent meta-analysis.

Fewer studies have explicitly considered *international performance* outcomes in this context. Blesa and Ripolles (2008) show that higher depth of control has a positive effect on the international performance of Belgian firms but a negative effect in the case of Spanish firms. Ripollés and Blesa (2012) reveal that higher depth of control has a positive effect on the international performance of INVs with strong marketing capabilities. Unlike expected, Hollender, Zapkau and Schwens (2017) demonstrate that no operation mode per se has a significant effect on the foreign performance of German SMEs. Instead, international experience and product adaptation moderate this relationship, making performance outcomes context dependent. Cui and Xu (2019) indicate that emerging market firms benefit from high depth of control especially when they have high levels of organizational slack and originate from locations with market-supporting institutions. Amankwah-Amoah et al. (2022) additionally reveal that high depth of control mediates the effects of foreign market knowledge on firms' international performance. Kalinic and Brouthers (2022) indicate an analogous pathway of SMEs' entrepreneurial orientation via higher depth of control on export performance. Similarly, Li, He and Sousa (2023) argue that product development capabilities increase international performance through aligned depth of control, contingent on entrepreneurial orientation.

In terms of the *breadth of control*, fewer studies exist that all examine *overall firm performance* as an outcome. In an early study, Delios and Beamish (1999) already report positive effects of increasing breadth of control on firm profitability. Goerzen and Beamish (2003) report similar results, indicating a positive effect of control across countries on performance. Lu and Beamish (2004) provide evidence for an S-shaped relationship between increasing breadth of control and firm performance. This link is moderated by firms' intangible assets related to technology and advertising. Nath, Nachiappan and Ramanathan (2010) show that higher breadth of control as part of international diversification has a positive effect on firm performance, while product/service diversification has the opposite effect. These results are supported by Khavul, Pérez-Nordtvedt and Wood (2010), who also report a positive effect of increasing breadth of control on INVs' performance. Drawing on meta-analytic procedures, Kirca et al. (2011) synthesize previous findings and show an overall positive effect of higher breadth of control on performance. This relationship is moderated by firm-specific assets such as R&D and advertising intensity. Building on this, Kirca et al. (2012b) suggest that these effects further depend on, for example, firms' strategic motivations, industry characteristics, and home country factors. Yang, Martins and Driffield (2013) report that the positive effects of control on performance are even stronger across developing (vs. developed) countries. Substantiating these findings, Schwens et al. (2018a) again provide meta-analytic support for a positive effect of the breadth of control on performance. Moreover, knowledge intensity negatively moderates this relationship. Arte and Larimo (2022) go beyond a linear positive effect, providing evidence for an inverted U-shaped relationship between increasing breadth of control and firm performance. Finally, Elbanna et al. (2024) indicate that increasing breadth of control has a positive effect on internationalization outcomes such as productivity, competitiveness, and profitability. Notably, the authors consider entry mode learning (i.e., depth of control) to be an important moderator, which is not supported. However, no study has explicitly considered *international performance* in this context.

Author(s) and year	Research question	Theory/ framework	Sample and method	Core findings
Depth of International Control				
Amankwah-Amoah et al. (2022)	See Figure A—4.			
Blesa and Ripolles (2008)	See Figure A—4.			
Brouthers (2013)	See Figure A—4.			
Brouthers, Brouthers and Werner (2008)	See Figure A—4.			
Brouthers and Nakos (2004)	What drives SMEs' entry mode choice and what are consequences for performance?	- Transaction cost theory	- N=293, primary - SMEs/Greece, Netherlands - Logistic regression	- SMEs with more developed internal control systems that make greater asset-specific investments typically prefer equity modes of entry. - SMEs that enter countries characterized by high environmental uncertainty prefer non-equity modes of entry. - SMEs using (non) equity modes of entry when transaction cost theory predicts (non) equity modes perform better than those using (equity) non-equity modes of entry.
Chang, Chung and Moon (2013)	When do WOS perform better than JVs?	- Internalization theory - Transaction cost theory	- N=799, secondary - JVs/China - Probit regression	- Converted WOS have a higher performance than continued JVs in industries that are characterized by high levels of intangible assets (e.g., technology or brand). - This improvement is stronger in industries that are characterized by high R&D and advertising intensity. - In industries characterized by high levels of intangible resources, WOS perform better than JVs, after controlling the local knowledge or resources of JV partners.
Cui and Xu (2019)	How does conducting FDI affect the profitability of emerging economy firms?	- Resource dependence theory	- N=973, secondary - MNEs/China - Difference in difference analysis	- Emerging market MNEs can realize profitability gains by conducting FDI through diversifying from home resource dependence and enhancing critical resource supplies. - Firms that have more organizational slack acquire more intangible assets and benefit more from FDI than firms with a lower level of organizational slack. - For emerging market MNEs originating from home locations with market-supporting institutions, the motivation to diversify from resource dependence is stronger.
Giachetti, Manzi and Colapinto (2019)	How does entry mode choice influence firms' performance?	- Various internationalization theories	- N=133, secondary - MNEs/Worldwide - Meta-analysis	- Overall, entry mode degree of control has a positive effect on firm performance. - The relationship between entry mode degree of control and firm performance is strengthened for firms entering developing countries (vs. firms entering developed countries).
Hollender, Zapkau and Schwens (2017)	How does SMEs' foreign market entry mode choice influence foreign venture performance?	- Resource-based view	- N=133, primary - SMEs/Germany - Hierarchical linear regression	- SMEs' choice of foreign market entry mode has no direct effect on foreign venture performance. - International experience and product adaptation moderate the relationship between SMEs' foreign market entry mode choice and venture performance. - Non-equity entry modes may hinder foreign market monitoring and expose SMEs to external challenges and potential opportunistic behavior of foreign partners.
Holtbrügge and Berning (2018)	How do different entry modes affect performance and what is the role of home government support?	- Revisited Uppsala Model	- N=556, secondary - MNEs/Germany - Regression analysis	- Location choice, activity mode, establishment mode, and market presence differently affect the performance of MNEs in Germany. - Firms that enter Germany in locations with many Chinese investors have a higher post-entry performance than those that invest in locations with few Chinese investors. - Firms entering Germany through foreign production have a higher post-entry performance than those that enter through sales offices.

Figure A—6 to be continued.

Figure A—6 continued.

Kalinic and Brouthers (2022)	See Figure A—4.			
Kim and Gray (2008)	How does MNEs' entry mode choice affect foreign affiliate performance?	- Transaction cost theory	- N=215, primary - MNEs/South Korea - Logistic regression	- The cultural distance index as conceptualized by Hofstede has a positive effect on entry mode choice. - Foreign MNEs that follow the entry mode predicted by the extended transaction costs model exhibit poorer performance than those that do not follow this model in terms of non-financial performance. - There are no significant differences regarding firms' financial performance.
Li, He and Sousa (2023)	How do product development capabilities affect export performance via export channel selection?	- Resource-based view - Institutional theory	- N=294, primary - Export firms/China - Logistic regression	- Firms with stronger product development capabilities are more likely to use a hierarchical channel. - Firms with weaker product development capabilities are more likely to use a non-hierarchical channel. - Firms that use export channels aligning with product development capabilities have better export performance, depending on entrepreneurial orientation and cultural-cognitive distance.
Magnusson et al. (2008)	See Figure A—4.			
Rasheed (2005)	How do domestic and foreign environmental factors affect the relationship of entry mode and performance?	- None	- N=123, secondary - SMEs/USA - Hierarchical regression	- In growing domestic environments, firms have a higher international revenue growth when using non-equity-based (exporting) foreign market entry modes. - When foreign market risks are high, international revenue growth is higher for equity-based modes.
Ripollés and Blesa (2012)	How do marketing capabilities affect entry mode choice of INVs and international performance?	- Resource-based view	- N=135, primary - INVs/Spain - SEM	- The marketing capabilities of INVs have a positive effect on the choice of high commitment entry mode. - Higher commitment entry modes have a positive effect on the international performance of INVs with strong marketing capabilities. - INVs with better marketing capabilities benefit from higher international performance.
Tihanyi, Griffith and Russell (2005)	See Figure A—4.			
Wan et al. (2023)	See Figure A—4.			
Zhao, Ma and Yang (2017)	How does entry mode choice influence firms' performance?	- Various internationalization theories	- N=44, secondary - MNEs/Worldwide - Meta-analysis - Survival analysis	- Transaction cost theory offers the most consistent predictions for a positive relationship between entry mode choice and performance, in contrast to other theories that indicate contradictory findings. - MNEs' choice of WOS as an entry mode has a positive effect on firms' performance. - Industry type, the time span of data, data sources, and subsidiary age are contextual moderators for the relationships between entry mode and performance.
Breadth of International Control				
Arte and Laimo (2022)	How does product diversification affect the international diversification-performance relationship?	- None	- N=107, secondary - MNEs/Worldwide - Meta-analysis	- The breadth of geographic diversification overall has a positive effect on MNEs' performance. - The relationship between international diversification (as a composite measure) and firm performance is characterized by a non-linear inverted U-shape. - Product diversification moderates the relationship between international diversification and performance such that performance is higher in firms with low product diversity.
Delios and Beamish (1999)	See Figure A—2.			
Elbanna et al. (2024)	How does SMEs' level of foreign market involvement (i.e., intensity and scope) affect internationalization outcomes?	- Organizational learning theory	- N=180, primary - SMEs/Three developed/emerging countries - Regression analysis	- A direct relationship between levels of foreign market involvement and internationalization outcomes exists (e.g., increased efficiency, increased overall competitiveness, increased sales profitability, market access). - Entry-mode learning potential moderates the relationship between intensity but not scope of foreign market involvement and internationalization outcomes.
Goerzen and Beamish (2003)	How does MNEs' geographic scope affect economic performance?	- Internalization theory	- N=580, primary - MNEs/Japan - SEM	- MNEs' geographic scope can be distinguished by two related elements: international asset dispersion and country environment diversity. - MNEs' international asset dispersion has a positive effect on economic performance, while the country environment diversity has a negative effect.
Khavul, Pérez-Nordtvedt and Wood (2010)	How does organizational entrainment affect the link between degree, scope, speed and performance of INVs?	- Entrainment theory - INV theory	- N=166, primary - INVs/China, India, South Africa - Hierarchical regression	- An increased scope of INVs' internationalization has a positive effect on INVs' performance. - Entrainment (i.e., temporal fit and synchronization of activity cycles with customers) with INVs' most important international customers positively moderates the relationship between international scope and performance. - With a certain level of internationalization, the benefits of entrainment emerge as costs are more efficiently spread.

Figure A—6 to be continued.

Figure A—6 continued.

Kirca et al. (2011)	See Figure A—2.			
Kirca et al. (2012b)	How do firm-, industry-, and (home) country-level factors moderate the multinationality-performance relationship?	- None	- N=152, secondary - MNEs/World-wide - Meta-analysis	- The positive effects of multinationality on performance depend on the type of multinationality, firm strategic motivations, industry characteristics, and home country development. - Unlike expected, firm size and the stage of internationalization are not significant moderators. - Different research contexts, measurement issues, and firm characteristics should be considered as moderators.
Lu and Beamish (2004)	How does multinationality affect firm performance?	- None	- N=1,489, secondary - MNEs/Japan - Regression analysis	- The relationship between geographic diversification and firm performance takes a horizontal S-shape. - Firms' intangible assets, i.e., technology and advertising skills, have a positive moderating effect on the relation between geographic diversification and firm performance. - Across different stages of internationalization, the costs and benefits of international diversification differ.
Nath, Nachiappan and Ramanathan (2010)	How do firms' functional capabilities and diversification strategies affect financial performance?	- Resource-based view	- N=102, secondary - Logistics firms/UK - Regression analysis	- Marketing and operations capabilities have the strongest effects on financial performance. - International diversification (i.e. geographic scope) has a positive effect on logistics firms' performance. - Product/service diversification has a negative effect on logistics firms' performance.
Schwens et al. (2018a)	How does the degree, scope and speed of internationalization affect firm performance?	- None	- N=43, secondary - MNEs/World-wide - Meta-analysis	- The degree and scope of internationalization overall have a positive effect on performance. - Knowledge intensity has a positive moderating effect on the relationship between speed and performance. - Knowledge intensity has a negative moderating effect on the relationship between the scope of internationalization and performance.
Yang, Martins and Driffield (2013)	How does the location of FDI affect the multinationality-performance relationship?	- Eclectic paradigm	- N=16,000, secondary - MNEs/World-wide - Regression analysis	- Multinationality (i.e., increasing number of FDI across countries) has a positive effect on firm performance. - FDI in developing countries has a larger effect on performance than in the case of such investments in developed countries. - The relationship between firms' FDI and return to investment is U-shaped in developing countries.

Note: FDI=Foreign Direct Investment; INV=International New Venture; JV=Joint Venture; MNE=Multinational Enterprise; R&D=Research and Development; SEM=Structural Equation Modeling; SMEs=Small and Medium-Sized Enterprises; WOS=Wholly Owned Subsidiary.

Figure A—6: Selected Studies on Manufacturing and Service Firms' International Control Decisions as Independent Variable

Source: Own Creation

2.4.2. Commerce Firms' International Control Decisions

Several studies have examined the effects of commerce firms' international control decisions on overall firm or international performance, but no respective studies exist in the context of online firms or ECFs (see Figure A—7).

Only two studies have analyzed the effect of *depth of control* in terms of operation mode choice on performance. Evans, Mavondo and Bridson (2008) provide mixed results for the effect of higher depth of control on *overall firm performance*. While the choice of high control operation modes has a positive effect on strategic effectiveness, they have a negative effect on financial performance. Gielens and Dekimpe (2001) have explicitly studied commerce firms' *international performance* as an outcome of depth of control. Retailers entering early with full control operation modes at larger scale, while offering a store format new to the host market and familiar to the parent, perform better internationally.

Concerning commerce firms' *breadth of control* in terms of their subsidiary network or related conceptualizations, studies report contradictory findings. Chan,

Finnegan and Sternquist (2011) show a negative effect of higher breadth of control on sales growth. However, there is no effect on commerce firms' return on investment. In contrast, Oh, Sohl and Rugman (2015) indicate (inverted) S-shaped relationships between the breadth of control and performance as part of commerce firms' intra- or interregional diversification. An S-shaped relationship is also supported by Dimitrova, Kim and Smith (2019). However, the effects are reinforced by firms' foreign market growth and reversed by store format diversification. Focusing on geographic regions instead, Dimitrova, Rosenbloom and Andras (2014) find that commerce firms operating subsidiaries in fewer regions perform better than those operating in more geographic regions. Shi et al. (2018) find that higher breadth of control as part of geographic diversification has a positive effect on commerce firms' financial performance. Finally, Nath, Kirca and Kim (2021) suggest a curvilinear relationship between increasing breadth of control and commerce firms' performance. This relationship is positively moderated by the level of brand standardization. Finally, the only study on *international performance* by Tolstoy, Jonsson and Sharma (2016) has analyzed commerce firms' online sales channel adoption and increasing breadth of control. They find that higher breadth of control has a positive effect on international sales performance but negatively affects the effect of online sales channel adoption.

Author(s) and year	Research question	Theory/ framework	Sample and method	Core findings
Depth of International Control				
Evans, Mavondo and Bridson (2008)	See Figure A—4.			
Gielens and Dekimpe (2001)	How do the scale, mode and order of entry or format adaptation, affect retailers' foreign sales performance and what are moderators?	- None	- N=75, secondary - Top grocery retailers/Europe - Growth curve analysis	- Early entry with large scale, lack of partners or acquired assets, while offering a store format, which is both new to the host market and familiar to the parent firm has a positive effect on post-entry sales in the long run. - Characteristics of the foreign operations' retail mix, the parent firm's resources, and host-market characteristics such as the population or wealth moderate the relationships to different degrees.
Breadth of International Control				
Chan, Finnegan and Sternquist (2011)	How do external and internal factors affect the sales growth and ROI of international retailers?	- Resource-based view	- N=200, secondary - International retailers/ Worldwide - Regression analysis	- Surprisingly, neither external nor internal factors have a significant influence on retail firms' ROI. - Retail portfolio management (i.e., number of formats) and experience (i.e., number of foreign markets served) have a negative effect on sales growth. - The development level, country income, and expansion speed have positive effects on sales growth, while population and country risk have no significant effect.
Dimitrova, Kim and Smith (2019)	How does degree of internationalization affect retailers' performance?	- Internationalization process theory	- N=18, secondary - International retailers/ Worldwide - Fixed-effects regression analysis	- The relationship between the degree of retailer internationalization and their performance follows an S-Curve. - After initiating international expansion, retailers tend to face a decline in performance, turning into increasing performance with further expansion. - As internationalization continues, retailers again face decreasing performance as complexity increases. - This relationship is reinforced by foreign market growth (of the firm) and reversed by increasing store format diversification.
Dimitrova, Rosenbloom and Andras (2014)	How does a retailer's international involvement affect retailer performance and which factors moderate this relation?	- Corporate diversification theory	- N=16, secondary - International retailers/ Worldwide - Fixed-effects panel regression analysis	- Retailers operating in fewer regions have stronger performance than retailers operating in more regions. - Retailers benefit from sales and management synergies when they have operations in fewer geographic regions, which can result in competitive advantages. - Cultural distance between home and host countries moderates the relationship between a retailer's degree of international involvement and their performance.

Figure A—7 to be continued.

Figure A—7 continued.

Nath, Kirca and Kim (2021)	How does internationalization affect the performance of retailers and do brand standardization and cultural diversity moderate this?	- Organizational learning theory	- N=73, secondary - International retailers/ Worldwide - Random-effects hierarchical model	- The internationalization of retailers has a positive effect on their firm performance, which curvilinearly increases as internationalization advances. - This relationship is quadratically moderated positively by the degree of brand standardization. - With increasing cultural diversity of foreign markets, the moderating effect of brand standardization becomes weaker.
Oh, Sohl and Rugman (2015)	How do inter- and intra-regional diversification affect firm performance?	- Internationalization process theory	- N=65, secondary - International retailers/ Worldwide - Regression analysis	- Intra-regional diversification has an inverted S-curve relationship with firm performance. - Inter-regional diversification has an S-curve relationship with firm performance. - Product diversification (i.e., across retail formats) has a negative moderating effect on the relationship between inter-regional diversification and firm performance.
Shi et al. (2018)	How do geographic and format diversification affect financial performance?	- Corporate diversification theory	- N=172, secondary - International retailers/ Worldwide - Regression analysis	- Geographic diversification has a positive effect on the financial performance of international retailers. - Format diversification has a negative effect on the financial performance of international retailers. - Format diversification has a negative moderating effect on the relationship between geographic diversification and retailers' financial performance.
Tolstoy, Jonsson and Sharma (2016)	How do retailers' online sales channel adoption and geographic scope affect their international sales performance?	- None	- N=562, secondary - Retail firms/Sweden - Regression analysis	- Online sales channel adoption has a positive effect on the international sales performance of retailers. - Retail firms' geographic scope has a positive direct effect on their international sales performance. - Geographic scope negatively moderates the effect of online sales channel adoption on sales performance.

Note: ROI=Return on Investment.

Figure A—7: Studies on Commerce Firms' International Control Decisions as Independent Variable

Source: Own Creation

2.4.3. *Effects of E-Commerce Firms' Internationalization on Performance*

As highlighted in Section 2.4.2., there is currently a lack of research examining the international control decisions of ECFs. Therefore, this section incorporates additional studies on the effects of ECFs' capabilities and further internationalization decisions on performance outcomes. While these studies initially concentrated on the overall firm performance of ECFs as a dependent variable, more recent research has shifted its focus more towards examining international performance as an outcome (see Figure A—8).

Three early studies have explored the effects of various specific capabilities, which affect the overall performance of ECFs. Saini and Johnson (2005) find that strategic flexibility has a negative effect on the performance of proactive market-oriented firms, while information technology capability has a positive effect. Website performance (e.g., website visitors and conversation rate) has a positive effect on ECFs' overall performance as well. Joong-Kun Cho, Ozment and Sink (2008) further highlight the positive effects of ECFs' logistics capability on firm performance, while unlike expected, logistics outsourcing does not affect their performance. Likewise, there is no moderating effect of outsourcing on the relationship between logistics capability and performance unlike expected. From a resource-based perspective, Colton, Roth and Bearden (2010) show that ECFs' market orientation has a positive effect on their brand strength and relations to suppliers. These resource variables in turn have a positive effect on firm performance regardless of their headquarter location. More than a decade later, only Swoboda and Sinning (2022) have analyzed performance outcomes of ECFs' international decision-making. The authors reveal positive effects of an irregular rhythm and high speed of internationalization on ECFs' growth. However, these effects are negatively moderated by both cultural-cognitive and regulative distances but not normative distances.

Several studies have specifically examined ECFs' international performance as an outcome. Investigating SMEs active in online internationalization, Sinkovics, Sinkovics and Jean (2013) were among the first to study the export performance in an e-commerce context. Although they provide evidence for a positive effect of the internet as a complementary sales channel on export performance, they conclude that it is not an alternative to a physical presence. Focusing on the online channel alone does not lead to better export performance but instead carries the risk of a "virtuality trap" by neglecting critical onsite interactions. Goldman et al. (2021) find a positive effect of the use of digital marketing tactics on international performance of ECFs in both developed and emerging markets. However, this effect appears to be stronger for ECFs originating from emerging vs. developed countries. Tolstoy, Nordman and Vu (2022) have studied effects of online marketing capability but find no direct effect on performance but a partial mediation via market orientation. Both market-driving orientation (i.e., exploration of opportunities) and market-driven orientation (i.e., exploitation of customer needs) drive ECFs' international performance. Tolstoy, Hånell and Özbek (2023) additionally show that effectual market creation has both a direct and an indirect positive effect on ECFs' international performance. The indirect effect is mediated by ECFs' insidership in international markets, i.e., activities related to international marketing analytics and international networking. Taking a closer look at host country contexts, Eduardsen et al. (2023) reveal negative effects of various export barriers on ECFs' online export performance. These effects are moderated by the home country's level of digital infrastructure and the host country's internet penetration such that the main negative effects are weakened.

Author(s) and year	Research question	Theory/ framework	Sample and method	Core findings
Overall Firm Performance				
Colton, Roth and Bearden (2010)	How do firm orientations and strategic resources affect international ECFs' performance?	- Resource-advantage theory - Resource-based view	- N=174, primary - ECFs/World-wide - SEM	- Market orientation has a positive effect on ECFs' brand strength and supplier relations. - Brand strength and supplier relations as firm resource variables have a positive effect on firm performance. - The headquarters' location does not moderate relationships, indicating that the results can be generalized across countries.
Joong-Kun Cho, Ozment and Sink (2008)	How do ECFs' logistics capability and logistics outsourcing affect their performance?	- None	- N=117, primary - ECFs/USA - Regression analysis	- Firms' logistics capability has a positive effect on firm performance in the e-commerce market. - Surprisingly, outsourcing of logistics and firm performance are not significantly related. - There is no significant relationship between firms' logistics capability and outsourcing and no interactive effect of logistics outsourcing on the relationship of logistics capability and performance.

Figure A—8 to be continued.

Figure A—8 continued.

Saini and Johnson (2005)	How do e-commerce capabilities affect ECFs' performance?	- None	- N=122, primary - Pure online/ brick-and-mortar ECFs/USA - OLS regression	- Strategic flexibility has a negative effect on the performance of proactive market-oriented firms. - IT capability has a positive effect on the performance of proactive market-oriented firms. - Website performance (i.e., website visitors, attraction/conversation rate, and frequency of account access) has a positive effect on ECFs' performance.
Swoboda and Sinning (2022)	How do internationalization rhythm and speed affect ECFs' annual growth and how do institutional distances moderate these effects?	- Internationalization process theory	- N=228, secondary - ECFs/Worldwide - Multilevel regression	- An irregular internationalization rhythm and high internationalization speed have a positive effect on ECFs' annual firm growth. - The focus of ECFs' internationalization has shifted from opportunity recognition to opportunity exploitation. - Regulative and cultural-cognitive distances diminish the time-based internationalization process decision effects. - Surprisingly, normative distance has no moderating effect on any relationship.
International Performance				
Eduardsen et al. (2023)	How do export barriers affect online export performance and how do digital infrastructure and host market internet penetration moderate this relationship?	- None	- N=1,256, primary/secondary - CBEC exporting firms/Europe - SEM	- Export barriers are more prevalent in the case of firms with smaller sizes that lack experience and have no affiliation with other companies. - All different types of CBEC barriers, i.e., financial complexities, coping with foreign markets, supplier restrictions, technical difficulties, and product limitations, have negative effects on online export performance. - The home country's level of digital infrastructure and the foreign market's internet penetration rate have a strong moderating effect on the relationship between CBEC barriers and export performance.
Goldman et al. (2021)	How do strategic orientations affect the use of digital marketing tactics and international performance of small ECFs?	- Traditional theoretical marketing frameworks	- N=446, primary - Small ECFs/Europe - Multigroup SEM	- Using digital marketing tactics has a positive effect on ECFs' international performance across markets. - The effect of digital marketing tactics on international performance is stronger for emerging market ECFs. - Growth orientation has a positive effect on digital marketing tactics only for ECFs from developed markets. - Customer orientation has a negative effect on digital marketing tactics only for ECFs from emerging markets.
Sinkovics, Sinkovics and Jean (2013)	How does the adoption of the internet as an alternative to physical presence contribute to export performance?	- Resource-based view - Transaction cost theory	- N=115, primary - E-Commerce SMES/UK - PLS SEM	- The use of the internet as an alternative to a physical presence does not lead to better export performance. - Using the internet as a complementary sales channel to physical presence has a positive effect on firms' export performance. - Firms with relatively low internet experience benefit more from the internet as a complementary sales channel in terms of better export performance.
Tolstoy, Hånell and Özbek (2023)	How does effectual market creation affect the international performance of small and medium-sized ECFs?	- Effectuation theory	- N=99, primary - E-Commerce SMEs/Sweden - Regression analysis	- Effectual market creation has both a direct and an indirect positive effect on ECFs' international performance. - The positive effect of effectual market creation is mediated by insidership in international markets. - Insidership activities relate to international marketing analytics and international networking of ECFs.
Tolstoy, Nordman and Vu (2022)	How do online marketing capabilities affect the international performance of small and medium-sized ECFs?	- Dynamic capabilities theory	- N=99, primary - E-Commerce SMEs/Sweden - Regression	- Online marketing capability alone does not drive international performance of e-commerce SMEs. - Online marketing capabilities are necessary, however, not alone sufficient to drive the international performance of SMEs using e-commerce as a sales channel. - Marketing ambidexterity (i.e., market-driven and stronger market-driving orientation) partially mediate the effect.

Note: CBEC=Cross-Border Electronic Commerce; ECF=Electronic Commerce Firm; IT=Information Technology; OLS=Ordinary Least Squares; PLS=Partial Least Squares; SEM=Structural Equation Modeling; SMEs=Small and Medium-Sized Enterprises.

Figure A—8: Selected Studies on E-Commerce Firms' Performance as Dependent Variable

Source: Own Creation

2.5. General Research Objectives

The preceding literature review highlights the sustained scholarly interest and dynamic debates in IB research. Despite this, research on ECFs' international decision-making, especially in terms of geographic scope, operation modes and FDI, and international control effects, remains underdeveloped. Likewise, critical questions concerning the role of specific host country contexts in the internationalization of digital firms are left unresolved. This thesis therefore seeks to resolve three major research gaps.

The *first research gap* relates to the specific antecedents of ECFs' geographic scope online, which remain unexplored. Extant research on the antecedents of geographic scope has almost exclusively focused on manufacturing and service firms (e.g., Kirca et al. 2011; Mansion and Bausch 2020). Only one study has considered commerce firms' geographic scope decisions, but not the impact of their unique resources or capabilities tied to the specific business model (Batsakis and Mohr 2017). The same applies to only one study on internet firms (Kotha, Rindova and Rothaermel 2001), leaving the drivers of ECFs' specific geographic scope decisions largely unclear. Scholars have repeatedly called for studies on the role of ECFs' specific digital resources and capabilities in shaping their geographic expansion (e.g., Chabowski and Samiee 2020; Jean and Kim 2020). Furthermore, environmental factors influencing geographic scope decisions are rarely studied, even in the context of manufacturing firms (e.g., Jiménez 2010; Mansion and Bausch 2020). While some scholars suggest that country context may actually lose relevance for digital firms (e.g., Chen et al. 2019), others argue its importance remains critical for ECFs' international decisions (e.g., Schu and Morschett 2017; Swoboda and Sinning 2022). However, research calls indicate the need to explain how specific country contexts affect such decisions of digital firms (e.g., Liu, Zhang-Zhang and Ghauri 2020; Tolstoy et al. 2021). Therefore, Study 1 aims to identify the specific intangible resources ECFs leverage to increase their geographic scope online and examine the moderating role of specific contextual factors in shaping these decisions.

The *second research gap* addressed by this dissertation pertains to the specific determinants affecting the likelihood of ECFs choosing wholly owned FDI. Extensive research has examined firm- and country-level factors affecting operation mode and FDI decisions for manufacturing and service firms (e.g., Wan et al. 2023). Some findings, for example, regarding the impact of international experience, remain inconsistent (e.g., Dow and Larimo 2009, Hernández and Nieto 2015, Tang and Gudergan 2018). Research specific to commerce firms is scarce, with only two studies addressing their antecedents (e.g., Evans, Mavondo and Bridson 2008; Picot-Coupey, Burt and Cliquet 2014) and one offering theoretical insights (Huang and Sternquist 2007). In the online context, just one empirical study considers institutional distances as a determinant of digital firms' FDI (Stallkamp, Chen and Li 2023). This comes as a surprise, as scholars have recently suggested the emergence of new (virtual) presence modes unique to ECFs (Brouthers et al. 2022), which others strongly debate (Hennart 2022). Consequently, scholars have called for studies on the specific mode decisions of ECFs, including their physical presence (e.g., Swoboda and Sinning 2022). Moreover, the role of (online) experience as a traditional antecedent has been questioned (e.g., Pezderka and Sinkovics 2011), which needs clarification. In addition, scholars emphasize the need to clarify the role of specific country factors that are critical for ECFs' business model and have also hardly been analyzed (e.g., Meyer et al. 2023). To address this shortcoming in the literature, Study 2 sheds light on ECFs' specific firm- and country-level antecedent of wholly owned FDI.

The *third research gap* identified by this dissertation concerns the impact of ECFs' depth and breadth of international control on their foreign sales performance, as well as the moderating effects of the market context. Many studies have analyzed the effects of depth and breadth of international control for manufacturing or service firms, but only separately (e.g., Kirca et al. 2011; Wan et al. 2023). Few existing studies on commerce firms indicate inconsistent findings regarding the effects of both depth and breadth of control on performance. For example studies report positive or negative effects of high depth of control (Evans, Mavondo and Bridson 2008; Gielens and Dekimpe 2001) and negative or positively S-shaped effects of high breadth of control (Chan, Finnegan and Sternquist 2011; Dimitrova, Kim and Smith 2019). Regarding ECFs, very few studies have addressed international performance outcomes of ECFs' specific capabilities (Goldman et al. 2021; Tolstoy, Hånell and Özbek 2023; Tolstoy, Nordman and Vu 2022). Only one has considered the impact of specific e-commerce market contexts (Eduardsen et al. 2023). The important mechanisms linking international control to ECFs' foreign sales performance or important market contexts remain unclear. However, scholars have called for such analyses to gain further insights into ECFs' successful international decision-making (Ipsmiller, Dikova and Brouthers 2022; Swoboda and Sinning 2022). To address this gap, Study 3 follows the research objective of examining the effects and possible trade-offs of ECFs' international control for foreign performance and the moderating role of local market contexts.

Building on these research gaps, three studies were designed to pursue the following three main research objectives:

- Analyzing whether and how (strongly) ECFs' intangible resources affect their geographic scope decisions and how host country factors, i.e., ROL, country development, and logistics performance, moderate these effects.
- Identifying whether and how (strongly) specific firm- and host country-level factors drive ECFs' choice of wholly owned FDI.
- Examining whether and how (strongly) ECFs' international control in terms of depth versus breadth drive their foreign sales performance and how host countries' e-commerce market size and growth moderate these effects.

Each of these three main research objectives is examined within a dedicated study. Based on these objectives, all three studies aim to answer important research questions concerning ECFs' specific internationalization decisions across diverse host countries. In Study 1, specific antecedents and contextual moderators of ECFs' online geographic scope decisions are investigated. Study 2 deals with the specific antecedents of ECFs' wholly owned FDI decisions at the firm and country level. Finally, Study 3 builds on the insights of the first two studies, examining the performance outcomes of ECFs' international control decisions and the moderating role of e-commerce market contexts. Finally, in Chapter E, the findings are discussed regarding the contributions to theory and practice, followed by an outlook on further research opportunities. The following section delves into the structure and contributions of each study in greater detail.

3. Structure and Contribution of the Studies

3.1. Antecedents of E-Commerce Firms' Geographic Scope

Driven by ongoing digitalization, ECFs may internationalize with a greater geographic scope than most offline firms (e.g., Yang et al. 2025). Reduced online entry barriers allow for instant and rapid market entry through a virtual presence at low cost (e.g., Schu and Morschett 2017). This allows ECFs to leverage specific intangible resources without the requirement for physical market entry (e.g., Ipsmiller, Dikova and Brouthers 2022). Consequently, ECFs can increase their geographic scope virtually rather than physically, in contrast to commerce firms, for example (e.g., Schu, Morschett and Swoboda 2016). However, whether and how ECFs leverage their unique online resources abroad to operate in an increasing number of online markets remains unclear. Therefore, it is critical to study how ECFs leverage specific intangible resources for their geographic scope decisions and whether and how the transfer of these resources is affected by specific host country context factors.

Building on the above, Study 1 has two motivations. First, there is a lack of theoretical and empirical insights into ECFs' specific internationalization decisions, particularly in terms of geographic scope. Research has studied the antecedents of geographic scope mostly for manufacturing firms (e.g., Kirca et al. 2012a). Scholars have only once addressed this decision in the context of commerce firms (Batsakis and Mohr 2017). While research on ECFs has focused on antecedents of market selection and internationalization speed (e.g., Luo, Zhao and Du 2005; Schu and Morschett 2017; Schu, Morschett and Swoboda 2016), only one study on digital firms has implicitly considered online geographic scope (Kotha, Rindova and Rothaermel 2001). However, the antecedents of ECFs' online geographic scope likely differ from those affecting offline firms due to their virtual presence (e.g., Chabowski and Samiee 2020; Jean and Kim 2020). Second, it is unclear whether and how the value and transfer of ECFs' resources is affected by specific context factors (e.g., Liu, Zhang-Zhang and Ghauri 2020; Tolstoy et al. 2021). Respective insights are also highly important to managers of ECFs aiming to expand their virtual presence. Managers may learn how to leverage unique online resources such as international online experience, website traffic, or social media use (Kotha, Rindova and Rothaermel 2001; Shaheer and Li 2020). Moreover, ECFs may learn how to deal with changing country contexts that may affect their scope decisions differently. Therefore, Study 1 follows two research questions:

- Whether and how (strongly) do intangible resources affect ECFs' geographic scope?
- Whether and how do host country factors, i.e. ROL, country development, and logistics performance, moderate these effects?

Extending the RBV in a digital context, Study 1 proposes a conceptual framework analyzing intangible resources as specific antecedents of ECFs' geographic scope decisions (e.g., Kotha, Rindova and Rothaermel 2001). Moreover, the moderating role of different country contexts is theorized. Traditionally the RBV suggests that firms achieve competitive advantages, also abroad, based on the transfer of valuable, rare, inimitable, and nonsubstitutable resources (Barney 1991). In contrast to offline firms, ECFs leverage new online resources based on real-time data to achieve competitive advantages online (Yang et al. 2025), requiring refinement of the RBV (e.g., Elia et al. 2021). The geographic scope of ECFs still likely depends on important experience and consumer-related resources (Pezderka and Sinkovics 2011). However, new digital resources are intangible, highly scalable, and data-driven (e.g., Gong, He and Lengler 2024). Thus, in Study 1, ECFs' geographic scope is theorized to depend on their international online experience, website traffic, and social media use. Moreover, extensions of the RBV assume the value and transferability of resource advantages to be dependent on specific host country environments (e.g., He, Brouthers and Filatotchev 2013; Priem and Butler 2001; Wan 2005), while their continued role is debated for digital firms (e.g., Chen et al. 2019). Therefore, the effects of ECFs' intangible resources on online geographic scope are theorized to depend on host countries' ROL, country development, and logistics performance (e.g., Oxley and Yeung 2001; Schu and Morschett 2017). These factors are expected to strengthen the effects of ECFs' international online experience, website traffic, and social media use on geographic scope.

To test the hypotheses, multilevel modeling with cross-level interactions is applied to a sample of the 263 leading ECFs in Europe in 2018 that made 2,632 market entries over a period from 1994–2018 across 64 host countries. A foreign market entry was defined as the launch of an online shop in a country with a country-specific domain, language, and currency (e.g., Schu, Morschett and Swoboda 2016; Shneor and Flåten 2008). Only ECFs operating in at least one foreign market with an online shop were considered, while each firm's internationalization path was carefully reconstructed and verified. Cases for which the geographic scope decisions could not be fully obtained over time were excluded.

The results reveal positive effects of international online experience, website traffic, and social media use on ECFs' geographic scope. As expected, ECFs' may leverage their specific intangible experience and consumer-related resources to expand their virtual presence (e.g., Kotha, Rindova and Rothaermel 2001). Applied to a digital context, the RBV can explain ECFs' geographic scope based on valuable, rare, inimitable, and nonsubstitutable online resources (Elia et al. 2021; Schu, Morschett and Swoboda 2016). Social media use is the strongest digital resource and more valuable than online experience (e.g., Knösel, Cheng and Shiu 2025). However, the value and transfer of these resources depends on specific host country context factors (e.g., Kirca et al. 2012b). ECFs can best transfer their international experience and social media use to increase geographic scope by entering countries with a strong ROL, high degree of country development and, most importantly, high local logistics performance. Surprisingly, the effects of website traffic are not moderated. Important implications can be drawn for managers of ECFs interested in the value of intangible online resources for virtual expansion and the still critical role of host country context in this decision.

3.2. Antecedents of E-Commerce Firms' Foreign Direct Investments

Despite their digital nature, many globally leading ECFs establish a physical presence in selected markets over time (e.g., Schu and Morschett 2017). While research has assumed the internet to promote virtual expansion, only a physical presence enables ECFs to transfer their hybrid (i.e., digital and physical) business model and implement full local operations and management (e.g., Batsakis, Konara and Theoharakis 2023; Hua and Wu 2024). This is realized by wholly owned investments in own physical assets such as warehouses and subsidiaries, which are fundamentally different from production-based FDI of manufacturers (e.g., Brouthers et al. 2022). However, little is known about the specific antecedents at the firm and country level that are relevant to ECFs' FDI decisions (e.g., Swoboda and Sinning 2022). Therefore, studying the role of ECFs' specific online experiences and specific country barriers or locations advantages is important to understand their mode decisions and FDI.

Study 2 has two motivations. First, the study adds to the theoretical discussion on operation mode and FDI decisions of digital firms. The business model of ECFs differs from manufacturers' production-based FDI abroad, small manufacturers' online presence, and even i-business firms with purely digital offers (e.g., Lee, Pattnaik and Gaur 2023; Tolstoy, Hånell and Özbek 2023). Scholars have called for studying new virtual operation modes and developing new theory (Brouthers et al. 2022; Ipsmiller, Dikova and Brouthers 2022); which others question (Hennart 2022). Second, while scholars have focused on antecedents of ECFs' virtual internationalization decisions (e.g., speed, Luo, Zhao and Du 2005; market selection or entry; Rothaermel, Kotha and Steensma 2006; Schu and Morschett 2017), only one study has analyzed the physical presence of born digital firms (Stallkamp, Chen and Li 2023). However, the role of (online) experience, for example, has been debated for digital firms' internationalization (e.g., Gabrielsson, Raatikainen and Julkunen 2022). Moreover, the additional role of specific country barriers or location advantages in digital markets for ECFs' hybrid business is unclear. This holds important implications for ECF managers interested in the drivers of FDI but also for manufacturers (e.g., Gong, He and Lengler 2024). The latter increasingly use ECFs for their own international expansion, while policymakers aim to attract growing ECFs to establish their own presence in host countries in order to expand their virtual presence (e.g., Cumming et al. 2023). Therefore, Study 2 aims to answer the following research question:

- Whether and how (strongly) do specific firm- and host country-level factors drive ECFs' choice of wholly owned FDI?

Study 2 proposes a conceptual framework based on capability and refined internationalization process reasonings to analyze the effects of ECFs' online experiences on their wholly owned FDI decisions (e.g., Cahen et al. 2025; Vahlne and Johanson 2017; Yang et al. 2025). Traditional internationalization process theory has characterized firms' expansion as a gradual, path-dependent, and rather slow process (Johanson and Vahlne 1977). However, this process has to be adapted to modern and ECFs' specific capabilities (Vahlne and Johanson 2017). Although digitalization has reduced the need for gradual and slow internationalization, ECFs' physical presence is argued to still require path-dependent online learning. Moreover, their focus has shifted from opportunity recognition to opportunity exploitation (e.g., Coviello, Kano and Liesch 2017; Swoboda and Sinning 2022). Therefore, in Study 2, ECFs' wholly owned FDI decisions are theorized to depend on three types of international online experience that are distinct from traditional offline experience. As both theories only implicitly consider the role of host country factors, complementary business model-specific rationales on barriers and location advantages for ECFs are considered (e.g., Dunning and Wymbs 2001). In particular, additional effects of host countries' logistics performance, internet user population, and ROL are theorized (e.g., Benmamoun et al. 2019; Meyer et al. 2023). All these firm- and country-level factors are expected to have a positive effect on ECFs' propensity to choose wholly owned FDI rather than a virtual presence only.

Multilevel logistic regression is applied to test the hypotheses based on a sample of the 241 leading ECFs in Europe from 2010–2020 that made 1,726 mode decisions across 144 host countries. Wholly owned FDI was defined as the opening of ECFs' wholly owned fulfillment centers, logistics units, and sales/service centers in a country. A usual period of one year between the decision and its implementation is considered (e.g., Schu, Morschett and Swoboda 2016; Swoboda, Schwarz and Hälsig 2007). Again, only ECFs operating in at least one foreign market were included and each firm's operation mode choices were carefully reconstructed and verified over time. Cases for which the firm- or country-level data were missing over time were excluded.

The results support most hypotheses, showing positive effects of international and host country online experience as well as logistics performance, internet user population, and ROL on ECFs' propensity to choose wholly owned FDI. Surprisingly, FDI online experience has no significant effect. Contrary to assumptions that experience may be less important in digital firms' internationalization (e.g., Gabrielsson, Raatikainen and Julkunen 2022; Pezderka and Sinkovics 2011), ECFs' unknown international and host country online experience are shown to be critical capabilities for their physical presence decisions. These online experiences represent unique capabilities that ECFs as digital firms build, scale, and transfer by learning through virtual presence (Schu and Morschett 2017). Although ECFs no longer require a physical presence or sequential entry, their FDI decisions are still path-dependent and based on distinct online learning mechanisms. However, specific host country factors, i.e., logistics performance, internet user population, and ROL are critical to ECFs' FDI as well, as they provide new location advantages (Dunning and Wymbs 2001). The study has important implications for ECFs' managers interested in the firm- and country-level antecedents of successful ECFs' FDI but also manufacturers using ECFs to expand or policymakers aiming to attract FDI.

3.3. *Effects of E-Commerce Firms' International Control on Performance*

While some leading ECFs focus on virtual presence, others increase their international control through physical presence within countries to improve customer services and across markets to gain scale effects. However, which ECFs achieve higher foreign sales performance is unclear (e.g., Batsakis et al. 2023; Swoboda and Sinning 2022). Higher depth of control within a country facilitates the implementation of locally adapted offers or quick delivery (e.g., Eduardsen et al. 2023), whereas a higher breadth of control enables the global scaling of ECFs' offers or management (e.g., Batsakis, Konara and Theoharakis 2023). Certain trade-offs may arise between local and central decision-making. Moreover, the important role of contextual differences in local e-commerce markets for ECFs' foreign success is poorly understood (e.g., Meyer et al. 2023). Thus, understanding whether ECFs benefit from increased international control in terms of higher foreign performance and how local e-commerce contexts shape this relationship is critical.

Study 3 pursues two motivations. First, studies on manufacturing and service firms have studied the effects of the depth and breadth of control on performance only separately (e.g., Kirca et al. 2011; Wan et al. 2023). Research in a context of commerce firms is scarce and yields inconsistent findings (e.g., positive or negative effects of depth of control, Evans, Mavondo and Bridson 2008; Gielens and Dekimpe 2001; or breadth of control, Chan, Finnegan and Sternquist 2011; Dimitrova, Kim and Smith 2019). Moreover, theoretical insights into successful internationalization of ECFs remain sparse, often focusing on consumer-related capabilities (e.g., Tolstoy, Hånell and Özbek 2023; Tolstoy, Nordman and Vu 2022). Only one study has explored how ECFs' international decisions affect overall firm performance (Swoboda and Sinning 2022). None have analyzed the effects of international control in terms of either depth or breadth of control on digital or ECFs' performance, despite calls for such research (e.g., Ipsmiller, Dikova and Brouthers 2022; Swoboda and Sinning 2022). However, this is especially important, as ECFs may face unknown trade-offs between both decisions due to their business model. Second, whether and how the effects of international control on performance are affected by local e-commerce market contexts remains also unknown (e.g., Eduardsen et al. 2023). Respective insights are highly relevant to ECFs and their managers possibly struggling with foreign sales performance. Certain trade-offs may arise that managers should be aware of when aiming to increase sales abroad. Therefore, Study 3 pursues two research questions:

- Whether and how (strongly) does ECFs' higher (vs. lower) international control in terms of depth versus breadth drive their foreign sales performance?
- Whether and how do host countries' e-commerce market size and growth moderate these effects?

Study 3 builds on three theoretical perspectives—internationalization process theory, network theory, and the dynamic capability view—recently adapted to the internationalization of digital firms (e.g., Yang et al. 2025). These refined perspectives question the role of physical control in the successful internationalization of digital firms (e.g., Birkinshaw 2022; Monaghan, Tippmann and Coviello 2020). Thus, a conceptual framework is developed to clarify the effects of ECFs' depth and breadth of international control on their foreign performance, while also considering the local e-commerce market context. Theoretically, ECFs benefit from digital learning and market entry, online networks to expand the customer base, and digital capabilities based on real-time data (e.g., Cumming et al. 2023). However, applying a purely digital theory lens may fail to explain digital and ECFs' performance, as it neglects onsite learning, local network relationships, and key operational capabilities (Batsakis et al. 2023; Gong, He and Lengler 2024). Consequently, in Study 3, increased depth and breadth of control are assumed to be associated with better foreign performance. These rationales are extended by the local e-commerce market size and growth as important contextual factors, posing further trade-offs to ECFs' depth and breadth decisions (e.g., Goldman et al. 2021). The effects of ECFs' depth and breadth of control are expected to be both positively and negatively moderated.

Multilevel modeling with cross-level interactions is applied for hypothesis testing based on a sample of 184 leading ECFs in Europe from 2015–2020 and 1,144 control decisions in 112 countries. ECFs had to operate in at least one foreign market and each firm's control decisions were carefully reconstructed over time. Depth of ECFs' control was defined by the level of hierarchical control and the operation mode chosen in a country (e.g., Brouthers et al. 2022; Evans, Mavondo and Bridson 2008). The breadth of control was defined by ECFs' full control across countries based on their network of WOS (e.g., Fleury et al. 2024). A time lag of one year between the control decision and performance was considered as these effects take about one year to manifest (e.g., Batsakis et al. 2023; Shi et al. 2018). Cases with missing firm- or country-level data were excluded.

The results support the assumed positive effects of both depth and breadth of control on ECFs' foreign sales performance. It is concluded that a purely digital approach to theory cannot sufficiently explain the performance of ECFs as important traditional mechanisms still apply. Instead, physical control is still critical for ECFs' successful business model transfer abroad, both in terms of depth and breadth, while the former is a stronger lever (e.g., Swoboda and Sinning 2022). This confirms a previously unknown trade-off for ECFs that must balance the depth and breadth of control and central or local decision-making (e.g., Evans, Mavondo and Bridson 2008). However, the effects further depend on the local e-commerce market context as well, which creates another trade-off (e.g., Kishore, Agrawal and Rao 2004). Surprisingly, the results show that ECFs' control decisions do not depend on local e-commerce market size (unlike their market selection, Schu and Morschett 2017). In contrast, the effects of depth of control are weakened in host country contexts of high market growth, whereas those of breadth of control are strengthened (e.g., Goldman et al. 2021). These insights allow new implications for ECF managers and emerging digital firms struggling with performance abroad.

4. Further Remarks

The structure of this dissertation is as follows: Addressing the research gaps and questions, this doctoral thesis builds on three separate studies, each presented in detail in Chapter B, Chapter C, and Chapter D. Study 1 analyzes antecedents of ECFs' geographic scope, Study 2 examines antecedents of ECFs' wholly owned FDI, and Study 3 analyzes the performance outcomes of ECFs' international control decisions. All three empirical studies, regardless of the theoretical and methodological approach, share the following consistent structure:

- Introduction
- Conceptualization and Hypothesis Development
- Empirical Study, including Sample, Measurement, Method, Results, and Stability Checks
- Discussion with Theoretical and Managerial/Practical Implications
- Limitations and Further Research

The three studies all refer to unique secondary datasets based on data from Digital Commerce 360 (2021), an agency tracking the leading ECFs in Europe since 2010. Regarding the methodology, all three studies build on multilevel modeling to account for the hierarchical data structure and to capture firm- and country-level effects (Hox, Moerbeek and Van de Schoot 2018, p. 215).

To conclude, Chapter E aims to answer the research questions by summarizing the findings of this dissertation and ends with an outlook on further research.

B. Study 1: E-Commerce Firms' Geographic Scope. Roles of Intangible Resources and Country-Specific Moderators[1]

1. Introduction

International ECFs, which provide physical goods to consumers through own online shops and marketplaces, rapidly expand their geographic scope, i.e., number of foreign markets (with country-specific online shops in terms of domain, language, and currency), and globally account for 20% of total retail sales (Swoboda and Sinning 2022; Young 2021). They profit from internet-based technologies and acquire resources over time that ease their expansion (e.g., Elia et al. 2021). However, firms develop distinct geographic scopes: Zalando or Esdemarca, both founded in 2008, established 17 or four country-specific online shops respectively (Esdemarca 2021; Zalando 2021b). Esdemarca has weaker international experience, has acquired less website traffic, and has a smaller social media network. Zalando has stronger respective resources, but its expansion is restricted to Europe; this restriction seems to be important for Zalando, while the role of country-specific context barriers is assumed to lose relevance for e-businesses (Chen et al. 2019). Therefore, this study examines how intangible resources affect ECFs' geographic scope and whether the degree of country development, ROL, or logistics performance are important contexts for these links.

Scholars have broadly studied the antecedents of geographic scope (or related constructs like geographic diversification; see Figure B—1). A wide geographic internationalization scope has often been attributed to firms' resources (e.g., experiential knowledge, Beleska-Spasova, Glaister and Stride 2012; intangible assets, Delgado-Gómez, Ramírez-Alesón and Espitia-Escuer 2004). However, almost all studies have addressed manufacturing firms. Only Kotha, Rindova and Rothaermel (2001) have linked internet firms' resources, like website traffic or reputation, to the number of foreign domains (Batsakis and Mohr 2017 study offline commerce). It is important to analyze the effects of traditional intangible resources, like international experience, and e-business-specific resources, like website traffic or social media networks, on geographic scope. Moreover, few studies have studied the role of external factors (e.g., risks, Jiménez 2010, country development, Mansion and Bausch 2020). Insights into the role of country-specific factors on this effect are important, as environmental factors are expected to lose relevance in e-business (e.g., Chen et al. 2019). In summary, most studies have addressed firms' resources as antecedents of geographic scope of manufacturing firms, but also have called for respective e-commerce

[1] This study was published as: Swoboda, B., & Mueller, M. (2022). E-Commerce Firms' Geographic Scope: Roles of Intangible Resources and Country-Specific Moderators. *Marketing ZFP–Journal of Research and Management*, 44(1), 3-22 (see also Section G, ESM).

M. Müller, *Strategic Management of International E-Commerce Firms*,
Handel und Internationales Marketing Retailing and International Marketing,
https://doi.org/10.1007/978-3-658-49680-7_2

studies (e.g., Chabowski and Samiee 2020; Jean and Kim 2020). Scholars have also called for analyses on the relevance of specific resources of ECFs regarding their geographic scope and the country-specific contexts that facilitate their geographic scope (e.g., Liu, Zhang-Zhang and Ghauri 2020; Tolstoy et al. 2021). Understanding the general and relative importance of major contexts for firms' resource effects on geographic scope helps managers successfully operate e-businesses internationally.

		Scope of Internationalization	Related Conceptualizations
Offline Firms	Internal Factors	*Beleska-Spasova, Glaister and Stride 2012*; Delgado-Gómez, Ramírez-Alesón and Espitia-Escuer 2004; Hitt et al. 2006; *Gallego and Casillas 2014*; *George, Wiklund and Zahra 2005*; *Kirca et al. 2011*; *Lin 2012*; *Lin 2014*; *Love, Roper and Zhou 2016*; Ruzo et al. 2011	Bauweraerts et al. 2019[1]; Felzensztein et al. 2015[1]; *Jean, Kim and Cavusgil 2020*; Kuivalainen, Sundqvist and Servais 2007[1]; Sambharya and Lee 2014[1]; Wiersema and Bowen 2008[1]
	Also external	*Jiménez 2010*; *Kirca et al. 2012a*; Mansion and Bausch 2020; Navarro-García 2016	–
Online/ Commerce	Internal	*Kotha, Rindova and Rothaermel 2001*	Batsakis and Mohr 2017[1]
	Also external	*This Study*	–

Note: Studies focusing scope only (vs. further decisions) in *italics*; [1] Diversification/Entropy Index.

Figure B—1: Literature Review on Antecedents of Geographic Scope

Source: Own Creation

Addressing these research gaps, this study analyzes two important research questions. First, whether and how do intangible resources affect the geographic scope of ECFs? Second, whether and how do host country factors, i.e., ROL, country development, and logistics performance, moderate these effects? We thus provide two important contributions for both theory and practice.

First, examining the antecedents of ECFs' geographic scope provides novel insights into their internationalization processes. In line with previous studies, we build on the RBV, which expects intangible resources to affect geographic scope (e.g., Kozlenkova, Samaha and Palmatier 2014). However, we contribute to the application of this theory in a digital economy by empirically capturing the effects of the intangible resources of ECFs (responding to calls, e.g., Chabowski and Samiee 2020). Therefore, quicker learning processes due to international online experience may affect geographic scope. Moreover, website traffic and social media networks built over time are suggested to facilitate additional market entries of ECFs (Kotha, Rindova and Rothaermel 2001; Shaheer and Li 2020). While international (offline) experience and consumer-related resources have been shown in meta-analyses to affect the geographic scope of manufacturing firms (Kirca et al. 2011), whether they are equally relevant in e-commerce remains unclear (e.g., Kotha, Rindova and Rothaermel 2001).

Second, we contribute to literature by following calls and analyzing the specific contextual factors relevant to ECFs (e.g., Jean and Kim 2020). We study interactions with the effects of intangible resources (not only independent effects, e.g., Navarro-García 2016). Applying multilevel modeling with cross-level interactions reveals explained variances of moderators and identifies the strongest levers (Hox, Moerbeek and Van de Schoot 2018, pp. 4-5). We also contribute to the application of the RBV for digital firms and the suggested role of contextual factors in this theory (e.g., Priem and Butler 2001; Wan 2005). We study host countries' ROL because of its strong importance for ECFs' expansion process and resource utilization (e.g., increasing ROL reduces risk of market entry or enhances transparency or transactional integrity, Oxley and Yeung 2001). The degree of country development is also important to study. Resource exploitation may be easier when entering developed countries (e.g., due to stable societal conditions, Kirca et al. 2011; Lu et al. 2014), but certain emerging markets have become increasingly interesting, as they report strong economic growth (Benmamoun et al. 2019). We finally study host countries' logistics performance because of its core role for ECFs and potential effects on the value of resources used to increase geographic scope (e.g., for the efficient, timely distribution of online orders, Zhang et al. 2019; Schu and Morschett 2017).

The remainder of this study is structured as follows. Based on theory, we derive and test hypotheses based on 2,632 market entries of 263 ECFs over 24 years. After the results are presented, we offer implications and opportunities for further research.

2. Conceptualization and Hypothesis Development

2.1. Definitions

To address our research aims, our conceptual framework proposes that ECFs' intangible resources—international online experience, website traffic, and social media use—affect these firms' geographic scope over time (see Figure B—2). These effects are conceptualized to depend on three contextual factors as continuous moderators at the country level.

Geographic scope is an important indicator of ECFs' international involvement and is commonly defined as the number of foreign markets entered by country-specific online shops (Kotha, Rindova and Rothaermel 2001; in contrast to the global diversity of firms' sales, for example, Bauweraerts et al. 2019). International online experience indicates ECFs' degree of knowledge about foreign markets (Batsakis and Mohr 2017), capturing firms' experience in operating country-specific online shops and gaining knowledge about foreign online markets over time. We define an ECF's website traffic as its customer base or interest in its website, as most repeat visitors become customers (also understood as users' general awareness, indicating current sales potential, Kotha, Rindova and Rothaermel 2001). Firms' social media use is a key resource reflecting their tacit digital communication skills and consumer interactions on social media (Elia et al. 2021; Shaheer and Li 2020). Followers on social media represent an engaged audience that can be reached and influenced by an ECF with the opportunity to gain additional knowledge of their needs and to convert them into customers (Katsikeas, Leonidou and Zeriti 2020). Therefore, social media followers are more indicative of firms' communication reach and future sales potential than a direct increase in orders or sales.

We study the roles of continuous national moderators reflecting the role of country environments: ROL (as the predominant part of a country's regulatory system indicating the extent to which a society's rules and regulations are enforced and freedoms are respected, e.g., Oxley and Yeung 2001), degree of country development (countries' economic growth and social and human conditions, e.g., Benmamoun et al. 2019; Çilingirtürk and Koçak 2018), and logistics performance (availability of logistical infrastructure for efficient and timely deliveries, e.g., Arvis et al. 2018).

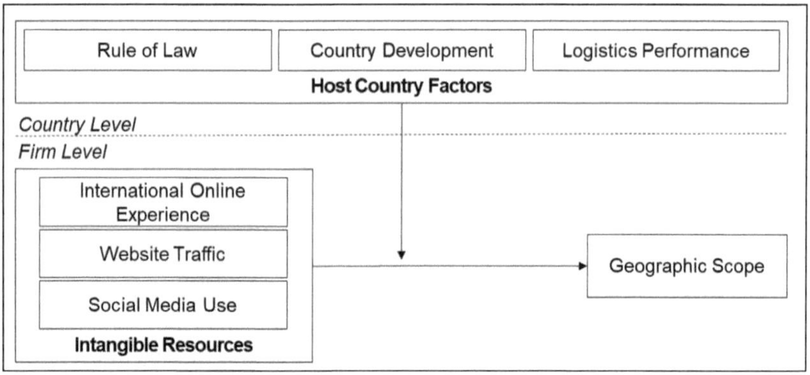

Figure B—2: Conceptual Framework

Source: Own Creation

2.2. Theory

Scholars have studied geographic scope based on various theories, while we build on the RBV because our antecedents are understood as valuable intangible resources and because this theory provides a stringent rationale for our research objectives. The RBV suggests that firms' assets, information, or knowledge are important for competitive advantages and strategic decisions, while intangible (vs. tangible) resources are particularly relevant (e.g., Barney 1991; Kozlenkova, Samaha and Palmatier 2014). Intangible resources do not deteriorate, can be used by firms simultaneously, and are difficult to imitate (they are typically valuable, rare, and nonsubstitutable, Molloy et al. 2011). Firms who own resources that meet these criteria can use them for successful international expansion (Brouthers and Hennart 2007; Hitt et al. 2006). However, not all intangible resources are equally relevant, and specific intangible resources in an e-environment are critical for internationalization (while traditional ones are questionable, Pezderka and Sinkovics 2011). We study important experiential and consumer-related resources. For ECFs, prior international experience is assumed to remain a critical intangible resource, i.e., a base for entry and geographic scope decisions (Samiee 2020). In a digital environment, firms' website traffic and social media use are expected to be important specific resources for ECFs (Elia et al. 2021). Website traffic is generally critical for firms' sales attributable mostly to customers accessing firm websites; social media is a central resource for digital communications and mutual interactions with consumers (Gao et al. 2018; Molla-Descals et al. 2014). All three resources acquired over time are seen as valuable, rare, inimitable, and nonsubstitutable and used to facilitate foreign market entry by ECFs. However, their relative importance for geographic expansion depends on how well they can be transferred to particular countries.

The use of firms' resources depends on the host country context, which is relevant for the geographic expansion of ECFs. We study country conditions because they create challenges for ECFs in better exploiting and transferring their resources (for differences to distances, e.g., Harzing and Pudelko 2016). We argue, for example, that the value of ECFs' resources critically depends on the actual degree of local regulations' effectiveness. We study countries' ROL, degree of development, and logistics performance as critical contextual factors in e-commerce. ECFs need effective local regulations that increase transactional integrity and transparency in a foreign market, for example (i.e., ROL may enable them to fully leverage their resources, Oxley and Yeung 2001). Likewise, highly developed host countries offer ECFs more stable environments, increasing the number of opportunities to make use of past experiences for example (Lu et al. 2014). Given the importance of timely delivery in e-commerce, national logistics performance is decisive for firms to derive competitive advantages from resources transferred to foreign markets (e.g., Schu and Morschett 2017). For firms, these factors are argued as having high potential in reinforcing the transfer of intangible resources to foreign markets.

Next, we derive hypotheses by referring to our current theoretical and empirical knowledge. First, we provide rationales for the hypotheses on the effects of firms' intangible resources on geographic scope. Second, we offer arguments for the role of each moderator in these effects.

2.3. Hypothesis Development

The RBV suggests that ECFs' geographic scope depends on their international online experience as an intangible resource. To achieve competitive advantages in a digital economy, the ability to use and transfer prior international online experience is no less important than are new digital resources (e.g., Pezderka and Sinkovics 2011; Schu, Morschett and Swoboda 2016).

ECFs with extensive international online experience possess general knowledge of how to operate in foreign markets and are skilled at using this knowledge as a valuable resource to enter and manage additional markets (e.g., Kirca et al. 2011; 2012b). Such experience is acquired mostly through the process of conducting business abroad and difficult to imitate or substitute by other means (e.g., Casillas, Barbero and Sapienza 2015). Firms with international experience have a more global orientation and are more likely to identify expansion opportunities, increasing their value and rarity (Mohr and Batsakis 2018). Due to these qualities, international online experience can be transferred and used in multiple host markets simultaneously. Therefore, international online experience enables ECFs to increase their geographic scope.

In summary, we expect ECFs to have a wider geographic scope if they can draw on previous international online experience. Empirical studies support our assumption indicating positive effects of experience on geographic scope, but only for manufacturers (e.g., Kirca et al. 2011; 2012b; Love, Roper and Zhou 2016).

We hypothesize the following:

H1. E-commerce firms' international online experience has a positive effect on their geographic scope.

Theoretically, ECFs' geographic scope is likely to depend on website traffic (e.g., Jean and Kim 2020). In a globalized digital economy, new intangible resources should be even stronger drivers of foreign expansion than traditional resources (e.g., like international experience, Liu, Zhang-Zhang and Ghauri 2020).

Website traffic, as an intangible resource, offers valuable analytical tools for

ECFs' customer relations, including information about the global distribution of total website access from outside the home market (Kromidha and Robson 2021). As website traffic increases, its value, inimitability and nonsubstitutability rise because international users are more attracted to highly popular online shops (Kotha, Rindova and Rothaermel 2001). High website traffic also reflects firms' promotional effectiveness, leading to a higher ranking in search engines, which can be transferred across countries, indicating firms' customer reputation (Molla-Descals et al. 2014). Likewise, firms may potentially benefit from entering partnerships to monetize website traffic and increase its value (Kotha, Rindova and Rothaermel 2001). We therefore argue that firms with high website traffic are able to benefit from their existing customer base as a valuable resource and more easily transfer it to foreign markets, thus increasing their geographic scope.

In summary, we expect ECFs with higher website traffic to have a wider geographic scope. Empirically, one study on internet firms finds positive effects of website traffic on geographic scope (Kotha, Rindova and Rothaermel 2001).

We hypothesize the following:

H2. E-commerce firms' website traffic has a positive effect on their geographic scope.

ECFs' social media use is another critical resource for foreign expansion (e.g., Shaheer and Li 2020). With consumers worldwide shifting towards digital information sources and sharing content across borders, transferring firms' social media as an important intangible resource is critical for their expansion (e.g., to address new customers, Gao et al. 2018).

In a digital age, ECFs derive value from being present on social media channels and analyzing consumers' needs and interacting with them through a variety of services (e.g., Katsikeas, Leonidou and Zeriti 2020). Firms gain access to sources of firm-specific knowledge about consumers' needs, which might be rare and difficult to copy or substitute, even if social media communication is considered challenging due to fierce competition. Using their social media presence built over time, firms may better transfer and establish important social communications in new host markets (e.g., Li, Larimo and Leonidou 2021). Moreover, this resource transfer may potentially profit from transnational consumer interactions as firms gain more followers interacting and sharing content with each other, inducing a domino effect across countries (Dolega, Rowe and Branagan 2021). ECFs, which are able to use social media as a resource to transfer their communications, therefore are more likely to increase their geographic scope.

In summary, ECFs with greater social media use realize a wider geographic scope. To the best of our knowledge, no empirical study has shown the role of social media in geographic scope. However, studies have highlighted the importance of social media for international market entry (e.g., Paniagua, Korzynski and Mas-Tur 2017).

We propose the following:

H3. E-commerce firms' social media use has a positive effect on their geographic scope.

Regarding the moderation hypotheses, theory suggests that the use of firms' resources may be affected by the legal and regulative conditions of foreign markets (He, Brouthers and Filatotchev 2013). Host countries with a strong (vs. weak) ROL reduce ECFs' difficulties conducting business in foreign environments (e.g., transactional integrity, Oxley and Yeung 2001). Firms can leverage the potential of their intangible resources and transfer them to foreign markets more easily. Thus, ROL is expected to affect the effects of intangible resources on geographic scope.

Regarding international online experience, host countries' legal systems affect the role of acquired knowledge of ECFs in their geographic scope decisions. International online experience helps firms understand foreign markets' regulatory systems, which affect the value of their resources in foreign contexts (Pezderka and Sinkovics 2011). In host countries with transparent rules and regulations firms' proprietary rights are protected, for example. Resources are more valuable, and firms can focus on exploiting experiences instead of having to deal with legal issues (e.g., Schu and Morschett 2017). An effective ROL allows ECFs to leverage their international online experience and increase their geographic scope.

Regarding website traffic, host countries' legal systems can affect the efficient use of firms' customer relationship management (CRM) across countries. Given the advancement of website tracking and analytics, the value of website traffic likely depends on firms' ability to legally make use of such resources (Luo 2022). Host countries with a strong ROL provide these conditions with transparent and codified laws, reducing online risks (Luo, Zhao and Du 2005). Customers trust in data protection rights, for example, enabling firms to transfer customer relations and to use their online shops to expand (Watson et al. 2018). Monetizing website traffic and entering advertising agreements is also easier, as parties can place their trust in contracts. An increasing ROL is argued to enable firms to better use their website traffic to increase their geographic scope.

Regarding social media, the ROL affects ECFs' ability to communicate with consumers in foreign markets and to use collected insights into consumers' needs from prior community interactions (Luo 2022). For firms to gain value from such interactions, consumers need access to such a platform, which is likely given in countries with a strong ROL. A weak ROL poses major hurdles for ECFs in replicating social media services in foreign markets (Katsikeas, Leonidou and Zeriti 2020). Social media use is easier when entering contexts where intangible resources are protected and where domino effects are more likely. Thus, an increasing ROL enables firms to better use social media to increase geographic scope.

Empirically, only Schu and Morschett (2017) have identified ROL as a factor driving the foreign market selection of ECFs.

We propose the following hypothesis:

H4. An increasing degree of rule of law in a country positively moderates the effects of e-commerce firms' (a) international online experience, (b) website traffic, and (c) social media use on their geographic scope.

We assume that the usefulness of intangible resources for expansion depends on the degree of host country development. Developed countries offer more predictable business environments for ECFs (e.g., volatility in economic systems), and resources may have higher value (e.g., Kirca et al. 2012b). The degree of country development will affect ECFs' use and transfer of resources abroad and thus the effect of intangible resources on geographic scope (Lu et al. 2014).

Considering firms' international online experience acquired over time, host countries' degree of development affects the value of this knowledge. In developed (vs. emerging) countries, the risks of unstable conditions (e.g., economic fluctuations) are much lower, making it easier for firms to rely on past experiences. Host countries with predictable economic or social conditions (e.g., purchasing power and living standards) increase firms' ability to more easily identify and exploit opportunities for expansion based on their international experience (Nuhu, Owens and McQuillan 2021). In predictable environments, firms can transfer knowledge more easily and can make better use of it to increase their geographic scope. ECFs can better exploit their international online experience with an increasing degree of country development.

Country development might affect the value of website traffic transfer to foreign markets. Firms' website traffic highly depends on the accessibility and use of the internet in host countries (Kardes, Flynn and Dugan 2020). Developed markets have the highest internet penetration rate worldwide and a more developed internet infrastructure (e.g., connection speed). ECFs' website traffic and popularity are more valuable in such contexts for increasing geographic scope, and their promotional effectiveness is easier to transfer (Watson et al. 2018). Firms in developed countries are able to better exploit website analytics to gain customer insights and leverage partnerships with advertisers from advanced digital economies. Increasing country development helps ECFs use website traffic as a resource to increase their geographic scope.

Country development also affects firms' ability to benefit from social media services and consumer interactions. In developed countries, ECFs may better analyze consumers' needs and behavior, as most of the population is reached through popular social media platforms (Vieira et al. 2019). Moreover, firms may better leverage possible domino effects resulting from high numbers of followers, increasing the value of firms' social media communications in terms of entering new foreign markets. As consumers become more aware of online scams, the value of firms' social media use for the purpose of expansion increases (Goyens 2020). Thus, ECFs can more easily build on social interactions and transfer their services to foreign markets. Increasing country development enables firms to better use social media as a resource to increase geographic scope. To the best of our knowledge, no previous study analyzed these moderations.

Therefore, we carefully hypothesize the following:

H5. An increasing degree of country development positively moderates the effect of e-commerce firms' (a) international online experience, (b) website traffic, and (c) social media use on their geographic scope.

Resource-based advantages also critically depend on efficient product deliveries by ECFs in host countries. Efficient host country logistics performance provides the infrastructural basis to deliver offerings and services (Arvis et al. 2018). Efficient logistics contexts in markets enable firms to better exploit and transfer their intangible resources. We expect logistics performance to affect the impacts of intangible resources on geographic scope.

Local logistics performance affects ECFs' ability to benefit from prior international online experience. Experienced firms possess valuable knowledge about foreign markets. Decreasing logistics performance may restrict the value of such knowledge and the ability to exploit it to expand (Pezderka and Sinkovics 2011). In contrast, increasing local logistics performance supports firms' knowledge transfer and opportunity recognition (e.g., not forcing them to build own logistics infrastructure, Douglas and Craig 2011). ECFs can partner with local logistics providers to exploit their know-how for foreign expansion. Host countries with high logistics performance allow firms to use and transfer their international experience to increase their geographic scope.

Local logistics performance might affect firms' ability to meet customers' online shopping expectations. High logistics performance is necessary to transfer firms' customer relations and leverage the full value of website traffic. In countries with efficient logistics infrastructure, customers are used to timely deliveries, leading to their high expectations of ECFs (Katsikeas, Leonidou and Zeriti 2020). Online shoppers might infer that since a firm has, in the past, delivered orders efficiently, it is therefore able to meet their current expectations, increasing the potential value of website traffic for expansion. Likewise, ECFs might be able to gain customers' trust and loyalty more easily (Schu and Morschett 2017). We assume that increasing logistics performance enables firms to benefit from their website traffic and increase their geographic scope.

Host countries' logistics performance affects the efficient transfer of social media interactions and their value for communicating services in foreign markets. Logistics is critical for the ability to deliver service quality as promised in social media communications. With the usual fulfilment time discussed on social media being a key promise, the value of firms' social media information increases (Zhang et al. 2019). In countries with weak logistics performance, firms may face the risk of social media interactions resulting in negative reviews and open complaints. Consequently, domino effects may become a disadvantage if firms gain a reputation for not delivering on their usual services (Luo 2022). Therefore, high logistics performance enables ECFs to transfer their social media services more easily to foreign markets and increase their geographic scope.

Empirically, one e-commerce study controlled for the effects of logistics performance and indicated its role in market entries (Schu and Morschett 2017).

We propose the following:

H6. An increasing degree of host country logistics performance positively moderates the effect of e-commerce firms' (a) international online experience, (b) website traffic, and (c) social media use on their geographic scope.

3. Empirical Study

3.1. Sample

For sample selection, foreign market entries of ECFs are commonly defined as the first launch of an online shop in a country with a country-specific domain, language, and currency (Shneor and Flåten 2008; Swoboda and Sinning 2022). A unique hierarchical database over a 24-year period was created based on different sources.

The selection of ECFs was based on the 2018 Internet Retailer's ranking of Europe's 500 largest ECFs (Digital Commerce 360 2018; Swoboda and Sinning 2022). This agency tracks ECFs' website traffic and social media platform data (based on information from firms or estimated by the agency and verified by each firm, Digital Commerce 360 2021). Firms on this list operate the leading European online shops but did not have to be founded in Europe and could be active worldwide. All firms included needed to be present in one foreign country at least. To the best of our knowledge, this database is the only one available providing expansion data or website and social media analytics on ECFs in Europe. Firms operating only in their home market (N=192) or solely offering international shipping through a "dot-com domain" (N=8) were excluded, resulting in 300 firms.

We subsequently collected data on each firm's expansion using data from websites, annual reports, official press releases, articles, or social media sites. Foreign market entries were matched to the respective year. At least two sources were used to verify seventy-five percent of the data, opening and double-checking their existence and requirements for every country's website (Swoboda and Sinning 2022). On this basis, in particular, the data on firms' international online experience were calculated (and some control variables). Firms' website traffic and social media followers, and some control variables, were obtained from the Digital Commerce 360 (2018) database. Firms for which market entries could not be fully reconstructed and verified over time were excluded (N=37).

Country-level data for ROL and logistics performance were obtained from the World Bank (2023a), and those on country development were obtained from the United Nations Development Programme (2020), matching the data to the respective years of market entry whenever possible.

In summary, the data include 2,632 market entries in 64 host countries over a period from 1994–2018 by 263 ECFs originating in 21 home countries (see Table B—1). The median shows eleven market entries per firm. The data were not normally distributed. Therefore, a maximum likelihood estimator with robust standard errors and chi-square test statistics was used (Maydeu-Olivares 2017).

Home Countries	Number of E-Commerce Firms	Number of Market Entries
Austria	1	13
Canada	1	2
China	5	99
Czech Republic	4	13
Denmark	5	55
France	50	417
Germany	41	422
Great Britain	74	698
Indonesia	1	1
Italy	5	58
Lithuania	1	1
Netherlands	13	49
Norway	1	4
Poland	6	33
Romania	1	2
Russia	1	1
Spain	6	108
Sweden	8	135
Switzerland	5	87
Turkey	3	13
United States	31	421
Total	**263**	**2,632**

Table B—1: Sample Distribution

Source: Own Creation

3.2. Measurement

Dependent Variable. We measured *geographic scope* dynamically over time as the number of ECFs' foreign-country-specific websites at the time of each new entry (Schu, Morschett and Swoboda 2016; Shneor and Flåten 2008). To reduce the natural skewness of the dependent variable, we used the natural logarithm, which is often applied in multilevel modeling (Hox, Moerbeek and Van de Schoot 2018, p. 103). The number of foreign markets is the most common indicator of firms' geographic scope. Relative to related concepts (e.g., indices of global sales distribution), we argue that this traditional measurement is well suited for modeling ECFs' geographic scope (e.g., Schu, Morschett and Swoboda 2016). Data on sales distribution over time is not available for ECFs to us.

Independent Variables. International online experience was measured as the number of years a firm operated an international online shop since its first foreign market entry (Batsakis and Mohr 2017). Firms' *unique website traffic* is an indicator of the customer base, who mostly accesses firms' websites, reflecting ECFs' current online sales potential (Molla-Descals et al. 2014). We measured this variable as the logarithm of firms' (unique) monthly website traffic (with data available for 2017, Kotha, Rindova and Rothaermel 2001). Firms' *social media* followers (we focused on Facebook, as it is a widespread social media marketing platform, e.g., Dolega, Rowe and Branagan 2021) represent the amount of reciprocal interactions with consumers in general (Shaheer and Li 2020). Consumers know and communicate with ECFs, often across nations, and thus represent future sales potential. This variable was measured using firms' logarithmmized number of likes on Facebook (with data available for 2017, Paniagua, Korzynski and Mas-Tur 2017).

Moderators. At the country-level, *ROL* was measured using the World Governance Indicators (WGI) of the World Bank (2022b, widely used in literature), reflecting regulative elements such as the quality of contract enforcement, property rights, the police and court system, and the likelihood of crime and violence (Oxley and Yeung 2001; World Bank 2022b). The ROL value was matched with the respective years of market entry.

Host country development was measured using the Human Development Index provided by the United Nations Development Program (2020; commonly used e.g., Çilingirtürk and Koçak 2018), which consists of three dimensions assessing a country's standard of living, i.e., life expectancy, education and knowledge, and national income (United Nations Development Programme 2020).

Due to missing data over time, we relied on the latest available reports. We measured *logistics performance* with the World Bank's six-dimensional logistics performance index (Arvis et al. 2018, Schu and Morschett 2017), the overall value of which reflected the quality of cross-border trade infrastructure, ease of logistics services and customs, tracking ability, and timely shipments (World Bank 2023b). We used the latest available and most complete data, which were published in 2018 and checked additional years in an alternative model.

Controls. We controlled variables at the firm and country level. Following studies on antecedents of geographic scope and e-commerce internationalization, we controlled for ECFs' *size* (Batsakis and Mohr 2017). Large-scale firms are expected to have more resources for expansion and argued to be more risk seeking, leading them to expand internationally (Kirca et al. 2012b). We measured the logarithm of firms' sales in 2017 because data on the number of employees were not available, and ECFs are known for hiring fewer employees while having high sales volumes (Digital Commerce 360 2018; Luo, Zhao and Du 2005).

We also controlled for *firm age* at the time of each market entry, measured as the number of years since foundation, which may affect firms' geographic scope (e.g., George, Wiklund and Zahra 2005). Firm age may drive geographic scope, as older firms have more time to acquire important resources and foreign market experience, which may be used for further expansion (Kirca et al. 2011). Moreover, older firms are more likely to face stagnant domestic sales, pressuring them to expand (Kirca et al. 2012b). Data on firm age were gathered from their websites.

Firms' *use of mobile sites* in 2017 was measured as a dichotomous variable (firms also offer mobile pages=1 or not=0) to account for the possible influences of multichannel merchants (Schu, Morschett and Swoboda 2016). Pure ECFs rely more strongly on the online channels than do those offering both offline and online channels, which might affect the expansion process and consequently the geographic scope of such firms. Data were acquired from Digital Commerce 360 (2018).

Home market size was controlled because it is known to influence firms' geographic scope. Firms originating in countries with large, developed home markets typically have acquired more resources, which can be used for expansion (e.g., Kirca et al. 2012b). It was measured using the logarithm of countries' gross domestic product (GDP) per capita, drawing on data from the World Bank (2023a) and matched to the year of each market entry (e.g., Schu and Morschett 2017).

At the host country-level, we controlled for *market size*, as attractive host markets were shown to affect firms' geographic scope (e.g., Kirca et al. 2012b). It may stimulate firms to enter markets with growth opportunities, where intangible resources can be applied effectively (e.g., Shahoor and Li 2020). Host market size was measured by the logarithm of the GDP per capita based on World Bank (2023a) data and matched to the year of each market entry.

Table B—2 shows descriptive statistics and bivariate correlations of all variables that do not exceed .575 and .917 at the firm and country-levels, respectively. We tested for variance inflation factors (VIF, e.g., Backhaus et al. 2023, pp. 111-113), which were below a common threshold of ten. Multicollinearity does not seem to be a serious problem.

	(1)	(2)	(3)	(4)	(5)	(6)	(7)	(8)	(9)	(10)	(11)	(12)
Mean	2.499	5.143	14.870	13.801	19.258	3.056	10.591	.985	10.155	1.054	3.634	.889
SD	1.064	5.050	2.125	2.257	1.536	1.104	.473	.122	.876	.811	.406	.063
VIF	-	1.127	1.846	1.763	1.453	1.258	1.143	1.090	6.906	5.591	3.025	8.020
	(1)	**(2)**	**(3)**	**(4)**	**(5)**	**(6)**	**(7)**	**(8)**	**(9)**	**(10)**	**(11)**	**(12)**
GeoScope (1)	1											
IntOnExp (2)	.292***	1										
WebTraff (3)	.186***	.147***	1									
SM (4)	.324***	.100***	.575***	1								
Firm Size (5)	.083***	.193***	.513***	.409***	1							
Firm Age (6)	.273***	.201***	-.012ns	.230***	.072***	1						
Home MS (7)	.114***	.106***	-.107***	.028ns	-.028†	.307***	1					
Mobsite (8)	.019ns	-.012ns	.182***	.250***	.018ns	.026ns	.013†	1				
Host MS (9)									1			
ROL (10)									.841***	1		
LP (11)									.717***	.809***	1	
CD (12)									.917***	.866***	.735***	1

Note: ***p<.001; **p<.01; *p<.05; †p<.10; ns=Not Significant. CD=Country Development; GeoScope=Geographic Scope; Home MS=Home Market Size; Host MS=Host Market Size; IntOnExp=International Online Experience; LP=Logistics Performance; Mobsite=Mobile Site; SD=Standard Deviation; SM=Social Media; VIF=Variance Inflation Factor; WebTraff=Website Traffic.

Table B—2: Correlations

Source: Own Creation

3.3. Method

To test the hypotheses, we adopted a multilevel modeling approach with cross-level interactions in Mplus 8.6. This hierarchical approach accounts for the nested data structure (firms active in multiple host countries) and simultaneously considers the interactions of firm- and country-level variables while accounting for the variance that occurs both between and within countries (Finch and Bolin 2017, p. 28). Intraclass correlation was calculated in a null model with no predictor variables to test whether multilevel modeling was appropriate. 32.6% of the variance in firms' geographic scope is attributed to country differences. Following Hox, Moerbeek and Van de Schoot (2018, p. 215), multilevel modeling is therefore highly appropriate.

We subsequently computed stepwise random intercept and random slope models (Finch and Bolin 2017, pp. 33-37; Swoboda and Sinning 2022). Model fit was assessed for each model via the Akaike and Bayesian Information Criteria (AIC; BIC). First, a baseline model including only firm-level control variables was calculated and supplemented by adding all additional firm-level independent variables. To increase the interpretability of the intercepts, we applied grand mean centering for all independent variables and moderators (e.g., Hox, Moerbeek and Van de Schoot 2018, pp. 61-63). The computed model can be described as follows:

$$GeoScope_{ij}=\beta_{0j}+\beta_{1j}\left(IntOnExp_{ij}\right)+\beta_{2j}\left(WebTraff_{ij}\right)$$
$$+\beta_{3j}\left(SocialMed_{ij}\right)+\beta_{controls}ILC_{ij}+r_{ij,} \quad (1)$$

where i denotes ECFs, and j denotes the host countries entered. $GeoScope_{ij}$ reflects firm i's geographic scope at the time of a new market entry. $IntOnExp_{ij}$ indicates firm i's international online experience, $WebTraff_{ij}$ indicates firm i's unique website traffic, and $SocialMed_{ij}$ represents firm i's social media use. ILC_{ij} includes firm-level control variables. β_{0j} denotes the first-level intercept, whereas β_{1j}, β_{2j} and β_{3j} indicate the regression scores of the independent variables at the firm level. The intercept β_{0j} and slopes β_{1j}, β_{2j} and β_{3j} were free to vary across countries. Finally, r_{ij} represents the first-level error term.

In a second baseline model, an additional country-level control was included, followed by separate models with the moderators added. All of these models served to predict variation in the β coefficients:

$$\beta_{0j}=\gamma_{00}+\gamma_{01}\left(CLV_j\right)+\gamma_{02}\left(CLC_j\right)+u_{0j}, \quad (2)$$

$$\beta_{1j}=\gamma_{10}+\gamma_{11}\left(CLV_j\right)+u_{1j}, \quad (3)$$

$$\beta_{2j}=\gamma_{20}+\gamma_{21}\left(CLV_j\right)+u_{2j}, \quad (4)$$

$$\beta_{3j}=\gamma_{30}+\gamma_{31}(CLV_j)+u_{3j}, \tag{5}$$

where γ_{00} denotes the second-level intercept of firms' scope. γ_{10}, γ_{20} and γ_{30} represent the intercept of the second-level random slope of international online experience, website traffic and social media use, respectively. CLV_j represents one of the three country-level variables, u_{qj} (q=0–3) represents country-level residual variances, and CLC_j represents the country-level control variable. For each moderator, a separate multilevel model was used for hypothesis testing. The following equation comprises equations (1–5) and shows the multilevel regressions including cross-level interactions:

$$\begin{aligned} GeoScope_{ij}&=\gamma_{00}+\gamma_{01}(CLV_j)+\gamma_{10}\left(IntOnExp_{ij}\right) \\ &+\gamma_{21}(CLV_j)\left(IntOnExp_{ij}\right)+\gamma_{20}(WebTraff_{ij}) \\ &+\gamma_{31}(CLV_j)(WebTraff_{ij})+\gamma_{30}(SocialMed_{ij}) \\ &+\gamma_{41}(CLV_j)(SocialMed_{ij})+\gamma_{ILC}ILC_{ij}+\gamma_{CLC}CLC_{ij}+error. \end{aligned} \tag{6}$$

3.4. Results

The results of the hypothesis tests are shown in Table B—3. Unstandardized coefficients are shown, because standardized coefficients cannot be computed in random intercept and slope models (e.g., Hox, Moerbeek and Van de Schoot 2018, pp. 17-18). Because of model convergence challenges in cross-level models and to prevent collinearity issues the moderating effects were tested separately (e.g., Kline 2015, p. 81; Swoboda and Sinning 2022). In addition, the effect sizes were computed to assess the relative strength of the independent variables (e.g., Marsh et al. 2009).

Firms' *international online experience* has a highly significant positive effect on geographic scope, as expected (b=.034, p<.001). The more international online experience ECFs have acquired over time in foreign online markets, the greater their geographic scope (e.g., similar to manufacturing firms, Kirca et al. 2011; 2012b). Therefore, *H1* is supported.

Increasing the *website traffic* of ECFs also has a positive effect on their geographic scope (b=.022, p<.05). The higher firms' cumulative website traffic is, the more foreign markets they enter with additional online shops (Kotha, Rindova and Rothaermel 2001). *H2* is therefore supported.

ECFs' *use of social media* has a highly significant positive effect on their geographic scope (b=.115, p<.001). The more social media followers a firm has acquired over time, the greater its geographic scope is. *H3* is also supported.

		Null Model	Baseline Model 1	Full Model	Baseline Model 2	Rule of Law	Country Development	Logistics Performance
		bp	bp	bp	bp	bp	bp	bp
Direct Effects								
International Online Experience	→ Scope			.034*** (.323)	.034*** (.323)	.035*** (.332)	.029*** (.275)	.026** (.247)
Website Traffic	→ Scope			.021* (.084)	.022* (.088)	.022* (.088)	.023** (.092)	.021* (.084)
Social Media Use	→ Scope			.116*** (.463)	.115*** (.459)	.112*** (.447)	.100** (.399)	.103*** (.411)
Cross-Level Interaction								
Rule of Law	→ Scope					-.266† (-.406)		
	x International Online Experience → Scope					.016*** (.024)		
	x Website Traffic → Scope					.005ns (.008)		
	x Social Media Use → Scope					.035** (.053)		
Country Development	→ Scope						-5.217* (-.618)	
	x International Online Experience → Scope						.188*** (.022)	
	x Website Traffic → Scope						-.043ns (-.005)	
	x Social Media Use → Scope						.377** (.045)	
Logistics Performance	→ Scope							-1.056*** (-.805)
	x International Online Experience → Scope							.043*** (.033)
	x Website Traffic → Scope							.004ns (.003)
	x Social Media Use → Scope							.043* (.033)
Controls (Company Level)								
Firm Size	→ Scope		.011ns	-.087***	-.086***	-.087***	-.081***	-.080***
Mobile Site	→ Scope		.117ns	-.428***	-.426***	-.426***	-.452***	-.451***
Home Market Size	→ Scope		.088*	.086*	.086*	.086*	.100**	.099**
Firm Age	→ Scope		.156***	.093***	.094***	.094***	.092***	.089***
Control (Country Level)								
Host Market Size	→ Scope				-.180***	.008ns	.186ns	.149*
Residual Variance (Country Level)		.389	.391	.287	.252	.227	.221	.143
Explained Variance (Country Level)					12.2%	9.9%	12.3%	43.2%
AIC		7,077.671	6,968.819	6,665.555	5,857.148	1,552.682	5,699.280	5,753.300
BIC (Adjusted)		7,085.766	6,987.706	6,692.537	5,886.828	1,593.155	5,739.753	5,793.773

Note: ***p<.001; **p<.01; *p<.05; †p<.10; ns=Not Significant; b=Unstandardized Coefficients. Effect sizes are shown in brackets.

Table B—3: Results

Source: Own Creation

An increasing degree of *ROL* positively moderates the effect of international online experience on firms' geographic scope ($b_{ROLxIntOnExp}$=.016, p<.001); *H4a* is therefore supported. However, ROL does not moderate the effect of website traffic on geographic scope ($b_{ROLxWebTraff}$=.005, p>.10); *H4b* is thus rejected. The value and transferability of website traffic (i.e., an implicit idea of existing customer relations) may not be affected by ROL, since it is hardly observable and thus does not require explicit adaptation (Kotha, Rindova and Rothaermel 2001). A weaker ROL might also facilitate the tracking of more sensitive customer data in foreign markets, which could cancel out the expected effects. ROL positively moderates the effect of social media use on geographic scope ($b_{ROL-xSocialMed}$=.035, p<.01). *H4c* is therefore supported. Overall, the ROL explains 9.9% of country-level variance.

Regarding the moderation of *host country development*, the results support *H5a*. Country development positively moderates the effects of international online experience on geographic scope ($b_{CDxIntOnExp}$=.188, p<.001). However, as above, *H5b* must be rejected, given that country development does not significantly moderate the effect of website traffic on ECFs' geographic scope ($b_{CDxWebTraff}$=-.043, p>.10). Firms' use and transfer of website traffic does not seem to be affected by host countries' degree of country development. As with ROL, we conclude that stable societal conditions do not increase the value of website traffic for expansion due to its implicit nature. However, we find support for *H5c*. Country development positively moderates the effect of social media on geographic scope ($b_{CDxSocialMed}$=.377, p<.01). Overall, this variable explains 12.3% of the country-level variance.

A host country's higher *logistics performance* positively moderates the effect of international online experience on geographic scope ($b_{LPxIntOnExp}$=.043, p<.001). *H6a* is therefore supported. However, logistics performance does not moderate the relationship between website traffic and geographic scope ($b_{LPxWebTraff}$=.004, p>.10). *H6b* is rejected. Logistics performance does not seem to affect firms' use of website traffic for expansion. In line with the previous nonsignificant results, the value of website traffic is in turn not affected by the logistics context in the host country. The effect of social media on geographic scope is positively moderated by logistics performance, which is in line with our expectations ($b_{LPxSocialMed}$=.043, p<.05); *H6c* is therefore supported. Logistics performance explains 43.2% of the country-specific variance.

Regarding our controls, we find additional significant negative effects exerted by *firm size*, whether the firm has a *mobile site*, and at the country level, *host country market size*. *Home market size* and *firm age* have significant positive effects on ECFs' geographic scope.

3.5. Stability Checks

A random split half test was used to ensure the robustness of the results (see Section G, ESM). This test supports our results for most hypotheses, indicating limited effects of website traffic.

Alternative models were tested (see Section G, ESM). *First*, we included host country online shops that did not offer local currencies to our sample, leading to 3,015 market entries in 125 host countries. This was done because the between-variance in country-level factors might differ. The results show stable positive effects of international online experience (b=.032, p<.001), website traffic (b=.031, p<.01), and social media use (b=.110, p<.001). The moderating effects of ROL ($b_{ROLxIntOnExp}$=.013, p<.01; $b_{ROLxWebTraff}$=-.004, p>.10; $b_{ROLxSocialMed}$=.034, p<.01), country development ($b_{CDxIntOnExp}$=.139, p<.01; $b_{CDxWebTraff}$=-.104, p>.10; $b_{CDxSocialMed}$=.399, p<.001), and logistics performance ($b_{LPxIntOnExp}$=.035, p<.001; $b_{LPxWebTraff}$=-.019, p>.10; $b_{LPxSocialMed}$=.051, p<.05) support our findings. The explained variances is 6.0–9.9% for ROL, 12.3–12.8% for country development, and 43.0–43.2% for logistics performance.

Second, we tested institutional distances (regulative, normative, and cultural-cognitive, according to Scott 2014, p. 56). Host-country distances are expected to affect the value of intangible resources and ECFs' expansion or geographic scope, respectively (Shaheer and Li 2020). High institutional distance might create additional obstacles for ECFs' expansion, as they lack important knowledge about foreign markets, limiting the value of their resources (Schu, Morschett and Swoboda 2016). Firms' resource transfer is likely more difficult when entering institutionally distant foreign markets. In line with our reasoning, international online experience (b=.039, p<.001), website traffic (b=.018, p<.10), and social media use (b=.115, p<.001) exhibit stable effects. However, we find mixed results on the moderations. Regulative distance negatively moderate the effects to some degree ($b_{REGDISxIntOnExp}$=-.004, p<.01; $b_{REGDISxWebTraff}$=.000, p>.10; $b_{REGDISxSocialMed}$=-.012, p<.001). Normative distance shows no moderating effects, and cultural distance shows marginal moderations for the effects of website traffic only. The explained variances for all three country-level variables do not exceed a value of 3.9%. We conclude that the role of institutional distances is less relevant for ECFs in our context.

Third, we checked whether measuring the degree of country development over time would produce stable results despite a smaller sample of 2,479 market entries due to missing data over time. In line with our main model international online experience (b=.034, p<.001), website traffic (b=.020, p<.05), and social media use (b=.112, p<.001) show the same effects in support of our hypotheses. The same is true for the moderating hypotheses, which also mirror our main findings for ROL ($b_{ROLxIntOnExp}$=.016, p<.001; $b_{ROLxWebTraff}$=.008, p>.10; $b_{ROLxSocialMed}$=.042, p<.001), the degree of country development ($b_{CDxIntOnExp}$=.155, p<.01; $b_{CDxWebTraff}$=.050, p>.10; $b_{CDxSocialMed}$=.381, p<.05), and logistics performance ($b_{LPxIntOnExp}$=.042, p<.001; $b_{LPxWebTraff}$=.010, p>.10; $b_{LPxSocialMed}$=.050, p<.05). Therefore we conclude that a static measurement of country development is not an issue in our data.

4. Discussion

4.1. Theoretical Implications

This study extends our limited understanding of how experiential and consumer-related digital intangible resources affect the geographic scope of ECFs (referring to calls, e.g., Liu, Zhang-Zhang and Ghauri 2020; Tolstoy et al. 2021). Our study further advances research by showing that the effects of intangible resources depend on important local host country contexts (e.g., Jean and Kim 2020). Based on these new insights, we carefully provide theoretical and managerial implications below.

Regarding the *first research question*, the results reveal positive effects of ECFs' international online experience, website traffic, and social media use on their geographic scope. These firms' unique intangible resources are critical drivers of their foreign expansion in a digital environment (e.g., Schu, Morschett and Swoboda 2016). In line with theory, our results support the notion that the examined intangible resources are valuable, mostly rare, inimitable, and nonsubstitutable in the online context. Building on these properties, firms may transfer these resources to foreign markets efficiently and exploit them to achieve competitive advantages internationally (e.g., Molloy et al. 2011). Additionally, referring to research on manufacturing and commerce firms, this study extends the scarce literature on ECFs' specific geographic scope decisions (Kotha, Rindova and Rothaermel 2001). Focusing on each independent variable allows for the identification of more nuanced theoretical implications.

We emphasize the relevance of international (online) experience. Knowledge acquired over time is an important base for ECFs' ability to transfer their business to foreign markets and exploit opportunities more effectively. As experience can be used in multiple markets simultaneously, it is valuable for increasing geographic scope. Our results are consistent with those of studies on manufacturing firms and the role of international experience, which is important in e-commerce as well (despite some scholars questioning this, e.g., Pezderka and Sinkovics 2011). Moreover, we contribute to the application of such theory by examining consumer-related intangible resources that are unique to the online context (more recently introduced in the literature, e.g., Samiee, Katsikeas and Hult 2021). Website traffic, i.e., firms' customer relations and online shop popularity, is found to be a valuable digital resource for international expansion. Using website traffic, firms can leverage their analytical tools in foreign markets, transfer their customer reputation, or benefit from better access to advertising partnerships (e.g., Molla-Descals et al. 2014). Firms' social media use is the strongest resource in terms of geographic scope in this study (due to the highest effect size), enabling firms to exploit and transfer their communications and promoted services across borders. Despite fierce competition, social media interactions induce beneficial cross-border domino effects as firms gain followers who share their experiences (e.g., Li, Larimo and Leonidou 2021). Surprisingly, this is a stronger driver than is international online experience, underlining the importance of digital resources for e-commerce expansion (e.g., Chabowski and Samiee 2020). Moreover, website traffic, as the weakest independent variable in our study, underscores our conclusions. Notably, the effects of website traffic are not affected by country-level moderators, and consequently less relevant to scope decisions in general.

In summary, we find support for one prior study on the important role of specific intangible resources in driving ECFs' geographic scope online (Kotha, Rindova and Rothaermel 2001). ECFs may focus on their international online experience and social media use in particular. We advance the prior research by accounting for both traditional and new digital consumer-related resources acquired over time. Studying the effects of intangible resources on geographic scope, we also empirically add to the application of RBV in a digital economy (e.g., Bhandari et al. 2023; Schu, Morschett and Swoboda 2016).

Regarding our *second research question*, we shed light on the overlooked but important role of local host country contexts, which affect ECFs' resource transfer to foreign markets (referring to calls, Jean and Kim 2020; Liu, Zhang-Zhang and Ghauri 2020). Host countries' ROL, degree of country development, and logistics performance have been identified as critical contextual factors in e-commerce. We empirically confirm the importance of these factors for the RBV by using appropriate multilevel modeling and accounting for important cross-level interactions (e.g., in contrast to independent effects, Navarro-García 2016). Our theoretical implications are threefold.

First, in line with theory, the value and transferability of firms' international online experience and social media use is affected by local regulatory conditions (e.g., He, Brouthers and Filatotchev 2013). An increasing ROL offers higher transparency and transactional integrity to ECFs operating in foreign online markets (e.g., Oxley and Yeung 2001). Instead of facing legal issues due to weak ROL, firms can transfer their international online experience and use it to better exploit opportunities. With proprietary rights being protected by a strong ROL, firms may better use social media to transfer communications and services to foreign markets (e.g., Katsikeas, Leonidou and Zeriti 2020). Insights from community interactions are more valuable for increasing geographic scope, and cross-border domino effects are more likely to occur in contexts where societal rules and freedoms are enacted.

Second, the degree of host countries' development is a more important context factor that affects the value of ECFs' international experience and social media for expansion. Firms' international experience is more valuable, and relying on past experiences is less risky in stable and predictable environments. Promising opportunities can be identified and exploited more effectively, as consumer needs fluctuate less in developed countries (e.g., Nuhu, Owens and McQuillan 2021). Moreover, firms may better reach consumers and analyze their needs on social media in contexts with broad access to the internet and popular social media platforms (e.g., Vieira et al. 2019). In developed contexts, social interactions are even more valuable, as consumers who are aware of online fraud are able to interact with a firm via social media.

Third, we show a strong impact of logistics performance on the value of international experience and social media use in foreign markets. Sufficient logistics performance is a necessary condition for firms' ability to use valuable international experience in foreign markets and exploit opportunities. Firms may cooperate with local logistics partners rather than investing in their own logistics infrastructure (e.g., Douglas and Craig 2011). The value of social media as a communication tool for firms' services is higher, as high logistics performance enables firms to optimize their fulfillment, which provides them with a critical competitive advantage (Zhang et al. 2019). Finally, the risks of detrimental domino effects and reputational damage are decreased, enabling firms to take full advantage of social media.

In summary, ECFs can best transfer their resources to increase geographic scope by entering host countries with a strong ROL, a high degree of country development and, most importantly, high local logistics performance. Specifically, logistics performance is the most relevant lever for ECFs' effective expansion (explaining 43.2% of the country-level variance, e.g., Schu and Morschett 2017). Figure B—3 graphically shows the linear moderating cross-level interaction effect of logistics performance on social media use and international online experience. The higher the degree of logistics performance in a country is, the better ECFs can leverage their past international experience and, in particular, social media use to increase geographic scope.

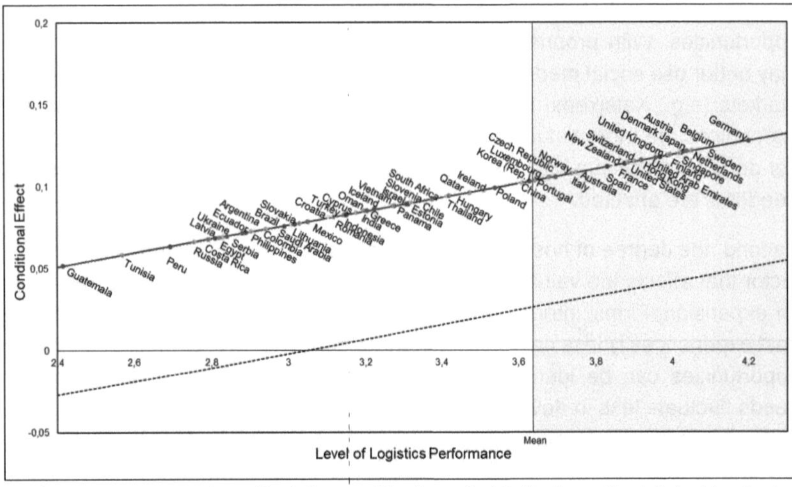

Note: Continuous line represents the conditional effect on social media use, the dotted line the conditional effect on international online experience. The graph indicates the 64 host countries examined in this study. The grey box indicates, starting from the mean of logistics performance, in which countries e-commerce firms can best use their social media or international online experience.

Figure B—3: Moderating Cross-level Interaction Effect of Logistics Performance

Source: Own Creation

4.2. Practical Implications

Managers in ECFs need to be aware of which intangible resources are most valuable for international country expansion. Importantly, understanding host country environments is relevant for leveraging and transferring these resources to increase geographic scope.

Given our findings, firms are advised to gain critical knowledge through international online experience and build online-specific consumer-related resources. Managers may expect that international online experience affects the geographic scope of online expansions, which might be relevant for further international decisions (e.g., speed, Luo, Zhao and Du 2005). However, in particular, firms' website traffic—not affected by any local contextual factor—and social platform interactions—the strongest lever—are of major importance for international geographic expansion. Managers focusing on only one adjustment should prioritize social media use because social media not only plays an important role in geographic expansion but also is known as a key touchpoint that may offer unique services to consumers (Dolega, Rowe and Branagan 2021). The important role of social media is underlined through the top 10% of firms in terms of geographic scope in our sample, which have an average of 9.635 million followers on Facebook alone. Moreover, ECFs like Zalando have strongly invested in social media, with the number of their followers rapidly increasing (Zalando 2021a). Zalando is one of the leading fashion commerce firms in Europe due to its communications being shared and services being discussed across digital borders. This example highlights the important role of large and interactive social communities in increasing geographic scope in a digital age.

Moreover, managers need to be aware of the role of host country local contexts to exploit firms' intangible resources for geographic expansion. Host countries' ROL, degree of country development, and logistics performance are important levers for ECFs. To increase the value of international online experience and social media use, firms should focus on contexts with a strong ROL, high country development, and especially high logistics performance. The latter explains by far the highest country-level variance and is most important. Quick delivery is known to affect ECFs' performance and regional expansion, which can possibly explain the focus of fashion commerce firm Zalando being on European countries. When facing a choice, we carefully advise ECFs to enter contexts where they can benefit from high logistics performance (explaining 43.2% of country variance). Moreover, countries with both a high degree of logistics performance and country development most strongly facilitate ECFs' resource-based geographic expansion (e.g., in Europe, Germany, Sweden, or Belgium, see Figure B—3). Ultimately, these insights may provide an important basis for linking geographic scope decisions with the successful expansion of ECFs (e.g., Liu, Zhang Zhang and Ghauri 2020).

5. Limitations and Further Research

This study has some limitations, suggesting directions for further research.

We refer to a unique longitudinal, geographically diversified database, but broader data would allow further conclusions (e.g., Schu and Morschett 2017). We calculated geographic scope, international online experience and most controls dynamically over time, but respective data on website traffic and social media are missing. Data for country development and logistics performance could not be matched with the years of market entry, but our results provide initial insights for further research. A worldwide database will improve generalizability but, to the best of our knowledge, is not yet available (Swoboda and Sinning 2022). We focus on country-specific online shops, but insights into local presence with logistic investments or studying emerging market ECFs are promising approaches (e.g., Benmamoun et al. 2019).

Regarding our measures, we refer to geographic scope as the number of foreign markets entered. Capturing geographic scope in terms of regional spread (vs.

individual countries) will reveal additional insights (e.g., Bauweraerts et al. 2019). Related multidimensional measures (e.g., degree of internationalization) might allow for a more refined view of ECFs' expansion decisions. We also use the available number of Facebook followers as a common proxy for social media use, while social media includes a variety of elements that may be relevant (e.g., Samiee, Katsikeas and Hult 2021). Moreover, we suggest measuring further important variables in e-commerce that were not available to us (e.g., competitive intensity and home market development), as they are known to affect the geographic scope of offline firms (e.g., Kirca et al. 2012b).

Concerning our conceptual framework, scholars may view geographic scope as a mediator of ECFs' performance, as this topic is unexplored in e-commerce (e.g., Kirca et al. 2011). ECFs' performance is expected to grow, but only to a certain level. We focused on the important intangible resources of ECFs, but the role of firm ownership, team characteristics, or transaction-related website functions should be studied (e.g., Bauweraerts et al. 2019; Love, Roper and Zhou 2016). Our alternative models show that institutional distances explain less country-level variance, but studying further moderators is interesting (e.g., social media strategies and environmental uncertainties, Li, Larimo and Leonidou 2021). However, to draw valid conclusions, future research needs to methodologically account for nested data structures.

C. Study 2: Determinants of Wolly Owned Foreign Direct Investments in E-Commerce Firms: A Hierarchical Country- and Firm-Level Analysis[2]

1. Introduction

Dynamic digitalization has sparked a debate on its impact on IB research and theory (e.g., Stallkamp, Chen and Li 2023; Yang et al. 2025). While most firms are affected, virtual expansion strategies are particularly evident among ECFs, i.e., firms selling physical goods via own online shops or marketplaces to consumers (reaching 23% of global retail sales in 2027; ITA 2024). They mostly internationalize virtually, have immediate access to markets at low cost, and also offer new digital expansion opportunities for manufacturers (e.g., Gong, He and Lengler 2024). However, leading ECFs add selective physical presences over time. For example, serving 150 countries virtually, Amazon (2025), is present in 21 countries with wholly owned FDI, i.e., websites with a local domain, language, currency, and additional investments in own physical assets, such as warehouses and subsidiaries. Alibaba (2024) has FDI in 11 countries; Rakuten (2024) has FDI in four countries. Such selective choices offer ECFs local advantages such as penetration of markets through adapted offers and same-day-delivery services, local images, or management (e.g., Batsakis, Konara and Theoharakis 2023; Hua and Wu 2024). IB research assumes that digitalization reduces the importance of firms' experience or country barriers and facilitates rapid virtual internationalization (e.g., Schu, Morschett and Swoboda 2016). However, this nascent research has hardly addressed ECFs' FDI, which is also important to digital firms.

This study provides a first theory based understanding of ECFs' FDI and helps establish an empirical baseline for research on digital firms' internationalization (Stallkamp, Chen and Li 2023; Verbeke, Coeurderoy and Matt 2018). ECFs' specific digital and physical business model affects ECFs' FDI differently than the production-based FDI of manufacturers does (e.g., Brouthers et al. 2022). Thus, we seek novel insights by linking ECFs' virtual and physical business model elements, i.e., yet unknown specific online learning capabilities and host country barriers in FDI. Extending refined internationalization process models, we explore why ECFs pursue FDI despite virtual options or low country barriers and whether virtual presence provides sufficient learning to make FDI decisions (e.g., Swoboda and Sinning 2022).

---

[2] This study is accepted for publication as: Mueller, M., & Swoboda, B. (2025). Determinants of Wolly Owned Foreign Direct Investments in E-Commerce Firms: A Hierarchical Country- and Firm-Level Analysis. *Management International Review*, In Press (acceptance letter 14.03.2025, see Section G, ESM).

M. Müller, *Strategic Management of International E-Commerce Firms*,
Handel und Internationales Marketing Retailing and International Marketing,
https://doi.org/10.1007/978-3-658-49680-7_3

Empirical studies have mainly addressed FDI among manufacturers (e.g., meta-analyses by Cuervo-Cazurra et al. 2023; Wan et al. 2023) and service or IT firms. The latter, for example, highlight traditional antecedents of FDI, such as institutional distance (Picot-Coupey, Burt and Cliquet 2014; Sánchez Peinado and Pla Barber 2006), host country or FDI experience (Evans, Mavondo and Bridson 2008; Pla-Barber, Villar and León-Darder 2014), and firm size or market attractiveness (Czinkota et al. 2009; Ekeledo and Sivakumar 2004a). For digital firms, especially ECFs, only a few studies exist on various decisions. Examples include the roles of distances or capabilities in ECFs' internationalization speed (Luo, Zhao and Du 2005; Schu, Morschett and Swoboda 2016) or of distances in market selection (Schu and Morschett 2017). For entry choice, distances have been shown to be relevant (Lee, Pattnaik and Gaur 2023; Rothaermel, Kotha and Steensma 2006), alongside reputation for geographic scope (Kotha, Rindova and Rothaermel 2001). Country-level antecedents were addressed by three studies on speed (e.g., legal factors, internet use; Luo, Zhao and Du 2005), market selection (e.g., ROL, market attractiveness; Schu and Morschett 2017), and market entry (culture; Rothaermel, Kotha and Steensma 2006). Virtual presence, i.e., dot-com vs. local domains, was shown to be influenced by the entrepreneurial orientation of small exporting manufacturers only (Ipsmiller, Dikova and Brouthers 2022); FDI vs. other modes were linked to the institutional distances of digital firms only (Stallkamp, Chen and Li 2023). No study on ECFs has considered virtual vs. physical presence. Conceptual papers refer to new theoretical antecedents and virtual modes (Brouthers et al. 2022), whereas other papers question the novelty of both for ECFs (Hennart 2022).

Despite this controversy, a surprising research gap exists in the literature on digital firms' FDI. While earlier studies expected the internet to replace physical presence (e.g., Sinkovics, Sinkovics and Jean 2013), scholars have recently argued that ECFs and platforms can obviate market-seeking FDI (Stallkamp, Chen and Li 2023; Yang et al. 2025). However, practical evidence reveals that ECFs establish selected physical presences over time, which few scholars have noted, leading to calls for closer examination of ECFs' local asset decisions owing to their growing relevance and specific hybrid (digital and physical) business model (e.g., Batsakis, Konara and Theoharakis 2023; Swoboda and Sinning 2022). We address this gap by analyzing an important research question: Whether and how strongly do specific firm- and host country-level factors drive ECFs' choice of wholly owned FDI? In theorizing respective effects, we add to mode choice research of digital firms and offer two contributions to literature.

First, in light of ECFs' specific business model, we expand theoretical discussions of physical market presence in the emerging research on digital firms.

Their market-seeking FDI differs from manufacturers' FDI focus on wholly owned production subsidiaries abroad or the online presence of small manufacturers often studied in IB (e.g., Tolstoy, Hånell and Özbek 2023; Ipsmiller, Dikova and Brouthers 2022), as those lacking online knowledge or commerce skills also turn to ECFs abroad (Gong, He and Lengler 2024). Although ECFs can ship from abroad, only a physically present business can facilitate locally adapted goods, prices or services, management, or relationships with customers, authorities, or suppliers (Batsakis, Konara and Theoharakis 2023; Mueller and Swoboda 2025). As ECFs physically move goods, they also differ from IT firms such as Google or Oracle and i-business firms such as Netflix or eBay (Paul and Gupta 2014; Lee, Pattnaik and Gaur 2023). Such firms' offers and customer interactions are usually digital with different FDI requirements that support a scaling of platforms via data centers or cloud infrastructure (Brouthers et al. 2022). ECFs' specific hybrid business model requires an analysis of specific FDI decisions. This calls for developing theoretical rationales on the antecedents of ECFs' decisions to add a physical presence in a country or not (Meyer et al. 2023).

Second, we contribute novel insights to the literature on digital internationalization concerning the joint role of firm- and country-level antecedents of FDI (which is generally rarely done in FDI research, e.g., Wan et al. 2023). We address research calls to clarify to what extent ECFs' FDI depends on specific online capabilities and external barriers (e.g., Meyer et al. 2023; Tolstoy et al. 2021). In particular, at the *firm level,* we know that distances affect various decisions of ECFs, whereas the role of experience in digital firms' internationalization has been debated (e.g., Gabrielsson, Raatikainen and Julkunen 2022; Pezderka and Sinkovics 2011). We challenge skeptics by highlighting ECFs' specific online capabilities and path-dependent virtual learning over time (e.g., in general and in host countries; Swoboda and Sinning 2022). We newly theorize that, unlike offline firms, ECFs gain experience digitally from successful offers, promotions, or local online interactions with consumers that allow them to exploit FDI opportunities, for example. We provide a first understanding of such unknown online learning mechanisms for a physical presence, as research on this topic has been limited, despite the growth of digital businesses (e.g., Gong, He and Lengler 2024). At the *country level,* specific antecedents of ECFs' business model abroad seem obvious: host countries' logistics, internet users, or ROL. We theorize that these match the logic of specific barriers or location advantages in digital markets for ECFs' hybrid business model (e.g., Dunning and Wymbs 2001; in difference to those most often studied for manufacturers, e.g., Pezderka and Sinkovics 2011). Only macroeconomic studies have discussed specific logistics or internet barriers, with contradictory findings for export vs. FDI flows. Finally, we also respond to calls for adopting hierarchical modeling when analyzing firm- and country-level drivers of digital firms' internationalization (e.g., Surana et al. 2024).

The remainder of this study proceeds as follows. Drawing on conceptualizations and theory, we derive and test hypotheses based on 1,726 mode decisions over 11 years corresponding to 241 ECFs originating in 22 home countries. After the results are presented, we provide theoretical and practical implications as well as directions for further research.

2. Conceptualization and Hypothesis Development

2.1. Operation Modes of ECFs

Operation modes represent governance structures that allow firms to implement their business model in host countries differently (e.g., Brouthers et al. 2022). We conceptualize ECFs' decisions regarding virtual vs. physical presence (export-based vs. wholly owned FDI) for several reasons that are specific to ECFs. The business model and internationalization of ECFs are based on a virtual presence with digital learning but require physical distribution, such as "last-mile" logistics and locally adapted offers (e.g., Meyer et al. 2023). While IB research has discussed many drivers of manufacturers' FDI, we rethink this decision for digital firms and advance theory on how ECFs' operation mode decisions are made. ECFs may simplify (mode) decisions to practical decisions (e.g., Pan and Tse 2000). The latter, we argue, ultimately focus on whether a physical presence should be added or not and define whether the business model can be fully transferred abroad.

Virtual presence among international ECFs refers to country-specific websites (e.g., dot-uk domain, language, currency) where goods are shipped from abroad (whereas dot-com domains do not indicate a clear market entry and are not host country-specific; Hua and Wu 2024; Ipsmiller, Dikova and Brouthers 2022; Swoboda and Sinning 2022). This also applies to ECFs' *cooperation with* contractual partners or local service providers that are partly strategically controlled (e.g., licensing, networks), which remain export-based (e.g., Hennart 2022). JVs with shared operational control are rare and atypical of digital firms and ECFs (e.g., Brouthers et al. 2022; Mueller and Swoboda 2025, and in our data). *Physical presence* refers to wholly owned FDI that is specific to ECFs' business needs, i.e., local domains and long-term investments in physical assets that facilitate the local replication of the business model (e.g., Stallkamp, Chen and Li 2023). Specific examples include wholly owned warehouses that focus on last-mile delivery and marketing subsidiaries that facilitate local customer relationship management and offers (e.g., assortments, prices, customer service, Tolstoy et al. 2021). However, establishing such a physical presence depends on local market knowledge and specific infrastructure (e.g., Ahi, Sinkovics and Sinkovics 2023).

2.2. Theory and ECFs' Specific Antecedents

The only study on digital firms' FDI theoretically explains the role of distance for FDI on the basis of the transferability of complementary resources abroad (Stallkamp, Chen and Li 2023). We extend this view and refer to capability and redefined internationalization process reasoning (major theories in research on the internationalization of digital firms, e.g., Cahen and Borini 2020; Vahlne and Johanson 2017; Yang et al. 2025). We theorize that ECFs can scale and transfer online capabilities and leverage digital learning as a path-dependent process in FDI (Schu and Morschett 2017). ECFs' experiences from virtual presence, which are distinct from traditional learning through the physical presence of manufacturers, for example (e.g., Coviello, Kano and Liesch 2017), determine their decisions to add physical presence in selected countries over time. We make both theories useful for explaining ECFs' FDI decisions, offering novel rationales for facilitating digital capability transfer and opportunity recognition via virtual presence and focused exploitation with FDI (e.g., Swoboda and Sinning 2022; Vahlne and Johanson 2017). In particular, we offer rationales on the relative value and limits of different types of online experience capabilities and clarify the questionable role of experience in digital firms (Pezderka and Sinkovics 2011). As both theories only implicitly consider country factors, we complementarily theorize business model-specific rationales on barriers and location advantages for ECFs (Dunning and Wymbs 2001). This supports a joint view of the firm- and country-level antecedents of FDI. We argue that a lack of specific logistic and internet infrastructure or ROL in a country may be a barrier to FDI (i.e., force virtual presence, Meyer et al. 2023), whereas their presence offers specific location advantages for ECFs' business model.

In line with capability and process theories, we conceptualize virtual location- and nonlocation-bound online knowledge (e.g., Cahen and Borini 2020; Vahlne and Johanson 2017). *Nonlocation-bound online knowledge* pertains to ECFs' learned routines in dealing with foreign customers virtually to exploit FDI opportunities in foreign markets over time (opportunity identification is likely simplified virtually; Tang and Gudergan 2018). Such knowledge also pertains to prior FDI online experience, which may affect subsequent FDI in other countries (Schwens et al. 2018b). It can be transferred as an online capability across foreign markets virtually. *Location-bound knowledge* pertains to ECFs' insights into a specific country's needs from virtual presence over time (not transferable to other markets; He, Brouthers and Filatotchev 2013). However, ECFs may rely too much on online capabilities and run the risk of falling into a "virtuality trap" (Sinkovics, Sinkovics and Jean 2013). We thus identify knowledge based on or learning via virtual presence as an important but controversial basis for FDI among digital firms.

We conceptualize ECFs' specific host country infrastructure and ROL as specific barriers to ECFs' hybrid business model and sources of specific location advantages (Dunning and Wymbs 2001; Meyer et al. 2023). While many external antecedents affect manufacturing and service firms' FDI (e.g., Wan et al. 2023), obvious local barriers or advantages for digital firms' or ECFs' FDI remain largely unexplored (e.g., Cumming et al. 2023). Countries' logistics infrastructure, commonly referred to as "logistics performance", and internet users or infrastructure, for example, have been linked to both FDI and exports by macroeconomic studies only (Halaszovich and Kinra 2020; Latif et al. 2018). Despite the high logistics costs of ECFs (over 25% of total costs; Reuters 2023; Janjevic and Winkenbach 2020) or their reliance on sufficient internet users in a country, the critical role of host country logistics performance or internet users for ECFs needs theorization. Similarly, the critical role of ROL in digital business models has been highlighted (e.g., Schu and Morschett 2017), but its role in mode choices has not. Addressing this theoretically, we propose that ECFs may face strong local barriers and costs for FDI if specific e-commerce infrastructure is lacking, while its presence could be a specific location advantage. For example, a country's low logistics performance can be a barrier for ECFs' ability to ensure quick delivery from warehouses, whereas high performance can make delivery more efficient. A lack of internet users can be a barrier to reaching customers, while the opposite offers location advantages with a latent broad customer base (e.g., Meyer et al. 2023). ECFs may also face local legal barriers and compliance-related risks or increased coordination costs due to a lack of ROL (e.g., Luo, Zhao and Du 2005).

Additionally, a systematic literature review supports our choices of relevant antecedents to ECFs' FDI (see Figure C—1, for a detailed description see Section G, ESM). We study experience as an important antecedent according to offline mode research, whereas the role of (online) experience is unknown and questioned for online businesses (e.g., Sinkovics, Sinkovics and Jean 2013). At the firm level, some antecedents of ECFs' internationalization (e.g., mainly distances or market capabilities) have been explored, but no types of online experience. At the country level, ECFs' business model-specific antecedents have mostly not been considered empirically. This review highlights the lack of knowledge and joint theoretical consideration of firm- and country-level antecedents of digital firms' mode decisions.

		Firm Level				Country Level			
	Industry	International Experience	Host Country Experience	FDI Experience	Other (see meta-analyses)	Logistics	Internet	ROL	Other (see meta-analyses)
Offline	Manufacturing	*Dow and Larimo 2009*; Hernández and Nieto 2015; Tang and Gudergan 2018; etc.	*He, Brouthers and Filatotchev 2013; Wan et al. 2023*; etc.	*Cui, Li and Li 2013*; Schwens et al. 2018b; etc.	Beugelsdijk et al. 2018; *Klier et al. 2017*; *Wan et al. 2023*; etc.	–	–	*Bailey 2018*; *Stoian and Filippaios 2008*, etc.	*Cuervo-Cazurra et al. 2023; Kostova et al. 2020; Morschett, Schramm-Klein and Swoboda 2010*; etc.
Offline	Services /IT	*Czinkota et al. 2009*; *Ekeledo and Sivakumar 2004a*; Evans, Mavondo and Bridson 2008	*Pla-Barber, Villar and León-Darder 2014*	*Pla-Barber, Villar and León-Darder 2014*	Picot-Coupey, Burt and Cliquet 2014; *Sánchez Peinado and Pla Barber 2006*; etc.	–	–	–	Picot-Coupey, Burt and Cliquet 2014; *Sánchez Peinado and Pla Barber 2006*; etc.
Online	Manufacturing		–	–	*Ipsmiller, Dikova and Brouthers 2022*	–	–	–	–
Online	Services /IT[1]	–	–	–	*Stallkamp, Chen and Li 2023*	–	–	–	–

Note: *Italics*=Studies on binary mode choice, e.g., FDI vs. other modes. Etc.=Further studies not listed here. [1] Including i-business and ECFs.

Figure C—1: Literature Review on Antecedents of Operation Mode Decisions

Source: Own Creation

Next, we derive hypotheses for each relationship based on theoretical rationales and clarify our current empirical knowledge first. We control and test traditional antecedents in stability checks (e.g., firm size or age and market attractiveness factors such as size, growth, population, or development).

2.3. Hypotheses Regarding Online Experience Factors

As mentioned, we argue that specific online capabilities emerge from ECFs' path-dependent virtual learning processes in foreign markets that are used to make decisions on physical presence (e.g., Swoboda and Sinning 2022). ECFs can transfer general, country-specific, or FDI-related online experience capabilities differently based on virtual learning to enhance their ability to recognize and particularly exploit selected FDI opportunities (e.g., Vahlne and Johanson 2017).

International online experience refers to ECFs' degree of general nonlocation-bound knowledge regarding virtual operations in foreign markets, which is acquired via local domains over time (as an empirically established proxy; e.g., Wan et al. 2023). Empirical studies have often identified international experiences as antecedents of manufacturers' FDI (e.g., inconclusively, Dow and Larimo 2009, Hernández and Nieto 2015, Tang and Gudergan 2018; see Figure C—1) and that of service and IT firms (e.g., Czinkota et al. 2009; Ekeledo and Sivakumar 2004a). However, we argue that virtually gained international experience differs from the experience of manufacturing or service firms (e.g.,

Pezderka and Sinkovics 2011). Online experience pertains to ECFs' digital capabilities, which enable them to provide offers and services or interact with authorities in different countries over time and can be used to exploit FDI opportunities abroad. While offline experience may be used to promote virtual expansion in other countries (as indicated for local domains of small manufacturing firms; Ipsmiller, Dikova and Brouthers 2022), it is unclear whether online experience is sufficient for deciding on the physical presence of ECFs (e.g., Coviello, Kano and Liesch 2017), as we argue.

We theoretically argue that *high international online experience* facilitates learning and the recognition of market opportunities for FDI. ECFs accumulate knowledge and transfer their online capabilities abroad in terms of digitally successful offers, services such as products or promotions, or relations to foreign authorities (e.g., Schu and Morschett 2017; Vahlne and Johanson 2017). Over time, ECFs recognize sales opportunities more easily in certain growing e-commerce markets and especially exploit them with FDI and local supply chain processes such as logistics and purchasing (e.g., Swoboda and Sinning 2022). This may be less risky even if physical processes are not established abroad. For example, with nearly 20 years of international online experience, Amazon recognized opportunities for FDI in Australia and Singapore in 2017. This was based on the firm's digital capabilities from a long virtual presence abroad and learned potential to establish supply chain processes in these growing markets (Pash 2017). We thus argue that ECFs with high international online experience have a better sense of where to exploit FDI and may be less reluctant to invest in new physical and adapted virtual processes.

In the case of a *low international online experience*, few virtual capabilities to transfer or recognize opportunities abroad exist (e.g., Tolstoy et al. 2021). Firms have less knowledge of how to promote digital offers or which products are successful abroad or how to deal with authorities in different countries. Such ECFs' ability to recognize investment opportunities is limited. ECFs are especially limited in exploiting market opportunities in a foreign country (e.g., developing new supply chain processes alongside adapted market offers, Stallkamp, Chen and Li 2023). Their risks of FDI are greater, and missed opportunities may hinder success (e.g., Swoboda and Sinning 2022). ECFs may even underestimate such experience, which could cause their business models to fail abroad (e.g., Pezderka and Sinkovics 2011).

We propose the following hypothesis:

H1. International online experience has a positive effect on an ECF's propensity to choose wholly owned FDI.

Host country online experience is acquired through virtual presence over time and pertains to the degree of a firm's location-bound knowledge regarding virtual operations in a particular foreign market. Empirical studies have often shown the role of host country experience for manufacturers' FDI (e.g., He, Brouthers and Filatotchev 2013; see Figure C—1) but only once for service firms (Pla-Barber, Villar and León-Darder 2014). These studies have argued that firms with such experience identify more local opportunities, overcome local obstacles, and increase their control in countries (e.g., Wan et al. 2023). In contrast, for digital firms, we only know that such market (but not online) knowledge affects market selection (Schu and Morschett 2017). We argue that ECFs with host country online experience can transfer their capabilities and knowledge of local customers or business practices more easily, especially to exploit FDI opportunities in a country (e.g., Ipsmiller, Dikova and Brouthers 2022). This location-bound knowledge is likely a major online capability to exploit FDI opportunities in a specific country (e.g., Colton, Roth and Bearden 2010).

We argue that *high host country online experience* provides unique knowledge from ECFs' country-specific virtual interactions over time. This includes especially knowledge of local customer needs and preferences but also local business practices, competitors, or further conditions. ECFs with such knowledge develop country-specific online capabilities and can more easily recognize local market opportunities and a suitable time to exploit them with FDI in a country. For example, a country may exhibit strong local e-commerce growth but also specific payment or delivery conditions. Exploiting such local opportunities requires adapted virtual offers to customer needs and especially supportive physical investments (e.g., locally adapted delivery, returns, products, prices, or enterprise resource planning systems; Janjevic and Winkenbach 2020). This may help establish the ECF physically as a local business. For example, Amazon entered Brazil in 2012 but chose wholly owned FDI only in 2019. The firm's main reasons included different taxation rules across regions (e.g., specific taxation in each federal geographical unit) and complicated delivery conditions, which required extensive (online) learning (Mello 2019). High host country online experience may also increase the confidence or commitment of ECF managers to invest in a specific market (e.g., similar to host country offline experience among manufacturers, Luo, Zhao and Du 2005).

In contrast, *low host country online experience* implies lower familiarity with a specific country's online customers, competitors and other conditions and thus the absence of specific online capabilities in a country (e.g., Schu and Morschett 2017). The potential local customers, employees, or suppliers who are needed for a physical presence are likely unaware of the ECF and may be reluctant to engage with it (e.g., Coviello, Kano and Liesch 2017). This may result in considerable liabilities of foreignness that may prevent the recognition and critical exploitation of local opportunities with wholly owned FDI (e.g., Swoboda and Sinning 2022).

We therefore propose the following hypothesis:

H2. Host country online experience has a positive effect on an ECF's propensity to choose wholly owned FDI.

FDI online experience is defined as ECFs' degree of nonlocation-bound knowledge about virtual and physical operations abroad acquired from previous FDI in foreign online markets over time. Empirical studies have reported that FDI experience among manufacturers increases their likelihood of further FDI (e.g., Cui, Li and Li 2013, see Figure C—1); one study reported the opposite result among service firms (Pla-Barber, Villar and León-Darder 2014). Manufacturers with FDI experience typically have established or refined routines for subsequent FDI in new foreign markets (e.g., Schwens et al. 2018b). For digital firms, such an experience has not yet been considered. We theoretically argue that FDI online experience allows ECFs to learn from both virtual and physical experience, i.e., develop hybrid capabilities. They can transfer their knowledge concerning successful products, customer relations, physical services, and management as capabilities abroad, thus facilitating further FDI.

Theoretically, ECFs with *high FDI online experience* draw not only on knowledge from previous virtual interactions abroad but also on previous FDI over time (e.g., Cui, Li and Li 2013). This knowledge represents ECFs' hybrid capability to generally set up and operate a physical presence (e.g., warehouses, subsidiaries, and management) in addition to a virtual presence abroad, thus replicating their hybrid business (e.g., Batsakis et al. 2023). For example, Zalando (2015) first implemented FDI in Italy in 2015, followed by wholly owned FDI in France and Poland, thereby drawing on its previous experience with establishing fulfillment centers and subsidiaries. High FDI online experience may also help firms transfer knowledge of specific management skills to subsidiaries and the hybrid business model via closely linked virtual and physical processes (e.g., Batsakis, Konara and Theoharakis 2023). Specific management skills in digital firms and ECFs include an IT-driven and entrepreneurial firm structure and culture or data-driven decision making based on specific key performance indicators (e.g., Ipsmiller, Dikova and Brouthers 2022; Tolstoy, Hånell and Özbek 2023).

In contrast, ECFs with *no or low FDI online experience* lack knowledge from prior FDI and cannot use or transfer their capabilities to establish and operate subsidiaries abroad (e.g., Fleury et al. 2024). For such ECFs, establishing specific organizational structures and processes in foreign countries is more difficult, and their FDI-related decisions are more complex. In exploiting FDI opportunities, these firms have no or few capabilities or routines for establishing such structures or processes (e.g., Wentrup 2016).

We assume that FDI online experience increases FDI propensity and propose:

H3. FDI online experience has a positive effect on an ECF's propensity to choose wholly owned FDI.

2.4. Hypotheses Regarding Environmental Factors

Regardless of industry and firm type, a certain level of infrastructure is necessary for FDI. Studies have analyzed several country-level antecedents of mode choices (see Figure C—1), however, more seldom than firm internal antecedents and often as part of broader constructs (e.g., infrastructural quality or market attractiveness, e.g., Filatotchev et al. 2007; Morschett, Schramm-Klein and Swoboda 2010). We argue that specific infrastructural factors predominantly affect ECFs' establishment of the hybrid business model abroad next to their capability transfer and learning. Logistics infrastructure in a country is directly tied to ECFs' physical business model elements and internet use to the virtual ones, whereas ROL is critical with respect to customer data and regulatory compliance in different countries (e.g., Schu and Morschett 2017; Oxley and Yeung 2001).

A *host country's logistics performance* defines the quality of the infrastructure for moving physical goods within a country and across its borders (Arvis et al. 2018). Empirical studies on manufacturing or service firms have investigated, for example, cost advantages, regional characteristics, the quality of infrastructure, or economic factors as possible antecedents of mode choices (Du, Lu and Tao 2008; Demirbag, Tatoglu and Glaister 2008; Filatotchev et al. 2007; Nielsen, Asmussen and Weatherall 2017). Respective studies of logistics infrastructure do not exist for such firms (not being a primary infrastructural barrier in contrast to others; e.g., Kwon and Konopa 1993). Studies on digital firms are missing as well (see Figure C—1; Schu and Morschett 2017 only control countries' logistics performance). Macroeconomic studies show inconclusive insights into the relevance of logistics infrastructure for export but also FDI flows (e.g., Halaszovich and Kinra 2020; in e-commerce, He, Wu and Choi 2021). Blyde and Molina (2015) analyze such roles for manufacturers' FDI and state that most studies capture this only indirectly via distance measures. We argue that theoretically logistics performance in a host country might be either a barrier or a location advantage for ECFs' physical (vs. virtual) presence (especially with regard to supply chain processes; e.g., Arvis et al. 2018; Cumming et al. 2023).

High logistics performance in a country arguably reduces barriers and offers location advantages for ECFs' physical presence. Important logistics competencies are a basis for ECFs' competitive advantage (e.g., Janjevic and Winkenbach 2020). These include efficient storage and warehousing, order fulfillment, customer-centered last-mile delivery, or return management but also IT-support or automated inventory management systems, for example (e.g., Hua and Wu 2024). Logistics costs of ECFs are over 25% of total costs (e.g., Reuters 2023; Zalando 2023). The addition of specific supply chain processes, such as selecting, negotiating, and interacting with suppliers and procuring goods, increases these relative costs further to 70–80%. To control this specific cost situation abroad, ECFs seek logistics infrastructure in a country to reduce the barriers to business model replication and FDI (e.g., Meyer et al. 2023). We argue that ECFs can realize their logistics- and IT-based business model and obtain competitive advantages abroad and use infrastructure as a location advantage for FDI. High logistics performance is thus a key factor in the service quality offered to customers (e.g., timely delivery, free returns, or order tracking).

In contrast, *low logistics performance in a country* directly constrains ECFs' logistics competencies and the corresponding advantages and costs (Pezderka and Sinkovics 2011). Similarly, e.g., reliance on exports and logistics partners because of lower logistics performance likely increase ECFs' costs (e.g., Hua and Wu 2024). We also argue that ECFs that face greater barriers due to their inability to provide quality services that they have promoted via FDI are likely to offer a poor customer experience (e.g., Schu and Morschett 2017).

We propose the following:

H4. Logistics performance has a positive effect on an ECF's propensity to choose wholly owned FDI.

A country's *internet user population* reflects the size of the population using the internet, its familiarity with digital technology, its available technological infrastructure, and the potential demand for ECFs (e.g., Meyer et al. 2023). Empirically, internet use in general is not linked with manufacturing or service firms' mode choices (see Figure C—1). Studies on manufacturers' mode choices focus mostly on market attractiveness elements with mixed insights in meta-analyses and without agreement on an appropriate proxy but not on specific IT or internet infrastructure (Wan et al. 2023). However, internet use in a country does affect ECFs' decisions, such as market selection or internationalization speed (Luo, Zhao and

Du 2005; Schu and Morschett 2017). Macroeconomic studies have provided inconclusive insights into the effects of internet infrastructure. Most studies show effects on export intensity (Lin 2015; Visser 2019) and fewer on FDI flows (e.g., Arvin, Pradhan and Nair 2021; Latif et al. 2018). Internet use is generally relevant to ECFs' business model to address customers via virtual presence (Ekeledo and Sivakumar 2004b), and we argue that this factor may present a specific barrier or offer location advantages for ECFs' FDI (e.g., Dunning and Wymbs 2001). We also test traditional proxies for market attractiveness in our stability checks.

We argue that a *large internet user population* reduces ECFs' barriers for specific customer-related digital activities and offers location advantages for FDI. These activities are based on the real-time collection of customer data and a large potential online customer base. ECFs may use these to adapt their products or prices to individual needs via their unique one-to-one marketing (Janjevic and Winkenbach 2020). Many internet users lower the barriers for being able to control or leverage such customer-related virtual activities and respective location advantages with FDI. However, whether internet users drive FDI is questionable for ECFs. Amazon (1998), for example, first implemented FDI in countries with many internet users, such as the UK or Germany, whereas German About You (2021) implemented FDI in markets with fewer internet users but increased online spending, such as Slovakia or Poland (Scayle GmbH 2024). Moreover, a large internet population allows ECFs to leverage increased local demand through fully controlled subsidiaries that enable high-quality offers and services (e.g., Mueller and Swoboda 2025) and even economies of scale (e.g., lower unit costs; Luo, Zhao and Du 2005).

In contrast, in countries with a *smaller internet user population,* customers may engage more with traditional media (e.g., television, Brouthers, Geisser and Rothlauf 2016). Low virtual demand for offers makes establishing a physical presence less attractive, and a virtual-only presence may be preferable owing to a lack of location advantages. This situation may also indicate a country's low level of digital readiness and thus confront ECFs with greater barriers, increasing their reluctance to implement FDI (Ekeledo and Sivakumar 2004b). Such a condition may also signal a lack of government support for digital businesses, thus posing challenges to FDI (Ahi, Sinkovics and Sinkovics 2023).

We propose the following:

H5. The internet user population has a positive effect on an ECF's propensity to choose wholly owned FDI.

Rule of law defines the degree to which formal rules and regulations are enforced in a country (e.g., Oxley and Yeung 2001). Studies on manufacturing firms have shown that ROL, among other regulatory factors, attracts FDI (e.g., Bailey 2018; Stoian and Filippaios 2008). Studies on service firms do not exist (see Figure C—1), while legal protection or ROL reduce ECFs' barriers of market selection or internationalization speed (Luo, Zhao and Du 2005; Schu and Morschett 2017). Macroeconomic research has again reported mixed effects in favor of exports or FDI alongside negative effects on FDI (e.g., Contractor et al. 2020; 2021; Yu, Beugelsdijk and de Haan 2015). It remains unclear whether ROL drives digital firms' mode choices. Theoretically, ROL is a specific regulatory factor pertaining to ECFs' internationalization (e.g., Ahi, Sinkovics and Sinkovics 2023). We argue that countries' high ROL reduces barriers to local regulatory compliance and offers location advantages such as reduced coordination costs in the replication of the firm's business model through a physical presence and thus FDI (e.g., Cumming et al. 2023).

We argue that *high or increasing ROL* can create barriers for export-based ECFs and offer location advantages to ECFs that implement FDI in a country. ECFs face specific and dynamic regulations abroad, e.g., concerning online contracts, competition, prices, ethical or transparent supply chains, or the protection of customer and property rights (Meyer et al. 2023). Export-based Chinese ECFs such as Temu or Shein face increasing pressure from EU and US regulations such as the supply chain act (Financial Times 2024). The latter abolished the 150 euro limit up to which items could be shipped duty-free from China to the EU, thus preventing aggressive low-price exports. Thus, governments incentivize ECFs' physical presence. However, FDI can also confront ECFs with barriers resulting from local restrictions on FDI (Ahi, Sinkovics and Sinkovics 2023). Such barriers led Amazon to divest in China, which required local data storage by law, thus restricting the firm's own physical presence (ECDB 2024d). We argue that high ROL reduces the legal barriers faced by ECFs and offers them local advantages pertaining to FDI as a result of cooperation with local authorities, lower local coordination costs and more compliance with local laws with regard to offers and supply chains (e.g., Pezderka and Sinkovics 2011).

In contrast, *low or decreasing ROL* in a country may confront ECFs with FDI-related barriers due to a lack of specific regulations, thus favoring online activities. This situation may result in limited protection of ECFs' contracts with local stakeholders, unfair competition, and weak sanctions of violations of customer or property rights (e.g., Meyer et al. 2023). Moreover, in this context, ECFs' relationships with local governments may be unstable, the coordination of subsidiaries may be costly, and local compliance may be challenging, thus giving rise to barriers and local disadvantages to such firms' physical presence (e.g., Luo, Zhao and Du 2005).

We propose the following:

H6. Rule of law has a positive effect on an ECF's propensity to choose wholly owned FDI.

Figure C—2 illustrates our conceptual framework and hypothesized effects.

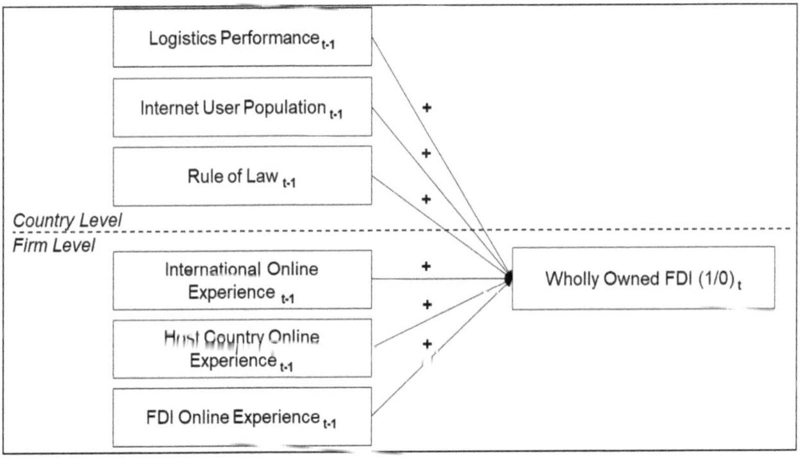

Figure C—2: Conceptual Framework
Source: Own Creation

3. Empirical Study

3.1. Sample

We developed a unique hierarchical database over time by referring initially to the only (to our knowledge) available and reliable secondary data concerning international ECFs (e.g., Swoboda and Sinning 2022). Longitudinal data capture trends and changes in internationalization, facilitate the interpretation of causal relationships, and reduce possible biases more effectively than cross-sectional data (e.g., Rindfleisch et al. 2008).

Our selection of ECFs was based on the 2010–2020 Internet Retailer's ranking of the 500 leading B2C ECFs in Europe (in terms of sales) provided by Digital Commerce 360 (2021), an agency that tracks firm-level data (e.g., website functions, traffic, and online sales) based on firms' information or estimations verified by each firm since 2010. This data source is suitable for the systematic selection of international ECFs (e.g., Schu and Morschett 2017), and this period is important, as e-commerce was one of the most rapidly growing industries during this time (e.g., U.S. sales increased by more than 400%, U.S. Census Bureau 2010; 2022, similar to major EU countries such as the UK or Germany, Centre for Retail Research 2023; HDE 2024). We used complete data from the time when it became available until the COVID-19 pandemic in 2021 (which had various impacts, e.g., on increased online sales, Cumming et al. 2023; this period also excluded the wars in Ukraine and Palestine) and tested our framework for possible differences between early and late FDI (2010–2015 and 2016–2020) in stability checks. We identified 804 ECFs that were not necessarily founded in Europe and may be active globally; however, they had to be present in at least one country abroad. A total of 215 ECFs that operated solely in their home markets were excluded, as were 147 ECFs that offered international shipping only via "dot-com domains." Moreover, 76 firms were not included among the leading firms in subsequent years, and 16 firms did not survive. This selection process identified 350 ECFs.

The database shows each foreign country entered by each ECF. We double-checked the presence of ECFs in each country by opening the host country website and verifying any possible presence in other countries in the following step. The chosen operation mode and market entry date were determined by the authors and trained graduate student assistants from annual reports, firm websites, press releases, public archives or articles, social media, business directories or recruitment sites. We verified 75% of these data through at least two sources. Wholly owned FDI was defined as the opening of ECFs' wholly owned fulfillment centers, logistics units, and sales/service centers in a country, i.e., investments related to the online business, in the respective year. A period of one year between the FDI decision and its implementation is common in IB research, whereas ECFs' decision-making is faster than that associated with offline commerce (which takes up to one year but entails decisions on urban real estate for store networks, for example; Schu, Morschett and Swoboda 2016; Swoboda, Schwarz and Hälsig 2007). We observed 27 parallel wholly owned FDI by ECFs in several countries in one year and only four brownfield (vs. greenfield) FDI, where only the home market of the acquired company was counted (not additional countries). We had to exclude 61 ECFs with investments only prior to 2010, mostly traditional brick-and-mortar food retailers, and fashion verticals entering Eastern European and Asian markets since the 1990s, and for 45 ECFs, we did not find information on the operation mode at all or could not reconstruct firm-level information over time (one year before FDI). The sample included 244 firms with 1,806 operation mode decisions in 169 host countries.

To include country-level independent variables (e.g., following Kostova et al. 2020), we had to obtain additional data from the World Bank (2022a; 2022b;

2023b, an established source in IB, e.g., Kostova et al. 2020) and the only one available providing these data over time, which we matched with the time-lagged decision years. We had to exclude 80 operation mode decisions in 25 very small host countries for which data on the WGIs and World Development Indicators or on the Logistics Performance Index were not available (19 or 61 decisions and 4 or 21 countries, respectively). Additional firm-level variables, such as international experience, firm size or platform business, were obtained from Digital Commerce 360 with a one-year time lag.

The final dataset included 1,726 mode decisions across 144 countries from 2010–2020; these decisions were made by 241 ECFs originating in 22 home countries (see Table C—1). We used multilevel modeling to account for our hierarchically structured data and employed a maximum likelihood estimator with robust standard errors and test statistics.

Home Countries	Number of ECFs	Number of Market Entries
Austria	1	8
Belgium	1	1
China	7	93
Czech Republic	3	7
Denmark	6	49
Finland	1	7
France	38	225
Germany	38	203
Great Britain	66	535
Ireland	1	2
Italy	11	270
Korea (Rep.)	1	12
Lithuania	1	1
Netherlands	9	28
Poland	5	18
Romania	1	3
Russian Federation	3	4
Spain	7	62
Sweden	6	19
Switzerland	4	11
Turkey	4	13
United States	28	155
Total	**241**	**1,726**

Table C—1: Sample Distribution

Source: Own Creation

3.2. *Measurement*

We used different sources for our measures, which were matched one year prior to mode implementation, because FDI is planned prior to its implementation (e.g., Swoboda, Schwarz and Hälsig 2007). This approach resulted in a time lag for the assessment of internal and external factors (e.g., Li et al. 2021).

Dependent Variable. We measured wholly owned FDI (=1) vs. non (wholly owned) FDI (=0) as a dichotomous variable capturing international ECFs' operation mode decisions in each host country over time (e.g., He, Brouthers and Filatotchev 2013; Stallkamp, Chen and Li 2023). The measurement of mode choices as binary decisions has commonly been used in IB (e.g., Kostova et al. 2020, showing often consistent effects to metric measurement). We used a successive data selection procedure involving several data sources and recorded the initial year of an ECF's country website alongside the local domain, language, and currency (as no exact day/month data were available in 80% of the cases). Wholly owned FDI includes typical forms of long-term investment in a country, such as warehouses and logistics or service/marketing subsidiaries that are wholly owned by an ECF (e.g., Cahen and Borini 2020). We carefully assessed each case of wholly owned FDI to ensure that it was predominantly related to the ECF's online activities by verifying its location and functions as an operation mode for online selling documented by the firm (e.g., logistics, fulfillment, online customer service). In contrast, modes without wholly owned FDI (e.g., country-specific domain only, local partnerships, partial ownership) in logistics/services of the online business were considered non (wholly owned) FDI.

Independent Variables. International online experience captured firms' overall knowledge about foreign market accumulated through virtual presence over time (e.g., Dow and Larimo 2009; Wan et al. 2023). We measured the number of years for which an ECF was internationally active online with regard to each mode decision (i.e., one-year lagged), which is the most frequently used proxy for international experience over time (e.g., Tang and Gudergan 2018; Wan et al. 2023). We referred to the entered country data provided by Digital Commerce 360 (2021) and collected the initial time of entry and subsequent operation mode decisions through the various abovementioned sources. We tested the alternative measure of the number of countries (which has been used less frequently) in our stability checks (Ipsmiller, Dikova and Brouthers 2022), while other measures, such as the diversity of experience ratios, were unavailable (e.g., Clarke, Tamaschke and Liesch 2013).

Firms' *host country online experience* was captured as a time-based indicator reflecting knowledge about a particular foreign market through virtual presence over time (e.g., Clarke, Tamaschke and Liesch 2013; Wan et al. 2023). This experience was measured by the number of years that an international ECF was active online in a specific country one year before a mode was implemented based on our collection of each operation mode decision through various sources. Alternative measures, such as the number of operations or locations in a country, were not available for most ECFs (e.g., Tang and Gudergan 2018).

ECFs' *FDI online experience* is considered a time-based measure of firms' knowledge about implementing FDI in foreign markets over time (e.g., Cui, Li and Li 2013). We measured this variable as the number of years since an ECF first implemented FDI in a country in addition to a country-specific domain (e.g., Schwens et al. 2018b). We referred to our (lagged) data on subsequent FDI over time provided by the above sources. Alternative measures, such as the number of FDI instances in a country or area over time, were not available (e.g., Barkema and Drogendijk 2007; Hong and Lee 2015).

We measured *logistics performance* in a country via the six-dimensional logistics performance index (Arvis et al. 2018, p. 8; Schu and Morschett 2017). This indicator reflects the quality of trade infrastructure, ease of logistics services and customs, tracking ability, and timely shipments within a country (World Bank 2022a). The data (one-year lagged) cover eleven years in two-year periods. We used the approximate mean values of two years to measure this variable in the interim years (e.g., 2010 and 2012 for 2011; Blomkvist and Drogendijk 2016).

We measured *Internet use* within a country as the logarithm of the total population using the internet on the basis of data obtained from World Bank (2023b). This measure was based on a country's internet penetration and the total population over the observed period of eleven years with a one-year time lag. Internet use is most often captured by internet penetration, which we tested in our stability checks (e.g., Batsakis, Konara and Theoharakis 2023). However, this factor uses only the proportion of internet users (rather than the actual number of users) to indicate ECFs' potential customers. For example, while a very small country characterized by high-level internet penetration may be initially appealing for FDI, the number of potential customers in this country may be very low, and FDI may hardly be worthwhile (e.g., Mueller and Swoboda 2025).

We measured *differences in countries' ROL* regarding the relevant dimension of the WGIs over eleven years with a one-year time lag (World Bank 2022b). This dimension represents the extent to which agents have confidence in and abide by the rules of society (i.e., the quality of contract enforcement, property rights, police, and courts as well as the likelihood of crime and violence) and is particularly relevant for ECFs (Oxley and Yeung 2001; Schu and Morschett 2017). However, regulatory institutions are broader and captured most frequently by an index of the institutional dimension of the Global Competitiveness Report (GCR; Kostova et al. 2020), followed by an index of all six WGIs. As WGIs were shown to be relevant to ECFs' internationalization speed (Swoboda and Sinning 2022), we tested both indices in stability checks but assumed them to be less relevant to FDI decisions.

Controls. At both levels, important variables were controlled and measured one year prior to FDI.

At the firm level, we controlled for *firm size* as a traditionally important capability for FDI (Pezderka and Sinkovics 2011). Firm size was measured by the logarithm of firms' online sales and obtained from Digital Commerce 360. Alternatives (e.g., number of employees) were not available to us; ECFs hire fewer employees (Luo, Zhao and Du 2005; Swoboda and Sinning 2022).

We controlled for firms' *online age*, which was measured as the number of years since an ECF started selling online, as not all ECFs founded their businesses online (which thus likely represents a digital capability). This factor may affect wholly owned FDI, as such ECFs may have more time to acquire digital resources to support FDI (e.g., Sinkovics, Sinkovics and Jean 2013). Data were collected, e.g., from ECFs' websites.

The *home market size* of an ECF was controlled as it might affect its expansion and wholly owned FDI (Swoboda and Sinning 2022). A small (vs. large) home market size offers limited domestic growth opportunities and may force international investment. Market size was measured by the country's logarithmized GDP per capita based on World Bank (2023b) data.

We controlled whether ECFs ran an online *marketplace* (i.e., a hybrid platform with physical delivery) in addition to their core retail business (Meyer et al. 2023). Wholly owned FDI may be required for such ECFs aiming to provide and control fulfillment services in foreign markets to attract local vendors or offer local customer service, not otherwise to be guaranteed (Brouthers et al. 2022). We used a binary measure: 1=yes (marketplace) and 0=no (Digital Commerce 360 2021).

Firms' *multichannel strategy* was controlled. Firms operating only online have a higher proportion of internet-based activities than do firms operating multichannel (e.g., offline channels, Schu, Morschett and Swoboda 2016). ECFs with additional offline channels are more flexible and can leverage existing organizational capabilities to make online related FDI and integrate offline and online supply chain activities (e.g., returning in-store purchases to warehouses; Swoboda and Sinning 2022). We measured this dichotomously: 1=also operating offline stores and 0=not (Digital Commerce 360 2021).

Prior *international* and *host country experience* with an offline store was included as a control because firms such as Apple may have gained experience in a country prior to online-related FDI (e.g., via offline stores), which they could use to scale and support further FDI regarding their online operations. This factor was measured dichotomously (1=prior international/host country experience and 0=no such experience). We also collected these data from various sources.

We controlled for *population density* at the country level as one possible indicator of market attractiveness (as a possible barrier or location advantage), particularly relevant for commerce firms, as it may affect their wholly owned FDI, which is often located in densely populated regions with high demand (Chan, Finnegan and Sternquist 2011). We measured this variable as people per sq. km of land area according to data obtained from World Bank (2023b) as these data cover all our host countries over time and avoid potential collinearity issues with the other country-level variables. We conducted additional analyses to test alternative measures of attractiveness in stability checks. Further measures, such as online market sales or numbers of online customers, were available only for certain European countries and only over the last five years.

Table C—2 shows descriptive statistics and bivariate correlations of all variables. Correlations at the firm level did not raise collinearity concerns, and all were assessed individually; however, we detected a high correlation of .857 between logistics performance and ROL at the country level. This may result from logistics performance relying to some degree on the ROL in a host country (e.g., as public investors rely on strong enforceable contracts, construction permits, or the timely implementation of infrastructure projects due to high ROL, e.g., Cumming et al. 2023; Janjevic and Winkenbach 2020).

	(1)	(2)	(3)	(4)	(5)	(6)	(7)	(8)	(9)	(10)	(11)	(12)	(13)	(14)	(15)
Mean	.140	3.210	.210	1.170	18.320	10.120	10.530	.150	.670	.050	.540	3.463	.846	16.167	281.998
SD	.350	4.405	1.153	3.070	2.320	0.140	.450	.050	.470	.222	.408	.520	.037	1.601	972.473
VIF (max.)	-	1.912	1.107	1.709	1.169	1.336	1.097	1.414	2.822	1.080	2.492	1.233	1.093	1.169	1.064
	(1)	**(2)**	**(3)**	**(4)**	**(5)**	**(6)**	**(7)**	**(8)**	**(9)**	**(10)**	**(11)**	**(12)**	**(13)**	**(14)**	**(15)**
FDI (1/0) (1)	1														
IOE (2)	.255***	1													
HCOE (3)	.407***	.270***	1												
FDIE (4)	.220***	.625***	.224***	1											
Size (log.) (5)	.113***	.218***	.097***	.230***	1										
OnAge (6)	.023ns	.350***	.058*	.268***	.269***	1									
HMS (log.) (7)	.077**	.141***	.052*	.126***	-.070**	.139***	1								
MP (1/0) (8)	.008ns	.018ns	-.018ns	.096***	.130***	-.105***	-.105***	1							
MC (1/0) (9)	-.077**	-.052*	-.064**	-.047†	-.039ns	.134***	.151***	-.502***	1						
PCE (1/0) (10)	.165***	.039ns	.004ns	.006ns	-.060*	.008ns	.111***	-.091***	.147***	1					
PIE (1/0) (11)	-.008ns	.076**	-.016ns	.008ns	-.022ns	-.002ns	.173***	-.408***	.739***	.204***	1				
LP (12)	.182***	.094***	.104***	.031ns	-.022ns	.029ns	.063**	.018ns	-.186***	.099***	-.081**	1			
INT (log.) (13)	.148***	.063**	.061*	.067**	-.011ns	.005ns	-.024ns	.073**	-.178***	.087***	-.132***	.319***	1		
ROL (14)	.156***	.071**	.100***	-.005ns	-.046†	.010ns	.085***	-.028ns	-.133***	.079**	-.046†	.857***	.009ns	1	
PopDen (15)	.079**	.059*	-.002ns	.048*	.046†	.063**	.004ns	.029ns	.010ns	.068**	.026ns	.172***	.149***	-.069**	1

Note: ***p<.001; **p<.01; *p<.05; †p<.10; ns=Not Significant. FDI(E)=Foreign Direct Investment (Experience); HCOE=Host Country Online Experience; HMS=Home Market Size; INT=Internet User Population; IOE=International Online Experience; LP=Logistics Performance; MC=Multichannel; MP=Marketplace; OnAge=Online Age; PCE=Prior Host Country Experience; PIE=Prior International Experience; PopDen=Population Density; ROL=Rule of Law; SD=Standard Deviation; VIF=Variance Inflation Factor.

Table C—2: Correlations

Source: Own Creation.

To avoid collinearity issues, these two variables were used only in separate regressions. We further included theoretically relevant controls and conducted numerous robustness checks (Kalnins 2022; Lindner, Puck and Verbeke 2022) by reference to independent theoretical rationales concerning the important roles played by both factors among ECFs' FDIs. We observed variance inflation factors below the usual threshold in all models, and the highest score remained below three (e.g., Backhaus et al. 2023, pp. 111-113; O'Brien 2007).

3.3. Method

Hypotheses were tested using multilevel logistic regression in Mplus 9 to account for nested data considering firm- and country-level effects and variance both between and within countries simultaneously (Hox, Moerbeek and Van de Schoot 2018, p. 215). Multilevel modeling accounts for our hierarchically structured data (e.g., experience is tied to a specific firm, while ROL is linked with a specific country, e.g., Hernández and Nieto 2015) and includes relevant information simultaneously in the analysis. The latter approach reduces the risk of biased results; thus, this method has been recommended in IB research (e.g., Surana et al. 2024).

We computed stepwise random intercept and slope models, and the AIC, BIC, and -2 log likelihood were used to assess model fit (Hox, Moerbeek and Van de Schoot 2018, p. 123, Kaufman 1996). First, a baseline model with only controls was calculated. We then added all country-level independent variables separately, which were included as cluster means to account for variation within clusters over time. Then, firm-level independent variables were tested separately before all variables were entered simultaneously into a model. All the independent variables were grand mean centered and standardized prior to estimation (increasing interpretability of intercepts and ensuring comparability of coefficient estimates; e.g., Hox, Moerbeek and Van de Schoot 2018, pp. 61-63; Stallkamp, Chen and Li 2023). The following equation describes the model with only controls and firm-level independent variables (IL_{ij}) first separately, then jointly:

$$Logit\ (FDI_{ij})=\beta_{0j}+\beta_{1j}(IL_{ij})+\beta_{controls}\,ILC_{ij}+r_{i}, \tag{1}$$

$$Logit\ (FDI_{ij})=\beta_{0j}+\beta_{1j}\left(IntOnExp_{ij}\right)+\beta_{2j}\left(HoCoOnExp_{ij}\right)$$
$$+\beta_{3j}\left(FDIOnExp_{ij}\right)+\beta_{controls}\,ILC_{ij}+\beta_{control}\,CLC_{j}+r_{ij} \tag{2}$$

with logit FDI_{ij}=logarithmized odds of the probability of ECF i choosing wholly owned FDI in country j; $IntOnExp_{ij}$= ECF's international online experience; $HoCoOnExp_{ij}$=host country online experience; $FDIOnExp_{ij}$=FDI online experience; β_{0j}=first-level intercept; β_{1j}, β_{2j}, β_{3j}=regression scores of firm-level independent variables; ILC_{ij}= firm-level controls; CLC_j=country-level control; r_{ij}=first-level error term. Equation (3) shows the model with a country-level independent variable (CL_j) only.

$$Logit\ (FDI_{ij}) = \beta_{0j} + \gamma_{03}(CL_j) + \gamma_{ILC} ILC_{ij} + \gamma_{CLC} CLC_j + \varepsilon \quad (3)$$

We then allowed the intercept *β values* to vary across countries as follows:

$$\beta_{0j} = \gamma_{00} + u_{0j} \quad (4)$$

$$\beta_{1j} = \gamma_{10} + u_{1j} \quad (5)$$

$$\beta_{2j} = \gamma_{20} + u_{2j} \quad (6)$$

$$\beta_{3j} = \gamma_{30} + u_{3j} \quad (7)$$

with γ_{00}=second-level intercept of the dependent variable; γ_{10} and γ_{20}=second-level intercepts of the random slopes of the firm-level predictors; u_{0j}=country-level residual variance; u_{1j}, u_{2j}, u_{3j}=random slopes of the firm-level variables at the country level. Substitution led to the following:

$$\begin{aligned} Logit\ (FDI_{ij}) = {} & \gamma_{00} + \gamma_{10}\left(IntOnExp_{ij}\right) + \gamma_{20}\left(HoCoOnExp_{ij}\right) \\ & + \gamma_{30}\left(FDIOnExp_{ij}\right) + \gamma_{03}(LP_j) + \gamma_{04}(INT_j) + \gamma_{05}(ROL_j) + u_{0j} \\ & + u_{1j}\left(IntOnExp_{ij}\right) + u_{2j}\left(HoCoOnExp_{ij}\right) + u_{3j}\left(FDIOnExp_{ij}\right) \\ & + \gamma_{ILC} ILC_{ij} + \gamma_{CLC} CLC_j + \varepsilon \end{aligned} \quad (8)$$

where LP_j= logistics performance of host country *j*; INT_j and ROL_j=countries' internet user population and ROL; γ_{03}, γ_{04}, γ_{05}=fixed effects coefficients of the country-level predictors; ε=residual variances and errors.

3.4. Results

The results of the hypothesis tests are presented in Table C—3. We standardized all the variables prior to the estimation to assess the relative effect sizes and magnitudes as well as the reported odds ratios (Exp(B), Backhaus et al. 2023, p. 270; Kaufman 1996). Owing to the strong correlation observed in this context, logistics performance and ROL were assessed in separate models.

		Model 1	Model 2	Model 3	Model 4	Model 5	Model 6	Model 7	Model 8	Model 9		Model 10	
		bp	*bp*	*bp*	*bp*	*bp*	*bp*	*bp*	*bp*	*bp*	Exp(B)	*bp*	Exp(B)
Intercept		-2.109***	-2.290***	-1.760***	-2.323***	-1.688***	-2.692***	-2.344***	-2.473***	-2.742***		-2.665***	
		(.146)	(.219)	(.164)	(.207)	(.178)	(.156)	(.136)	(.153)	(.212)		(.216)	
Firm Level													
International	→ Wholly owned		.675***			.381**				.420***	1.522	.420***	1.522
Online Experience	FDI (1/0)		(.085)			(.111)				(.110)		(.113)	
Host Country	→ Wholly owned			4.274***		4.256***				3.165***	23.689	3.305***	27.250
Online Experience	FDI (1/0)			(.770)		(.808)				(.627)		(.643)	
FDI Online Experi-	→ Wholly owned				.439***	.120ns				.125ns	1.133	.114ns	1.121
ence	FDI (1/0)				(.081)	(.088)				(.086)		(.086)	
Country Level													
Logistics Perfor-	→ Wholly owned						.633***					.526***	1.692
mance	FDI (1/0)						(.098)					(.103)	
Internet User Pop-	→ Wholly owned							.505***		.553***	1.674	.379***	1.461
ulation (log.)	FDI (1/0)							(.101)		(.102)		(.117)	
Rule of Law	→ Wholly owned								.466***	.515***	1.738		
	FDI (1/0)								(.091)	(.094)			
Controls (Firm Level)													
Firm Size (log.)	→ Wholly owned	.641***	.524***	.405**	.466***	.318**	.627***	.651***	.630***	.347**	1.415	.336**	1.399
	FDI (1/0)	(.139)	(.129)	(.134)	(.126)	(.113)	(.133)	(.138)	(.135)	(.115)		(.110)	
Marketplace (1/0)	→ Wholly owned	-.187*	-.172*	-.144†	-.233**	-.165*	-.131†	-.199*	-.132†	-.143 †	.867	-.151†	.860
	FDI (1/0)	(.076)	(.069)	(.079)	(.081)	(.077)	(.074)	(.080)	(.073)	(.079)		(.079)	
Multichannel (1/0)	→ Wholly owned	-.519***	-.290*	-.409**	-.464***	-.280*	-.404***	-.474***	-.439***	-.181ns	.834	-.181ns	.834
	FDI (1/0)	(.101)	(.118)	(.118)	(.109)	(.126)	(.098)	(.100)	(.097)	(.121)		(.119)	
Home Market Size	→ Wholly owned	.236*	.159†	.180ns	.166†	.123ns	.202*	.241***	.206*	.092ns	1.096	.095ns	1.100
(log.)	FDI (1/0)	(.100)	(.095)	(.112)	(.091)	(.106)	(.098)	(.099)	(.098)	(.101)		(.103)	
Firm Online Age	→ Wholly owned	-.098ns	-.435***	-.105ns	-.228*	-.317**	-.089ns	-.112ns	-.091ns	-.343**	.710	-.339**	.712
	FDI (1/0)	(.096)	(.120)	(.092)	(.105)	(.118)	(.103)	(.099)	(.098)	(.126)		(.125)	
Prior Host Country	→ Wholly owned	.335***	.344***	.387***	.355***	.389***	.304***	.300***	.322***	.319***	1.375	.322***	1.380
Experience (1/0)	FDI (1/0)	(.060)	(.064)	(.069)	(.063)	(.074)	(.060)	(.058)	(.059)	(.069)		(.070)	
Prior International	→ Wholly owned	.176ns	.016ns	.195ns	.271ns	-.020ns	.155ns	.183ns	.151ns	.084ns	1.088	.067ns	1.069
Experience (1/0)	FDI (1/0)	(.123)	(.274)	(.264)	(.262)	(.282)	(.127)	(.123)	(.125)	(.285)		(.285)	
Controls (Country Level)													
Population Density	→ Wholly owned	.135***	.136***	.158***	.139***	.153***	.049*	.161***	.075***	.131***	1.140	.111***	1.117
	FDI (1/0)	(.022)	(.024)	(.027)	(.022)	(.029)	(.021)	(.020)	(.021)	(.029)		(.030)	
-2 Log likelihood		1,302.166	1,226.798	1,050.880	1,260.122	1,024.316	1,265.178	1,273.650	1,277.798	985.378		989.492	
AIC		1,322.166	1,250.798	1,075.880	1,284.122	1,052.316	1,287.178	1,295.650	1,299.797	1,017.377		1,021.492	
BIC (Adjusted)		1,344.933	1,278.118	1,103.200	1,311.442	1,084.189	1,312.222	1,320.693	1,324.840	1,053.804		1,057.919	

Note: ***p<.001; **p<.01; *p<.05; †p<.10; ns=Not Significant; b=Coefficients of Standardized Variables; FDI=Foreign Direct Investment; Standard errors are shown in brackets.

Table C—3: Results

Source: Own Creation.

For ECFs with more international online experience, the results indicated an increasing likelihood of wholly owned FDI (b=.420, p<.001, Exp(B)=1.522), supporting Hypothesis 1. A one-standard-deviation increase in this experience increased the odds of FDI by a factor of 1.522 in Models 9 and 10. The more experience ECFs obtained online internationally, the more likely they were to choose FDI.

ECFs' *host country online experience* increased their likelihood of choosing wholly owned FDI (b_{Model9}=3.165, p<.001, Exp(B)=23.689; $b_{Model10}$=3.305, p<.001, Exp(B)=27.250). A one-standard-deviation increase in host country experience increased the odds of FDI by a factor of 23.689 in Model 9 and 27.250 in Model 10. The more experience ECFs have gained in specific foreign online markets, the more likely they chose FDI over time. Hypothesis 2 is supported.

ECFs' *FDI online experience* increased the likelihood of these firms choosing wholly owned FDI when assessed individually (b_{Model4}=.439, p<.001); however, no significant effect was observed when international and host country online experience were included (b_{Model9}=.125, p>.10; $b_{Model10}$=.114, p>.10). Therefore, Hypothesis 3 was rejected.

Logistics performance increased ECFs' likelihood of choosing wholly owned FDI (b=.526, p<.001, Exp(B)=1.692), supporting Hypothesis 4. A one-standard-deviation increase in host country logistics performance increased the odds of ECFs choosing wholly owned FDI by a factor of 1.692. The better a host country's logistical infrastructure was, the more likely ECFs were to choose FDI, such as through local warehouses or subsidiaries.

Internet user population increases the likelihood of ECFs choosing wholly owned FDI (b_{Model9}=.553, p<.001, Exp(B)=1.738; $b_{Model10}$=.379, p<.001, Exp(B)=1.461). A one-standard-deviation increase in internet use increases the odds of ECFs choosing FDI by a factor of 1.738 when ROL is accounted for and by 1.461 when logistics performance is accounted for. The higher a country's internet use is, the more likely ECFs are to use FDI for expansion. These results support Hypothesis 5.

ROL increases the likelihood of ECFs' wholly owned FDI (b=.515, p<.001, Exp(B)=1.674). A one-standard-deviation increase in the host country's ROL increased the odds of ECFs choosing the FDI mode by a factor of 1.674. The more transparent and effective a country's regulations were, the more likely ECFs were to opt for FDI. Thus, Hypothesis 6 is supported.

As controls, *firm size*, ECFs' *platform business*, and *prior host country experience* significantly and consistently affected the likelihood of ECFs choosing FDI.

3.5. *Stability Checks*

To ensure stability, alternative models were tested. *First*, a random split half test was conducted. The results of the firm- and country-level variables remained stable (see Section G, ESM).

Second, we replaced several independent variables with alternatives and tested further alternative models (see Section G, ESM).

We tested internet penetration (i.e., the percentage of the population using the internet) as an alternative measure of internet user population (Batsakis, Konara and Theoharakis 2023; World Bank 2023b). The results supported our model (b_{Model7}=.510, p<.001), but multicollinearity issues emerged when all the factors were tested in one model (b_{Model9}=.060, p>.10; $b_{Model10}$=-.043, p>.10). Our measurement was supported.

We tested the indices of GCR and WGIs (Kostova et al. 2020). The results indicated weaker effects concerning the GCR items but similar results regarding the WGIs, thus supporting our measurement choice.

We tested common measures of market attractiveness (i.e., further barriers and location advantages), e.g., GDP, GNI per capita or GDP per capita growth. The results were stable but partly nonsignificant (MA_{GDP}: b=.574, p<.001; MA_{GNI}: b=.587, p<.001; MA_{GROWTH}: b=-.062, p>.10). We tested the population, the percentage of the urban population, and country development, which produced largely similar results (e.g., Chan, Finnegan and Sternquist 2011).

We tested the number of countries (i.e., geographic scope) as an alternative measure of international online experience. The effect was slightly weaker (b_{Model9}=.416, p<.001, Exp(B)=1.516; $b_{Model10}$=.410, p<.001, Exp(B)=1.507). FDI online experience had a significant but weak effect in this context.

Third, we tested our framework over a ten-year period, but we measured the independent variables for the same year when FDI was observed. The results regarding the firm- and country-level variables were largely stable. We also tested independent variables at t_{-2}; the results remained stable for all the variables, albeit with considerably fewer observations. These findings supported the stability of our observations regardless of the timing chosen.

Fourth, we tested our framework for possible differences between early and late FDI (2010–2015 and 2016–2020). At the firm level, the impact of host country online experience was unchanged, but FDI online experience became marginally significant in the later period. Notably, logistics performance and, to some degree, ROL were significantly stronger from 2016–2020, as discussed later.

Fifth, we tested whether country-level variables moderate the effects of significant firm-level variables. Theoretically, the value and transfer of international experience may depend on the local environmental context of foreign markets (He, Brouthers and Filatotchev 2013). The results indicated that no effect of online experience was moderated by any country-level factor, whereas the direct effects supported our model.

4. Discussion

4.1. Theoretical Implications

This study provides novel evidence on the selective use of wholly owned FDI by ECFs as an emerging research area on digital firms requiring adapted theories and fresh thinking (responding to calls for respective analyses, e.g., Stallkamp, Chen and Li 2023; Swoboda and Sinning 2022). Considering the joint effects of firm- and country-level antecedents of physical presence, this study contributes to the limited knowledge on digital firms' operation mode decisions and the debate on the impact of dynamic digitalization on IB research and theory. Our results provide theoretical and practical implications for ECF managers, manufacturing firms undergoing digital internationalization, and policymakers.

Regarding our *first contribution*, we elucidated the specific business model employed by ECFs in contrast to IT or i-business firms and manufacturing firms. Further characterization is valuable to promote a broader theoretical conversation concerning the heterogeneity of digital firms' internationalization in an emerging IB research stream (Brouthers et al. 2022; Yang et al. 2025). We clarify that ECFs' virtual presence and physical (i.e., export-based) delivery of products from abroad represent a basis for internationalization, in contrast to i-businesses (e.g., Stallkamp, Chen and Li 2023). However, importantly, the general competencies of firms such as Amazon lie primarily in IT and physical supply chain management. The technological foundation enables a high level of integration of customer-specific data (e.g., from individual accounts, shopping baskets; Batsakis et al. 2023) and thus the ability to promote customer-centricity and exploit trends through various touchpoints (e.g., mobile apps, social media, user-generated content) which can serve as a primary decision database. Assortment, price and online services represent the core of one-to-one offers or simplified up- or cross-selling. However, all this strongly influences supply chain processes (e.g., Batsakis, Konara and Theoharakis 2023), which are consumer-driven, offer agility to new suppliers, products and services, and ensure efficiency of logistics costs (e.g., quick delivery, free returns, warehousing; Janjevic and Winkenbach 2020). We argue that a physical presence via wholly owned

FDI enables such a business model to be implemented strategically and operationally in host countries. Moreover, this depends on specific online experiences and infrastructure abroad, which differ from those of manufacturers, which can even use ECFs for expansion. Additionally, FDI allows the specific IT- and entrepreneurship-driven organizational structure and culture or specific key performance indicators to be implemented (e.g., Tolstoy, Hånell and Özbek 2023).

Our *second contribution* builds on practical observations that ECFs, despite being digital, establish selective physical presences potentially driven by specific firm- and country-level antecedents (to establish an empirical baseline in research on digital firms' internationalization, Stallkamp, Chen and Li 2023; Verbeke, Coeurderoy and Matt 2018). We thus advance FDI research in the digital era, which is still focused on manufacturing and service firms. We do so by providing novel systematic evidence on specific virtual and physical business model elements as a basis for FDI decisions and their antecedents. Accordingly, we contribute to empirical literature and theory concerning the role of ECFs' experiences and country factors in FDI as follows.

We contribute to the empirical literature with a first study on ECFs' FDI over time. We also empirically show for the first time that experiences are relevant for digital firms' physical presence, beyond our knowledge on the role of distances for digital firms shown in the only study on FDI (Stallkamp, Chen and Li 2023). This finding contradicts the critical assumption in the literature that experience might be less important in digital firms (e.g., Gabrielsson, Raatikainen and Julkunen 2022; Pezderka and Sinkovics 2011). Location-bound host country online experience and nonlocation-bound international online experience are highly relevant for ECFs' FDI. Moreover, we propose that such experiences are gained online based on successful offers, services, promotions, or local online interactions with consumers that allow ECFs to exploit FDI (e.g., Mueller and Swoboda 2025). These online experiences for physical presence are different from those known from manufacturers' FDI, which are mostly based on physical processes in production or distribution, for example. Online experience may also be highly relevant to i-businesses' FDI decisions; however, their acquisition of such experience and competitive or demand challenges, for example, strongly differ from those of ECFs (e.g., Gong, He and Lengler 2024; Mithani 2023). We thus contribute to the literature with a new conceptualization of online learning from experiences beyond known offline experiences. Finally, international and host country online experience affect ECFs' FDI positively, whereas among manufacturers, the effects of international experience remain inconclusive (e.g., non-significant by Dow and Larimo 2009, negative by Hernández and Nieto 2015, positive by Tang and Gudergan 2018), and host country experience among service firms has only been studied once (Pla-Barber, Villar and León-

Darder 2014; see Figure C—1). The roles of the three types of experience for FDI have also rarely been compared in literature (e.g., Wan et al. 2023). Further implications to literature can be drawn from our stability checks (e.g., geographic scope with similar results to our time-based measures of experience).

We contribute to theory by showing that ECFs require distinct online experience capabilities for FDI (different from physical capabilities) that need novel thinking and adapted rationales for digital firms' online capabilities and internationalization processes (e.g., Cahen and Borini 2020). We extend capability theory because different online experiences represent unique capabilities that ECFs as digital firms build, scale, and transfer by learning through virtual presence in general or in specific countries over time (e.g., Schu and Morschett 2017). Moreover, these capabilities are also critical elements of the refined internationalization process of modern firms (Vahlne and Johanson 2017). We extend these process rationales because ECFs no longer require physical presence or sequential entry (i.e., internationalize rapidly without physical constraints, Yang et al. 2025), but their decisions on physical presence are still path-dependent and based on distinct online learning mechanisms. While Vahlne and Johanson (2017) viewed risk and uncertainty as the basis of modern firms' rational decision-making and increasing commitment abroad, the focus of such firms has shifted to novel online capabilities and from opportunity recognition to exploitation (Coviello, Kano and Liesch 2017). We enhance this logic by showing that country-specific online experience is particularly related to ECFs' exploitation of FDI opportunities in select countries, going beyond ECFs' irregular, rapid online internationalization, which has thus far been linked only to a virtual presence (Schu, Morschett and Swoboda 2016). Furthermore, and surprisingly, hybrid FDI experience has no effect once ECFs' general and host country online experiences are accounted for, indicating a lower relevance of offline experience. Finally, in contrast to assumptions about digital firms, we conclude that experience and learning remain critical for establishing physical presence and foreign performance (Mueller and Swoboda 2025). As digitalization advances, researchers may reconsider capability and process theories and how opportunity exploitation through online experience changes competitive advantages through FDI (Swoboda and Sinning 2022). ECFs' online learning may even affect transaction cost rationales, as the level of risks and uncertainties may shift from reducing investment risks to exploitation of opportunities with FDI (Brouthers, Geisser and Rothlauf 2016; Swoboda and Sinning 2022). Moreover, we argue that theories need to be enhanced by the roles of external factors in ECFs' FDI.

This study initially contributes to the empirical literature on host country-specific factors as antecedents of ECFs' FDI. We reveal that business model-specific factors—a country's logistics performance, internet user population, and ROL—

critical to ECFs' virtual internationalization decisions (e.g., speed, Luo, Zhao and Du 2005; market selection or entry; Rothaermel, Kotha and Steensma 2006; Schu and Morschett 2017) are equally crucial for their physical presence decisions. Moreover, these factors are different from those relevant to manufacturing or service firms highlighted thus far in mode research (see Figure C—1). Only macroeconomic studies have reported ECF-specific but contradictory insights, as all three antecedents affect both export flows and FDI flows (logistics infrastructure, Halaszovich and Kinra 2020 vs. He, Wu and Choi 2021; internet use, Arvin, Pradhan and Nair 2021 vs. Visser 2019; ROL with even negative effects on FDI, Contractor et al. 2020; 2021 vs. Yu, Beugelsdijk and de Haan 2015). Our insights emphasize the need to examine these factors at the microeconomic level of firms' decision-making. Finally, we show that countries' logistics performance, internet use, and ROL positively affect ECFs' FDI decisions to a similar extent and tend to be stronger than international online experience. Further implications for the literature can be drawn from our alternative models (e.g., nonsignificant effects of known attractiveness factors, e.g., market growth or population size; nonsignificant moderations of our country-level factors).

With respect to theory, we argue that country-level factors must be considered important additional rationales to fully explain digital firms' internationalization processes. Firm- and country-level antecedents are seldom theorized jointly in studies on manufacturing or service firms' FDI (with few exceptions, Wan et al. 2023). Moreover, while research on country-level factors in ECFs' decisions strongly focuses on institution-based rationales (e.g., Cumming et al. 2023), we stress the role of novel infrastructural factors emerging in e-commerce (Agarwal and Wu 2015; Benmamoun et al. 2019). The latter complement ECFs' ability to exploit their online experience due to the specific location advantages these factors offer for ECFs' business model and FDI (in contrast to traditional supply-side location advantages, e.g., natural resources, labor costs, production infrastructure, Yang et al. 2025). For example, ECFs prefer markets that feature low barriers to the exploitation of the business model, e.g., in terms of the supply chain, digital infrastructure, or ROL (e.g., Gong, He and Lengler 2024). Finally, by theorizing the impacts of e-commerce-specific barriers, we contribute to the theorization of new location advantages for digital firms (while online experience could be conceptualized as a new ownership advantage, Dunning and Wymbs 2001). However, logistics performance and ROL use are correlated, which is surprising, as both factors are theoretically distinct barriers; logistics performance theoretically represents the physical supply side, whereas ROL represents both the supply and the virtual demand side of ECFs' business models. Further analyses are needed, as, for example, logistics performance becomes more important in later (vs. earlier) FDI decisions (2016–2020 vs. 2010–2015).

4.2. Practical Implications

This study has practical implications for managers, manufacturing firms internationalizing digitally and policy makers.

We explored existing FDI over time and thus focused on decisions that did not result in failure. Managers of ECFs may avoid implementing unsustainable FDI in the e-commerce sector (e.g., Wentrup 2016) and may decompose FDI decisions into manageable choices by considering important and specific antecedents (Brouthers et al. 2022). Thus, in their efforts to transfer business models and localize their offers, managers may focus primarily on acquiring host country online experience. This factor is not easy to change, as a firm either has market-specific online experience or not. However, we can propose focusing primarily on respective countries for FDI. We also propose at least three ways of increasing host country learning or compensating for a lack of such experience: leveraging analytics in local online markets, seeking reliable local professionals, or building relationships with local stakeholders (e.g., Luo, Zhao and Du 2005; Meyer et al. 2023; Mueller and Swoboda 2025). General international online experience represents a second requirement. Host country logistics performance, which offers considerable advantages regarding the full control of efficient supply chains, is also important, as are internet user population and ROL, which entail possible barriers or location advantages with respect to FDI.

Our insights also have implications for manufacturing firms' digital internationalization. As mentioned, small manufacturers start their virtual presence with own domains abroad and often subsequently turn to leading ECFs to benefit from their specific capabilities, for example (Cong, He and Lengler 2024). For those firms, knowledge of the antecedents that increase the likelihood of ECFs' FDI in a country is valuable. Increased physical presence among ECFs enables them to localize their business model and to tailor their offers and those of manufacturers more closely to customers, which may be beneficial to manufacturers. However, ECFs' search for local suppliers can make it more difficult for manufacturers to compete via ECFs. These manufacturers may be forced to establish their own presence in other countries (e.g., Meyer et al. 2023).

Policymakers seeking to attract growing ECFs to their country can facilitate the virtual presence of ECFs, which is the strongest driver of FDI. More importantly, politicians recognize that e-commerce-specific country-level factors are relevant drivers. Thus, implementing strong logistics infrastructure to support FDI (e.g., transportation, customs efficiency; Cumming et al. 2023), high-quality internet infrastructure (e.g., connectivity, cyber security; Eduardsen et al. 2023) and a transparent legal framework (e.g., advice on legal issues, taxation, data privacy; Ahi, Sinkovics and Sinkovics 2023) can be used as local policy levers to promote

ECFs' physical presence. However, politicians should be aware that promoting digitalization and ECFs is likely to increase competition in related industries. Offline firms may thus be under pressure. Moreover, societies face dynamic changes in IT that require regulation to enable the population and industries to keep pace with these shifts.

5. Limitations and Further Research

This study has limitations that suggest directions for future research.

We explore longitudinal data concerning leading ECFs, but an extended database will support further conclusions, e.g., regarding ECFs worldwide, business-to-business ECFs, or regional differences in wholly owned FDI (e.g., Yang et al. 2025). Examining smaller ECFs or the growing platform business within ECFs can provide new insights into FDI (our controls for *firm size* and the *marketplace* affect FDI both positively and negatively). The control of *previous experience in a host country* (beyond online) is also positive, suggesting further research on going vs. born digitals (e.g., Batsakis, Konara and Theoharakis 2023).

With respect to our measurements, we consider FDI but cannot identify acquisitions or cooperative modes (both and especially ECFs' various partnerships; e.g., Brouthers et al. 2022). Measuring ECFs' degree of control, mode switches, or learning from failure over time is challenging but could reveal stepwise decisions affected by antecedents (e.g., Mueller and Swoboda 2025). As noted, data on more ECF-specific antecedents across nations could become available for future research (e.g., ECFs' online marketing capabilities, such as social media usage or web traffic in countries). Online market potential, local e-commerce competition, or specific ROL and media barriers that affect ECFs' internationalization can be studied by reference to future data concerning e-markets (e.g., Batsakis, Konara and Theoharakis 2023; Pezderka and Sinkovics 2011).

In our framework, we capture the local environment with infrastructural factors and the ROL, while normative or cultural institutions may be studied (e.g., Lee, Pattnaik and Gaur 2023). We often refer to opportunities or customer needs, which are critical for ECFs, yet what drives the adaptation of online offers or services is unclear but important (e.g., assortment, payment options; Ipsmiller, Dikova and Brouthers 2022). It is also unclear how adaptation and standardization decisions affect ECFs' local and general performance or growth. The same applies to competition or digital capabilities (e.g., Fleury et al. 2024).

D. Study 3: Effects of International E-Commerce Firms' Depth versus Breadth of Control on Foreign Sales Performance and the Role of Market Size and Growth as Context Factors[3]

1. Introduction

The rise of international ECFs that sell physical goods via a virtual presence in country-specific online shops and marketplaces has supposedly reduced the need for physical presence abroad (Batsakis, Konara and Theoharakis 2023; Brouthers et al. 2022). In practice, however, Amazon, Zalando, or Rakuten added a physical presence within markets to improve customer service and across markets to gain scale effects. Amazon (2025), for example, set up local services and scaled its network of WOS across 21 larger e-commerce markets with modest growth. In contrast, ASOS, About You, or Trendyol are successful with relatively little local control (Meyer et al. 2023). About You (2021), for example, has WOS in only two growing e-commerce markets. It is unclear which ECFs achieve higher foreign sales performance and whether integrating a physical presence within a market or scaling it across markets increases performance (e.g., Batsakis et al. 2023). A higher (vs. lower) depth of control within a country enables the implementation of locally adapted offers or quick delivery (Eduardsen et al. 2020), whereas a higher (vs. lower) breadth of control enables the global scaling of ECFs' offers or management (Batsakis, Konara and Theoharakis 2023). Little is known about important e-commerce market contexts that reflect critical local demand or growth opportunities and may affect ECFs' control decisions. Therefore, the focus of our study is on the international depth and breadth of control effects on foreign sales performance and moderations of local e-commerce market size and growth.

Previous empirical studies have analyzed the effects of both depth and breadth of control on performance separately for manufacturing firms (e.g., meta-analyses by Giachetti, Manzi and Colapinto 2019; Kirca et al. 2011; 2012b; Wan et al. 2023). For international commerce firms with business models similar to ECFs, few studies show inconclusive results for performance (e.g., positive or negative for high control within markets, Evans, Mavondo and Bridson 2008; Gielens and Dekimpe 2001; negatively or positively S-shaped for high breadth of control, Chan, Finnegan and Sternquist 2011; Dimitrova, Kim and Smith

3 This study was published as: Mueller, M., & Swoboda, B. (2025). Effects of International E-Commerce Firms' Depth Versus Breadth of Control on Foreign Sales Performance and the Role of Market Size and Growth as Context Factors. *Management International Review*, In Press (see also Section G, ESM).

M. Müller, *Strategic Management of International E-Commerce Firms*,
Handel und Internationales Marketing Retailing and International Marketing,
https://doi.org/10.1007/978-3-658-49680-7_4

2019). With respect to ECFs, only three studies address international performance effects (of marketing tactics, market creation, or capabilities, Goldman et al. 2021; Tolstoy, Hånell and Özbek 2023; Tolstoy, Nordman and Vu 2022), but only one considers host country contexts (internet penetration on export effects, Eduardsen et al. 2023). No study has considered the effects of international control in terms of depth or breadth on ECFs' foreign sales performance or important market contexts (conceptually, Hånell et al. 2020), although scholars strongly call for research on the performance of important ECFs (e.g., Ipsmiller, Dikova and Brouthers 2022; Swoboda and Sinning 2022).

Surprising research gaps exist in the current IB literature on digital firms' control decisions and performance. Scholars see a need for new studies due to the rise of ECFs and their virtual presence (Cumming et al. 2023; Gong, He and Lengler 2024). Studies of the mechanisms behind "space–place relationships" are lacking but important, as firms face the risk of over-reliance on virtual presence (Sinkovics, Sinkovics and Jean 2013; Stallkamp, Chen and Li 2023). The benefits of control may also depend on the size or growth of local e-commerce markets as two indicators for assessing market potential ("must know", Kishore, Agrawal and Rao 2004; Schu and Morschett 2017).

In this study, two research questions are proposed: Whether and how strongly does ECFs' higher (vs. lower) international control in terms of depth vs. breadth drive ECFs' foreign sales performance? How do host countries' e-commerce market size and growth moderate these effects? This study offers two contributions to literature.

Regarding the first research question, we contribute to the IB literature on the importance of ECFs' control decisions for foreign performance in general and contrast the effects of depth vs. breadth of control and thus possible trade-offs. These decisions have been studied separately (e.g., Miller, Lavie and Delios 2016), although the trade-offs of local and central decision-making or mature and growing markets are crucial in commerce (e.g., Swoboda and Elsner 2013). We revisit three theories to explain performance through control that have recently been adapted to digital firms by challenging the impact of ECFs' physical control on performance (e.g., Cumming et al. 2023; Meyer et al. 2023). From an *internationalization process* view, digital firms' virtual presence requires no physical investments in countries and enables rapid market entry, digital learning, and scale (Birkinshaw 2022; Monaghan, Tippmann and Coviello 2020). Their internationalization and FDI have been argued to be less path dependent, requiring less control (Nambisan and Luo 2022, p. 132). However, the latter may still be critical for ECFs' business model and local adaptation (Surana et al. 2024; Swoboda and Sinning 2022). From a *network perspective*, virtual presence is defined by low embeddedness in local networks and exploitation of digital relationships (Brouthers et al. 2022). While offline firms rely on subsidiary networks within and across markets, ECFs may scale and leverage online networks to drive foreign sales without a physical presence (Batsakis, Konara and Theoharakis 2023). However, digital firms still opt for a physical presence in important markets to leverage local relationships, which may be more critical than leveraging online networks (e.g., Stallkamp, Chen and Li 2023). ECFs' digital nature also implies a reassessment of *dynamic capabilities* and being "global by default" (Meyer et al. 2023). Such capabilities enable basic adaptation within and can be scaled digitally across countries to increase sales. However, ECFs risk falling into a "virtuality trap" (i.e., overreliance on virtual capabilities/presence only, Surana et al. 2024) and failing to adapt or transfer offers and services (Batsakis, Konara and Theoharakis 2023; Sinkovics, Sinkovics and Jean 2013). Research assumes that virtual presence may obviate the need for physical presence to be successful, while we elucidate whether control of physical presence in general contributes to success and whether potential trade-offs arise within or across countries.

Regarding the second research question, we contribute to the IB literature as an initial longitudinal study considering cross-level interactions of international control effects with the local e-commerce market context by addressing calls for overlooked e-commerce-specific contextual differences (e.g., Eduardsen et al. 2023; Meyer et al. 2023). We view ECFs' internationalization depending on its context and argue that ECFs' advantages in terms of depth or breadth of control depend on the local e-commerce market size and growth (e.g., Kishore, Agrawal and Rao 2004). The latter defines the foreign sales potential of ECFs by reflecting local customer demand and market dynamics. We argue that both size and growth affect the advantages of both control decisions differently, which may entail a further trade-off. Market size may increase the learning benefits that ECFs can derive from local supply chains within countries (e.g., to provide local customer services) or may harm transfer across countries to scale assortments (e.g., due to procurement network coordination; Tolstoy, Jonsson and Sharma 2016; Wang, Mao and Archer 2012). Market growth may limit the benefits of local control, as ECFs face learning barriers due to volatile market conditions, but it may also increase opportunities for ECFs to scale the business model across markets. In the latter case, they may benefit from local FDI incentives that increase mutual learning, access to distribution networks or capability integration (e.g., Agarwal and Wu 2015).

The further structure of this study is as follows. Building on conceptualizations and theory, we develop and test hypotheses based on 1,144 control decisions corresponding to 184 ECFs originating in 22 home countries. After the results are presented, we provide theoretical and practical implications as well as directions for further research.

2. Conceptualization and Hypothesis Development

2.1. Conceptualization and Theory

We conceptualize *foreign sales performance* as an important outcome of ECFs' international decisions (e.g., Colton, Roth and Bearden 2010; Gregory, Ngo and Karavdic 2019; Tolstoy, Jonsson and Sharma 2016). ECFs and commerce firms refer to foreign sales as important industry benchmarks, e.g., when identifying and competing with competitors (e.g., Hånell et al. 2020). Further performance measures such as profitability or return on assets vary by commercial sector and are available for public firms only, while most ECFs are not required to report such data (Swoboda and Sinning 2022). We argue that foreign sales directly relate to ECFs' efforts to improve offers and management within countries with WOS (control depth) or to achieve cross-national network synergies between WOS (control breadth).

We conceptualize the depth and breadth of ECFs' internationalization, as is common in the literature (e.g., Miller, Lavie and Delios 2016). As mentioned, the level of control is relevant to ECFs' business model, which is based on learning from virtual presence, electronic networks, and digital market capabilities (Cumming et al. 2023; Eduardsen et al. 2023) but also requires local adaptation and distribution networks to ensure delivery or service quality (Batsakis, Konara and Theoharakis 2023; Tolstoy et al. 2021). We address potential trade-offs of control within and across markets (e.g., contrasting foreign sales intensity, Elbanna et al. 2024) that are generally faced by international commerce firms (Swoboda and Elsner 2013).

ECFs' *depth of international control* reflects the degree of hierarchical control over local operations, supply chains, and management within a host country. It is conceptualized on the basis of ECFs' usual virtual presence (e.g., passive or active) and traditional physical presence modes (e.g., alliances or WOS), representing degrees of control and enabling capabilities to be learned and transferred through different degrees of local embeddedness (Brouthers et al. 2022; Ipsmiller, Dikova and Brouthers 2022). Initially, ECFs can be present in a foreign market through a country-specific website (e.g., Brouthers et al. 2022) and thus through indirect/passive or *direct/active exports* (e.g., Sinkovics, Sinkovics and Jean 2013). The former represents the lowest degree of local control, as ECFs' websites are largely home country-centered (i.e., dot-com or dot-com/uk). The latter includes elements of adaptation in terms of the locally registered domain, language, and currency (e.g., dot-uk; Swoboda and Sinning 2022). While dot-com/uk domains offer global reach but low control with a standardized virtual presence, local domains offer more control but must comply with local legal requirements and domain management costs (e.g., Ipsmiller, Dikova and Brouthers 2022). Both present a low-risk entry strategy and allow ECFs to learn about customers online and leverage electronic networks or digital capabilities at low costs. However, both virtual presences allow limited control of product delivery and customer service quality, which limits ECFs' ability to respond to the local context. *Cooperative modes* (e.g., alliances) allow for more control over operational elements of the supply chain via contracts (seen as traditional options of physical presence, Brouthers et al. 2022). Typical, for ECFs are partly controlled contractual partnerships or strategic alliances with local goods suppliers or service providers (Benmamoun et al. 2019). This ranges from low operational control, in which partners adhere to contractual obligations, to high operational control in their own warehouses, which are operated by logistics partners (Hua and Wu 2024). It offers potential benefits of learning, network access, complementary assets and capabilities or the shared risk of the external context (Cha, Kotabe and Wu 2023). Depending on how much control an ECF maintains through governance mechanisms, firms may face complex coordination challenges (Kiohoro, Agrawal and Rao 2004). *WOS*, as a long-term investment in physical assets, allows for local management, services, and adaptation to consumer needs based on ECFs' experience. WOS offers full strategic and operational control of virtual and physical presence, which allows local operations and supply chain networks to replicate capabilities in foreign markets, fully adapt offers (e.g., assortments, promotions, Tolstoy, Nordman and Vu 2022) and achieve full control over service quality (e.g., next-day delivery, Hua and Wu 2024). However, ECFs face high initial costs, operational risks, and different external contexts (Fleury et al. 2024).

Theoretically, we expect that despite ECFs' rapid online internationalization process, greater depth of control within countries remains path dependent over time and requires local business networks and capabilities to realize successful local adaptation (Swoboda and Sinning 2022). ECFs' performance abroad is especially affected by high (vs. low) depth of control; otherwise, EFCs' requirements for critical adaptation for commerce firms cannot be met (Batsakis, Konara and Theoharakis 2023; Tolstoy, Jonsson and Sharma 2016).

ECFs' *breadth of international control* refers to firms' level of control across host markets and the potential for economies of scale, distribution networks, and synergies (e.g., Fleury et al. 2024). We conceptualize breadth as ECFs' full international strategic and operational control across countries on the basis of the network of WOS. Like offline commerce firms, ECFs rely on managing complex cross-national supply chain operations to ensure efficient delivery, maintain high-quality service, and adapt to local market contexts (e.g., Hua and Wu 2024). Unlike the international breadth of virtual presence, which captures only ECFs' digital operations and intangible assets (Tolstoy, Jonsson and Sharma 2016), ECFs' subsidiary network captures the combined scale benefits of virtual and physical presence. The latter captures the international scaling of ECFs' strategic and operational control and signals long-term commitment to a host country network and local stakeholders. ECFs may benefit from cross-country synergies by leveraging their subsidiary network as regional hubs (Schu and Morschett 2017; Schu, Morschett and Swoboda 2016).

Theoretically, we expect that while ECFs' virtual presence and learning can be used to scale across online markets (e.g., Mithani 2023), they require a physical network of subsidiaries and cross-country capabilities to realize network synergies (e.g., Batsakis, Konara and Theoharakis 2023). We assume that ECFs' foreign sales performance is affected by a higher breadth of control; otherwise, EFCs face increasing but critical coordination issues that may corrupt sales (e.g., Hua and Wu 2024).

We conceptualize local e-commerce market size and growth as critical market contexts for ECFs that reflect customer demand, market dynamics, and e-commerce infrastructure (Dong, He and Blut 2024; Schu and Morschett 2017). Market size offers direct contact with a large customer base and demand for additional services or local networks for adaptation, although managing an increasing number of such markets may be complex (Chan, Finnegan and Sternquist 2011). Market growth offers opportunities for scaling subsidiary networks or cross-country synergies (e.g., Kishore, Agrawal and Rao 2004), but it may constrain ECFs' local adaptation due to market volatility. Thus, ECFs may face another tradeoff, as the local market context may limit performance depending on ECFs' control decisions in terms of depth vs. breadth.

E-commerce *market size,* as a critical context for ECFs, reflects the local customer base and potential for additional offers or higher returns (Schu and Morschett 2017; Rothaermel, Kotha and Steensma 2006). ECFs may achieve higher sales by introducing local services (Batsakis, Konara and Theoharakis 2023). Amazon or Zalando, for example, have high control within and across markets in developed e-commerce markets to enable next-day delivery, local assortments, or management (Janjevic and Winkenbach 2020).

Theoretically, we expect that market size affects ECFs' international control over time, i.e., their learning, network management, and capability transfer. While ECFs can better leverage higher control in large markets for adaptation, additional FDI across such markets may limit the scale benefits of greater breadth due to high complexity (Tolstoy, Jonsson and Sharma 2016).

Market growth, as a critical context, reflects market dynamics particularly relevant for ECFs' risk of control in a country (Wan et al. 2023) vs. opportunities for growth (Cumming et al. 2023). While ECFs such as ASOS or Shein prefer virtual presence in growing markets, JD.com and About You invest across such markets. The volatility of growing markets may affect ECFs' control (Chan, Finnegan and Sternquist 2011) but presents opportunities to scale the supply chain.

Theoretically, we assume that market growth influences the effects of higher control differently than market size does (Kishore, Agrawal and Rao 2004). While rapidly growing markets can complicate the successful implementation of services (Janjevic and Winkenbach 2020), we argue that ECFs can gain opportunities for network synergies across such markets.

Figure D—1 depicts our conceptual framework.

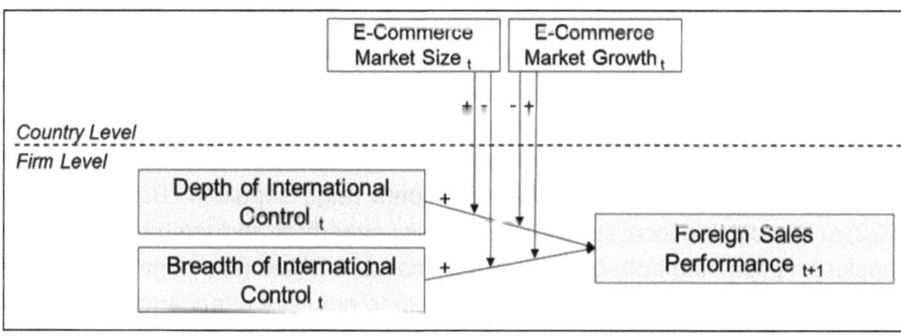

Figure D—1: Conceptual Framework
Source: Own Creation

Next, we derive hypotheses for each relationship based on theoretical rationales and clarify our current empirical knowledge. We consider a time lag of one year between the control decision and performance because that is usual, and such relationships also take approximately one year to manifest in commerce (e.g., Batsakis et al. 2023; Shi et al. 2018).

2.2. Hypotheses on the Performance Effects of International Control Decisions

We revisit ECFs' control decisions from a process, network and capability-theoretical lens and provide new mechanisms to explain performance abroad. We argue that physical control in general allows ECFs to leverage learning, business networks, and operational capabilities for local adaptation and international scaling to increase performance (Batsakis et al. 2023; Johanson and Vahlne 2009).

The depth of international control relates to ECFs' hierarchical control over local operations and management in a country based on their operation mode. While offline firms' control depends on exports, cooperation, or WOS, ECFs' virtual presence does not require physical presence to control country operations (e.g., Schu and Morschett 2017). Empirically, manufacturing firms' depth of control positively affects performance (e.g., Giachetti, Manzi and Colapinto 2019; Wan et al. 2023), whereas only two commerce studies show contradictory results (negative or positive, Evans, Mavondo and Bridson 2008; Gielens and Dekimpe 2001). The performance effects of digital firms, such as ECFs' depth of control, have not been studied.

We argue that *high depth of control* enables ECFs to identify and seize local opportunities to adapt offers and services to customer needs, leading to better sales. ECFs may use high control in a country to gain hands-on market-specific knowledge that can be used to adapt offers or services (e.g., Tolstoy, Nordman and Vu 2022). With local subsidiaries, ECFs may offer local assortments or faster delivery to ensure a better customer experience than outsourcing to partners (e.g., Hua and Wu 2024). ECFs may become embedded in local business networks and collaborate with local stakeholders (e.g., suppliers, Batsakis et al. 2023) to improve the local supply chain. Unlike exports or partnerships, ECFs can transfer and combine both digital and physical capabilities (e.g., digital marketing capabilities and physical logistics capabilities) to enhance offers and sales.

In contrast, *low depth of control* in a country allows ECFs to directly interact with or learn about local customers at low cost and identify local opportunities (e.g., Swoboda and Sinning 2022). However, the customer experience may be poorer because delivery time and quality, for example, depend on reliable logistics partners, whereas ECFs face liabilities of foreignness (i.e., lack hands-on experience with local cultures; Nambisan and Luo 2022, p. 55). Moreover, ECFs may rely on online networks and digital stakeholder relations but lack collaboration opportunities and enhanced productivity due to liabilities of outsidership (i.e., lack of local business networks, Johanson and Vahlne 2009). ECFs may not fully leverage their digital capabilities because they lack the operational or network capabilities to actually seize local opportunities (e.g., Batsakis et al. 2023).

Therefore, we propose the following:

H1. A higher degree of depth of an ECF's international control decisions is associated with higher foreign sales performance.

The breadth of international control relates to ECFs' level of control across countries and the potential for scaling offers and services or central management. While offline commerce requires FDI per se, ECFs may scale the presence virtually but may not standardize supply chain elements (Schu, Morschett and Swoboda 2016). Empirically, offline firms' breadth of control affects performance positively (Kirca et al. 2011), although two studies present contradictory results (negative or positive S-shaped, Chan, Finnegan and Sternquist 2011; Dimitrova, Kim and Smith 2019). The performance effects of ECFs' breadth of control have not been studied.

High breadth of control enables ECFs to leverage their network of WOS across countries to improve foreign sales performance through economies of scale, cross-country synergies, and centralized management (e.g., Dimitrova, Kim and Smith 2019). We argue that ECFs' process-related learning is path dependent because they may develop and transfer operational knowledge via WOS to reduce the risk of replicating and standardizing offers/services across countries (e.g., Swoboda and Sinning 2022). Expanding the network of WOS across countries enables synergies in ECFs' own supply chains and with cross-country business networks (Johanson and Vahlne 2009). As ECFs coordinate more activities centrally across WOS, they may better transfer operational capabilities to streamline assortments, promotions, CRM, or logistics and improve foreign sales performance (e.g., Nath, Nachiappan and Ramanathan 2010).

In contrast, with *low breadth of control* across countries, ECFs may replicate and learn through a virtual presence and thus increase foreign sales digitally. However, they may miss critical operational learning and the potential for standardization to increase long-term foreign sales (e.g., Mithani 2023). Firms may also leverage online networks to scale quickly and outsource logistics; however, ECFs lack potential synergies or access networks to improve offers or services (e.g., Benmamoun et al. 2019). Similarly, ECFs may transfer and apply digital capabilities virtually at low cost, although operational capabilities to standardize assortments or customer services across markets to increase foreign sales over time are lacking. Consequently, ECFs rely strongly on partners and are unable to control or improve sales performance abroad (Hua and Wu 2024).

We hypothesize the following:

H2. A higher degree of breadth of an ECF's international control decisions is associated with higher foreign sales performance.

We argue that higher (vs. lower) depth and breadth of control contribute differently to foreign sales performance. ECFs must prioritize if time and resources for expansion are limited (Eduardsen et al. 2023). ECFs are more flexible than offline commerce firms because of their virtual presence but still face the need to improve foreign sales through adapted offers in a country or efficient CRM across countries (Swoboda and Elsner 2013). Empirically, no study has considered such trade-offs regarding control for offline firms or ECFs. Only for manufacturers' higher foreign market involvement have scholars shown that international sales share drives performance more strongly than geographic reach does (e.g., Elbanna et al. 2024; Miller, Lavie and Delios 2016), whereas a meta-analysis shows the opposite (Schwens et al. 2018a).

We argue that for ECFs' sales, improving offers and services visibly within countries is more critical to performance abroad than scale advantages across countries. *Prioritizing depth of control* ensures local adaptation to cultural needs and leverages market knowledge, local network relationships, and combined digital and physical capabilities (Meyer et al. 2023). This allows for high-quality offers and services (e.g., next-day delivery, Janjevic and Winkenbach 2020), which is critical for customer satisfaction, experience and ECF competitiveness. Similarly, ECFs may implement local strategic and operational management dedicated to integrating virtual and physical presence to improve the customer experience and sales in and across countries (Batsakis et al. 2023).

In contrast, by *prioritizing breadth of control*, ECFs may learn to replicate assortments or services at reduced prices across countries to improve sales. However, commerce markets are often specific with respect to customers' needs, and knowledge of processes is less important for success than offers are (Swoboda and Elsner 2013). Large WOS networks also allow for synergies across countries, but access to local business networks may be limited, and the quality of collaboration with local stakeholders may vary (Hua and Wu 2024). A cross-border distribution network also enables more efficient and free delivery at the risk of volatile service quality and barriers due to specific regulations, especially in logistics (e.g., taxes, product safety, Meyer et al. 2023). Finally, ECFs may gain strategic and operational capabilities across WOS, even with a potentially dominant home market, but may develop weaker capabilities to fulfill local customer needs, which limits foreign sales (Batsakis, Konara and Theoharakis 2023; Nath, Nachiappan and Ramanathan 2010).

Thus, we argue the following:

H3. The association of the depth of international control with ECFs' foreign sales performance is stronger than the association of the breadth of international control.

2.3. Hypotheses on the E-Commerce Market Context

The effects of higher (vs. lower) control on ECFs' performance are likely to depend on alignment with external contexts (e.g., Giachetti, Manzi and Colapinto 2019; Kirca et al. 2012b). These are specific to ECFs' successful internationalization due to digitalization (e.g., Cumming et al. 2023; Eduardsen et al. 2023). We argue that ECFs' advantages in terms of learning, networks, and capabilities through control depend on the size and growth of the local e-commerce market (e.g., Dong, He and Blut 2024; Goldman et al. 2021). The extant research has not addressed such contexts in general or for digital firms.

E-commerce market size is related to the potential customer base for ECFs' offers in a country, which is crucial for assessing the attractiveness of an online market and opportunities for high returns (Schu and Morschett 2017). No empirical insights into the moderation effect of market size on firms' control decisions exist.

With respect to ECFs' depth of control, *a large market size* indicates highly developed e-commerce in a country with high local demand, income levels, and potential for ECFs to introduce adapted offers and customer service to achieve higher sales (e.g., Wang, Mao and Archer 2012). Large markets offer greater potential for ECFs to leverage local market knowledge in a country because perceived FDI risk is reduced, but this knowledge may also be more difficult to protect and use over time (Rothaermel, Kotha and Steensma 2006; Schu and Morschett 2017). Local business networks and embeddedness may become more valuable as experienced service providers and local partners are available to build and improve ECFs' local supply chains (Kishore, Agrawal and Rao 2004). ECFs may transfer and integrate their digital and operational capabilities more effectively, as large e-commerce markets support local infrastructure but also imply more intense competition that may inhibit it (Goldman et al. 2021). *A low* market size may limit ECFs' ability to leverage knowledge of local customer needs and benefit from networks, as demand is low and FDI for introducing additional offers is not worthwhile (Janjevic and Winkenbach 2020; Wang, Mao and Archer 2012).

With respect to ECFs' breadth of control, *high market size* may limit cross-country synergies and centralized management across countries. While ECFs may transfer their FDI experience and gain scale, effectively replicating knowledge across large markets may be highly complex and reduce benefits for foreign sales (Tolstoy, Jonsson and Sharma 2016). The same applies to standardizing assortments, prices, or CRM in a WOS network across many large markets and achieving synergies (e.g., Johanson and Vahlne 2009), which is challenging for offline commerce but may be less challenging for ECFs with lower WOS. Since physical presence in multiple large markets with specific demands requires different capabilities, transferring these across countries may be limited, resulting in the outsourcing of logistics, for example (Janjevic and Winkenbach 2020). *A low* market size may facilitate ECFs' internal knowledge and capability transfer or coordination of the WOS network for synergies because they face less complex markets (Agarwal and Wu 2015). We expect market size to strengthen the effect of high depth of control on ECFs' performance abroad but mitigate the effect of high breadth.

We hypothesize the following:

H4. Market size moderates the associations of (a) higher depth and (b) higher breadth of international control with ECFs' foreign sales performance (a) positively and (b) negatively.

E-commerce market growth reflects the dynamic development of an online market, which is crucial for assessing future potential for foreign sales but also increases risk (e.g., Cumming et al. 2023). Empirically, market growth has not been considered a moderator of depth or breadth of control in general. For ECFs, only Kishore, Agrawal and Rao (2004) indicates a positive moderating effect on the antecedents of depth of control.

With respect to ECFs' depth of control, *high market growth* may reflect a dynamic and fast-changing environment, making it difficult to reliably adapt offers due to fluctuating demand and volatile market trends (e.g., Wan et al. 2023). Acquiring and leveraging long-term market-specific knowledge may be more challenging in markets with a physical presence, and cooperation may be preferable to reduce volatility risk (Morschett, Schramm-Klein and Swoboda 2010). In growing markets, local networks may still be developing, and reliable business partners may be harder to find, challenging ECFs' ability to establish their own local supply chains, which is crucial for sales performance (Kishore, Agrawal and Rao 2004). It may be more difficult for ECFs to transfer and integrate their digital and operational capabilities in such markets because infrastructural barriers limit foreign sales (e.g., Agarwal and Wu 2015). In contrast, *low* market growth may enable ECFs to leverage market knowledge and local business networks because markets are more predictable and FDI for local offers is less risky (e.g., Ho, Kauffman and Liang 2007).

With respect to ECFs' breadth of control, *high market growth* offers opportunities for developing, testing, and refining supply chain elements that may improve foreign sales performance. The growth momentum in such markets may enable ECFs to scale assortments, prices, or CRM through FDI and benefit from diverse learning opportunities, as e-commerce infrastructure, for example, is still developing (e.g., Goldman et al. 2021). These markets attract new suppliers or partners that offer opportunities to scale ECFs' business networks, which can enable stronger collaboration and mutual learning (e.g., Agarwal and Wu 2015). High market growth may also encourage ECFs to continuously develop, test, and refine their operational capabilities or recognize new ways to streamline the supply chain across markets, fostering foreign sales performance (e.g., Janjevic and Winkenbach 2020). *Low* market growth may hold few FDI incentives or learning opportunities for ECFs to benefit from market changes and improve their operational capabilities (e.g., Kishore, Agrawal and Rao 2004).

We assume that market growth mitigates the effect of higher (vs. lower) depth of control on ECFs' foreign performance but strengthens the effect of higher (vs. lower) breadth and argue the following:

H5. Market growth moderates the associations of (a) higher depth and (b) higher breadth of international control with ECFs' foreign sales performance (a) negatively and (b) positively.

3. Empirical Study

3.1. Sample

To study performance over time, we developed a database from unique sources: a ranking of the leading ECFs by Digital Commerce 360 (2021) 2015–2020 and individual foreign sales performance data from ECDB (2024c) that are fully available only from 2016 to the beginning of the coronavirus pandemic in 2021. The independent, moderating and control variables were lagged by one year (e.g., Batsakis et al. 2023; Shi et al. 2018).

We selected ECFs on the basis of the rankings of the 500 leading B2C ECFs in Europe (in terms of sales, Digital Commerce 360 2021). This source collects firm-level data (e.g., firm size, foreign entries) based on firms' own information or estimations verified by each firm. Initially, 560 ECFs were found that were not necessarily founded in Europe and are active worldwide but had to be active in at least one foreign market. We excluded 193 ECFs that operated only in their home markets and 47 ECFs that operated only "dot-com domains" abroad because these do not indicate clear foreign market entries. This procedure resulted in 320 ECFs. For each ECF, local presence and further firm-level control variables were collected by the authors and trained master's student assistants. We examined the host country websites of each ECF to verify their existence and used annual reports, press releases, public archives or articles, social media, firm directories and job market sites to verify market entry dates and collect the operation mode in each country. At least 80% of the data were checked by two or more sources. Similarly, the industry, firm size and born digital characteristics of the firms were collected or double-checked against the databases. For 33 ECFs, the operation mode or firm size could not be obtained.

We expanded this database with foreign sales performance data from ECDB (2024c) on individual ECFs. To our knowledge, this is the only recently available database on ECFs' foreign sales over time, which is based on firms' own information and verified estimations. We attempted to verify these data and further firm-level controls such as online age, foreign sales share or offering a marketplace within the online business using the sources and procedures mentioned above. We matched these foreign sales data with the selected 287 EFCs and excluded 101 ECFs (often smaller firms not obliged to publish financial data), for which no sales data in general or over time were available. ECDB (2024b) was also used to obtain country-level e-commerce market data, which we matched to the year of the control decision. Data on B2C e-commerce market size were available for over 150 countries. We estimated these data based on the national chambers of commerce and UNCTAD's (2024) B2C e-commerce index and calculated e-commerce market growth over the investigated period. We excluded 50 mostly very small host countries (e.g., Afghanistan, Monaco, and Maldives) and two ECFs with entry decisions only in these countries.

The final dataset included 1,144 control decisions in 112 countries by 184 ECFs from 22 home countries (see Table D—1). We used a maximum likelihood estimator with robust standard errors and test statistics (Maydeu-Olivares 2017).

Home Countries	Number of ECFs	Number of Market Entries
Australia	1	3
Austria	1	1
Belgium	1	7
China	6	79
Czech Republic	2	4
Denmark	4	47
Finland	1	21
France	33	118
Germany	36	127
Great Britain	39	260
Ireland	1	3
Italy	10	182
Korea (Rep.)	1	27
Netherlands	5	17
Poland	3	9
Romania	1	1
Russian Federation	2	2
Spain	6	40
Sweden	3	47
Switzerland	3	15
Turkey	3	9
United States	22	125
Total	**184**	**1,144**

Table D—1: Sample Distribution

Source: Own Creation

3.2. Measurement

Dependent Variable. We measured ECFs' foreign performance as net first-party online sales after deducting returns, allowances, discounts, and third-party marketplace sales (ECDB 2024b). Foreign net sales are an important benchmarking tool for ECFs to assess their sales profitability and competitive positioning and are commonly used for industry rankings. We follow earlier studies on ECFs (Gregory, Ngo and Karavdic 2019; Tolstoy, Jonsson and Sharma 2016), as further performance measures (e.g., return on assets, net income, Batsakis et al. 2023) vary by commerce sector and are not required to be published by most ECFs (e.g., Swoboda and Sinning 2022). We tested foreign sales growth as a stability check (Colton, Roth and Bearden 2010).

Independent Variables. Firms' *depth of international control* was measured on a four-point scale to capture ECFs' level of hierarchical control over operations and management within a host country: 1= indirect/passive virtual presence, 2=direct/active virtual presence, 3=cooperative modes, and 4=WOS (covering ECFs' virtual and physical operation mode decisions in each host country over time; Brouthers et al. 2022). Because, to our knowledge, no alternatives exist, we oriented ourselves toward traditional mode scales (e.g., Evans, Mavondo and Bridson 2008; Hernández and Nieto 2015). We referred to studies on international ECFs to define forms of virtual presence similar to traditional exports (e.g., Ipsmiller, Dikova and Brouthers 2022; Sinkovics, Sinkovics and Jean 2013). An *indirect/passive* virtual presence was defined as operating in a dot-com/uk domain (i.e., a standardized website with no local adaptations beyond linguistic translation). A *direct/active* virtual presence was defined as a country-specific dot-uk domain (i.e., a locally registered domain, adapted language, and currency, Schu and Morschett 2017), which offers more control over operations in a country. *Cooperative modes* were defined as various forms of cooperation with shared control (i.e., contractual partnerships, alliances, or logistics networks); JVs are not common. *Wholly owned subsidiaries* for full operational control were defined as sales/service subsidiaries in a country. WOS unrelated to ECFs' core online commerce business were excluded (e.g., production/technology sites or offline stores). We subsequently interpret this scale and its effects only in terms of significance and sign (not in terms of the meaning of intervals in this metric, e.g., Lalla 2017; instead of a less informational dummy treatment, Winship and Mare 1984).

The breadth of international control was measured as the number of markets in which an ECF had its own subsidiaries and warehouses (i.e., full strategic and operational control) in addition to a virtual presence to capture ECFs' level of control across host countries. This measure captures ECFs' virtual and physical commitment to a country network of subsidiaries that enables firms to scale their international supply chain over time (e.g., Schu and Morschett 2017). Related measures, such as geographic diversification (i.e., the proportion of sales in a country, Oh, Sohl and Rugman 2015), were unavailable for ECFs over time. We tested the breadth of virtual presence (i.e., number of countries) in our stability checks.

Moderating Variables. Host country *e-commerce market size* was measured as market revenue in B2C sales of physical goods, including taxes and excluding returns, discounts or services (ECDB 2024b). This measure reflects ECFs' relevant market segment, which has recently become available and has been overlooked in previous studies (Schu and Morschett 2017). *E-commerce market growth* was measured as the year-over-year change in market sales (ECDB 2024b), which is most common in the literature (e.g., GDP growth, Morschett, Schramm-Klein and Swoboda 2010). It captures the sector-specific growth relevant for B2C ECFs. Alternative measures (e.g., online shopping expenditures, Ho, Kauffman and Liang 2007) are not yet available across countries.

Controls. We controlled important variables at the firm and country levels.

We controlled for *firm size* as an important indicator of firms' ability to increase performance (Oh, Sohl and Rugman 2015). We measured the logarithm of firms' online sales with data from Digital Commerce 360 (2021). This is a common indicator of ECF size because ECFs hire fewer employees, and the numbers are not available over time (Swoboda and Sinning 2022).

Firms' *online age* was measured as the number of years since an ECF first started selling online. Online age may affect ECFs' sales performance because more time is available to gain experience and digital capabilities (Sinkovics, Sinkovics and Jean 2013) and because not all ECFs start businesses online (Fleury et al. 2024). We collected these data from the ECDB (2024c).

We controlled for *home market size*, which may affect ECFs' foreign performance and expansion (e.g., Batsakis et al. 2023). Large home markets may limit ECFs' further domestic growth and drive increased foreign sales (Swoboda and Sinning 2022). Home market size was measured with the logarithmized GDP per capita via data from the World Bank (2023b).

The *foreign sales share* was controlled to account for ECFs' degree of internationalization, which affects performance (Bhandari et al. 2023), on the basis of ECDB (2024c) data. A high share of foreign sales also reflects ECFs' experience in international markets (Tolstoy, Nordman and Vu 2022).

We controlled for ECFs running an additional online *marketplace* (i.e., offering a platform for third-party sellers) in addition to their online shop (Gong, He and Lengler 2024). This may enable ECFs to expand their local network and attract more customers, which can lead to increased foreign sales (Cha, Kotabe and Wu 2023). We used a binary measure of 1=yes and 0=no (ECDB 2024c).

Born digital firms (i.e., ECFs with a virtual presence from inception, Monaghan, Tippmann and Coviello 2020) were controlled because firms that go digital (i.e., those that adopted digital channels later) can draw on legacy infrastructure and experience to increase performance (Birkinshaw 2022). Born digital ECFs may be less flexible and cannot integrate virtual and physical presence (Batsakis, Konara and Theoharakis 2023). We used a binary measure (1=born digital and 0=not, Digital Commerce 360 2021).

To control *industry* effects, we created dummy variables for the three most important industries in our sample, i.e., *fashion*, *electronics*, and *food* (i.e., 29%, 21%, and 8% of ECFs, respectively). We used industry classification data from Digital Commerce 360 (2021). Commerce firms' sales volume differs greatly across industries (e.g., grocery vs. fashion due to purchase frequency, Batsakis et al. 2023).

At the country level, we controlled for *host market size*, measured as the logarithm of host countries' GDP per capita (Batsakis, Konara and Theoharakis 2023), which is most often used to capture market attractiveness (Rothaermel, Kotha and Steensma 2006) and is available from the World Bank (2023b). A large market reflects high demand for ECFs' offers and thus opportunities to increase foreign sales performance (Swoboda and Sinning 2022).

Bivariate correlations of all variables at the firm and country levels did not raise any concerns about collinearity in our data (see Table D—2), as also indicated by the VIF values, which were all below two (e.g., Backhaus et al. 2023, pp. 111-113; O'Brien 2007).

To mitigate potential bias from possibly omitted variables, we addressed endogeneity concerns by employing the established instrumental variable approach (see Table D—3; e.g., following Antonakis et al. 2014). We chose *host country online experience* (measured by the number of years a firm has been virtually present in a specific country, e.g., Wan et al. 2023) as an instrumental variable (IV) theoretically related to ECFs' depth of international control. The host country's online experience reflects ECFs' market-specific knowledge acquired via virtual presence over time (e.g., Li and Meyer 2009). This experience relates to ECFs' ability to recognize or exploit specific location advantages for adapted offers in a country and choose to implement high control locally (e.g., Tang and Gudergan 2018).

	(1)	(2)	(3)	(4)	(5)	(6)	(7)	(8)	(9)	(10)	(11)	(12)	(13)	(14)	(15)
Mean	4.602	2.373	9.097	5.477	14.365	10.505	.072	.555	.171	.497	.139	.055	10.020	8.333	.217
SD	2.117	1.324	1.055	1.769	5.842	.515	.268	.326	.377	.500	.346	.228	1.010	1.986	.118
VIF (max.)	-	1.347	1.951	1.480	1.699	1.812	1.439	1.298	1.713	1.540	1.445	1.218	1.257	1.302	1.080
	(1)	**(2)**	**(3)**	**(4)**	**(5)**	**(6)**	**(7)**	**(8)**	**(9)**	**(10)**	**(11)**	**(12)**	**(13)**	**(14)**	**(15)**
ForPerf (log.) (1)	1														
DoC (2)	.313***	1													
BoC (3)	.553***	.378***	1												
Size (log.) (4)	.768***	.224***	.437***	1											
OnAge (5)	-.055ns	.030ns	.012ns	.014ns	1										
HoMS (log.) (6)	-.045ns	.212***	.100**	-.028ns	.570***	1									
MP (0/1) (7)	.083**	-.055ns	-.180***	.093**	-.177***	-.165***	1								
ForSh (8)	.471***	.115**	.300***	-.094**	-.092**	-.091**	-.016ns	1							
BD (0/1) (9)	-.036ns	-.155***	-.331***	.019ns	-.232***	-.164***	.521***	-.068*	1						
Fash (0/1) (10)	-.052ns	-.139***	-.097**	-.049ns	.104***	-.089**	-.053ns	-.130***	-.118***	1					
Elec (0/1) (11)	.121***	.055ns	.003ns	.057ns	-.002ns	-.087**	.016ns	.161***	-.096**	-.400***	1				
Food (0/1) (12)	.088**	.094**	.107**	.064*	-.016ns	-.091**	.111***	.142***	.063*	-.240***	-.097**	1			
HosMS (log.)(13)	-.094**	.089**	-.095*	-.009ns	.040ns	.110***	-.022ns	-.124***	.086**	-.013ns	.005ns	-.054ns	1		
ECMS (log.)(14)	-.083**	.194***	-.133***	-.065*	-.037ns	.061*	.079**	-.031ns	.176***	-.129***	.004ns	.071*	.374***	1	
ECMG (15)	.043ns	-.060*	.070*	.021ns	.013ns	-.052ns	.003ns	.063*	-.044ns	.011ns	.005ns	.015ns	-.374***	-.236***	1

Note: ***p<.001; **p<.01; *p<.05; ns=Not significant. BD=Born Digital; BoC=Breadth of International Control; DoC=Depth of International Control; ECMG=E-Commerce Market Growth; ECMS=E-Commerce Market Size; Elec=Electronics; Fash=Fashion; ForPerf=Foreign Sales Performance; ForSh=Foreign Sales Share; HoMS=Home Market Size; HosMS=Host Market Size; MP=Marketplace; OnAge=Online Age; SD=Standard Deviation; VIF=Variance Inflation Factor.

Table D—2: Correlations

Source: Own Creation.

We chose *international online experience* (measured as the number of years since an ECF's first online market entry, e.g., Dow and Larimo 2009) as an IV relevant to ECFs' breadth of international control. Firms may leverage general international online experience as a capability to scale their foreign operations and control across countries (Kirca et al. 2011; Schu, Morschett and Swoboda 2016).

		Random Intercept (Baseline) Model	
		Consistent Model	**Proposed/Efficient Model**
		b*p*	b*p*
Intercept		4.739*	4.695*
Firm Level			
Depth of Control	→ Foreign Sales Performance (log.)	.174***	.172***
Breadth of Control	→ Foreign Sales Performance (log.)	.013***	.013***
IV_1	→ Depth of Control	.184***	
IV_2	→ Breadth of Control	.816***	
Controls (Firm Level)			
Firm Size (log.)	→ Foreign Sales Performance (log.)	.891***	.892***
Online Age	→ Foreign Sales Performance (log.)	.019*	.019ns
Home Market Size (log.)	→ Foreign Sales Performance (log.)	-.637**	-.634**
Foreign Sales Share	→ Foreign Sales Performance (log.)	3.280***	3.282***
Marketplace (0/1)	→ Foreign Sales Performance (log.)	.264**	.266**
Born Digital (0/1)	→ Foreign Sales Performance (log.)	-.032ns	-.029ns
Fashion (0/1)	→ Foreign Sales Performance (log.)	.097ns	.097ns
Electronics (0/1)	→ Foreign Sales Performance (log.)	-.138ns	-.137ns
Food (0/1)	→ Foreign Sales Performance (log.)	-.581***	-.602***
Controls (Country Level)			
Host Market Size (log.)	→ Foreign Sales Performance (log.)	-.042**	-.014**
AIC		14,748.408	2,599.349
BIC (Adjusted)		14,787.611	2,627.338

Note: ***p<.001; **p<.01; *p<.05; ns=Not Significant; b=Unstandardized Coefficients; IV=Instrumental Variable.

Table D—3: Comparison of Consistent and Proposed Model

Source: Own Creation

We initially checked whether these IVs are strong predictors of depth and breadth of control using F-tests (Stock and Watson 2020, p. 270). The calculated F-values exceeded the recommended threshold of 10 (IV_1=36.36, IV_2=199.01), therefore the IVs can be considered strong predictors (Antonakis et al. 2014). Afterwards, we estimated a consistent model including these IVs in addition to our efficient (i.e., proposed) model and tested whether there was a change in effects using the Hausman (1978) test. The effects did not change significantly, suggesting a low probability of endogeneity issues (Swoboda and Sinning 2022). This finding indicates that both the depth and breadth of international control are exogenous (e.g., Hausman 1978).

3.3. Method

We tested our hypotheses using multilevel modeling with cross-level interactions in Mplus 9 to account for our nested data structure (i.e., ECFs made control decisions in multiple different host countries), considering firm- and country-level effects as well as variances between and within countries simultaneously (Hox, Moerbeek and Van de Schoot 2018, p. 215). To evaluate model fit, we employed stepwise random intercept and slope models, systematically refining the models and comparing them using the AIC and BIC values (Hox, Moerbeek and Van de Schoot 2018, p. 123, Kaufman 1996).

In the first step, a baseline model with only the control variables was calculated. We then subsequently added the independent variables separately and jointly, added country-level moderators, and finally all variables into one model. All independent and moderating variables were grand mean centered in order to increase the interpretability of intercepts and coefficient estimates (e.g., Hox, Moerbeek and Van de Schoot 2018, pp. 61-63; Stallkamp, Chen and Li 2023). The following equation describes the model predicting ECFs' foreign sales performance with only the controls and the firm-level independent variables:

$$
\begin{aligned}
For\_Perf_{ij(t+1)} &= \beta_{0j} + \beta_{1j}\left(Ctrl\_Depth_{ij(t)}\right) \\
&+ \beta_{2j}\left(Ctrl\_Breadth_{ij(t)}\right) + \beta_{controls}\, ILC_{ij(t)} \\
&+ \beta_{controls}\, CLC_{j(t)} + r_{ij} \qquad (1)
\end{aligned}
$$

where i denotes an ECF in the host country j, For_Perf_{ij}=ECF's foreign sales performance one year after the control decision in a country was made; $Ctrl\_Depth_{ij}$ =ECF's depth of international control; $Ctrl\_Breadth_{ij}$=ECF's breadth of international control; β_{0j}=first-level intercept; β_{1j}, β_{2j}=regression scores of firm-level independent variables; ILC_{ij}= firm-level controls; CLC_j=country-level control; r_{ij}=first-level error term. The intercept β_{0j} and the slopes β_{1j} and β_{2j} were free to vary across countries, whereas the CLC_j and country-level moderators CLV_j were assumed to predict variations in the β coefficients according to the following equations:

$$\beta_{0j}=\gamma_{00}+\gamma_{01}(CLV_{j(t)})+\gamma_{02}(CLC_{j(t)})+u_{0j}, \tag{2}$$

$$\beta_{1j}=\gamma_{10}+\gamma_{11}(CLV_{j(t)})+u_{1j}, \tag{3}$$

$$\beta_{2j}=\gamma_{20}+\gamma_{21}(CLV_{j(t)})+u_{2j}, \tag{4}$$

with γ_{00}=second-level intercept of the dependent variable; γ_{10} and γ_{20}=second-level intercepts of the random slopes of the firm-level predictors; u_{0j}=country-level residual variance; and u_{1j}, u_{2j}=random slopes of the firm-level variables at the country level. A substitution of equations (1) to (4) and inclusion of the two country-level moderators CLV_j as cross-level interactions resulted in the final equation:

$$\begin{aligned} For\_Perf_{ij(t+1)}&=\gamma_{00}+\gamma_{01}(CLV_{j(t)})+\gamma_{10}\left(Ctrl\_Depth_{ij(t)}\right)\\ &+\gamma_{11}(CLV_{j(t)})\left(Ctrl\_Depth_{ij(t)}\right)+\gamma_{20}\left(Ctrl\_Breadth_{ij(t)}\right)\\ &+\gamma_{21}(CLV_{j(t)})\left(Ctrl\_Breadth_{ij(t)}\right)+\gamma_{ILC}ILC_{ij(t)}+\gamma_{CLC}CLC_{ij(t)}+\varepsilon \end{aligned} \tag{5}$$

with ε=residual variances and errors.

3.4. Results

Table D—4 shows the results of our hypothesis testing with unstandardized coefficients (standardized coefficients cannot be computed for random intercept and slope models, e.g., Hox, Moerbeek and Van de Schoot 2018, pp. 17-18). We report additional effect sizes to assess the relative strength of the coefficients (e.g., Marsh et al. 2009).

In support of *H1*, the results show that greater (vs. lower) *depth* of international control is positively associated with ECFs' foreign sales performance (b=.165, p<.001). The greater ECFs' control within foreign markets is, the better they perform in terms of foreign sales. Similarly, a higher (vs. lower) *breadth* of ECFs' international control is positively associated with their foreign performance (b=.015, p<.001). Higher control across countries through subsidiaries leads to higher foreign sales performance by ECFs. *H2* is supported.

		Model 1	Model 2	Model 3	Model 4	Model 5	Model 6	Model 7	Differences (t-values)
		bp	bp	bp	bp	bp	bp	bp	
Intercept		4.473ns	4.723*	4.452ns	4.695*	4.556*	4.859*	4.695*	
Firm Level									
Depth of Control	→ Foreign Sales Performance (log.)		.193***		.172***	.173***	.155***	.165*** (.206)	
Breadth of Control	→ Foreign Sales Performance (log.)			.021***	.013***	.014***	.015***	.015*** (.143)	4.564***
Country Level									
E-Commerce Market Size (log.)	→ Foreign Sales Performance (log.)					-.015ns		-.019ns (-.048)	
	× Depth of Control					.001ns		-.004ns (-.010)	
	× Breadth of Control					-.001ns		.000ns (.000)	.447ns
E-Commerce Market Growth	→ Foreign Sales Performance (log.)						-.476*	-.456* (-.098)	
	× Depth of Control						-.360*	-.332* (-.074)	
	× Breadth of Control						.032*	.030* (.007)	2.271**
Controls (Firm Level)									
Firm Size (log.)	→ Foreign Sales Performance (log.)	.951***	.922***	.898***	.832***	.892***	.893***	.893*** (1.490)	
Online Age	→ Foreign Sales Performance (log.)	.018ns	.019ns	.019ns	.019ns	.019ns	.019*	.019ns (.105)	
Home Market Size (log.)	→ Foreign Sales Performance (log.)	-.663*	-.648**	-.636*	-.634**	-.630**	-.641**	-.634** (-.308)	
Foreign Sales Share	→ Foreign Sales Performance (log.)	3.471***	3.394***	3.279***	3.282***	3.288***	3.273***	3.283*** (1.010)	
Marketplace (0/1)	→ Foreign Sales Performance (log.)	.251*	.232*	.301**	.266**	.269**	.271**	.267** (.065)	
Born Digital (0/1)	→ Foreign Sales Performance (log.)	-.273**	-.131ns	-.086ns	-.029ns	-.026ns	-.036ns	-.027ns (.000)	
Fashion (0/1)	→ Foreign Sales Performance (log.)	-.020ns	.066ns	.046ns	.097ns	.094ns	.103ns	.099ns (.047)	
Electronics (0/1)	→ Foreign Sales Performance (log.)	-.244ns	-.197*	-.139ns	-.137ns	-.137ns	-.124ns	-.129ns (-.042)	
Food (0/1)	→ Foreign Sales Performance (log.)	-.559***	-.596***	-.567[illegible]	-.602***	-.594***	-.594***	-.588*** (-.127)	
Controls (Country Level)									
Host Market Size (log.)	→ Foreign Sales Performance (log.)	-.019ns	-.046**	-.014[illegible]	-.014**	-.028ns	-.055***	-.041** (-.052)	
AIC		2,717.561	2,604.448	2,68[illegible]27	2,599.349	2,601.594	2,594.326	2,600.985	
BIC (Adjusted)		2,741.819	2,630.572	2,71[illegible]150	2,627.338	2,635.181	2,631.645	2,640.170	

Note: ***p<.001; **p<.01; *p<.05; ns=Not significant; b=Unstandardized Coefficients. Effect sizes are shown in brackets.

Table D—4: Results

Source: Own Creation.

Comparing the relative strength of increasing depth vs. breadth of international control, we find the effect of depth to be significantly stronger than that of breadth (t=4.564, $p<.001$). The depth of control is more strongly positively associated with ECFs' foreign sales performance, supporting *H3*.

With respect to country-level interaction effects, *market size* does not moderate associations of either depth or breadth of control with foreign performance ($b_{MSIZExCtrl\_Depth}$=-.004, $p>.10$, $b_{MSIZExCtrl\_Breadth}$=.000, $p>.10$). Surprisingly, market size does not strengthen or weaken the effects of depth or breadth of control on foreign sales performance, which we address in the discussion. *H4a* and *H4b* are rejected. *Market growth* negatively moderates the associations of depth of control and performance ($b_{MGROWTHxCtrl\_Depth}$=-.332, $p<.05$), supporting *H5a*. The results also show a positive moderation effect of market growth on the associations of breadth of control and performance ($b_{MGROWTHxCtrl\_Breadth}$=.030, $p<.05$), supporting *H5b*.

Among the firm-level controls, *firm size*, *foreign sales share*, and *marketplace* are positively associated with foreign performance, whereas *home market size*, and *food industry* are significantly negatively associated with ECFs' foreign performance. At the country level, *host country market size* is surprisingly negatively associated with ECFs' foreign performance.

3.5. Stability Checks

We tested several alternative models to check the stability of our results.

First, we tested a randomly split half sample with identical results for the independent variables and the moderations (see Section G, ESM).

Second, we tested several alternative models (see Section G, ESM). We tested the stability of the international control–performance relationship by adding several ECFs for which two more years of performance data, but no e-commerce market data, were available (221 ECFs with 1,691 control decisions). The results remained stable.

Third, we tested foreign sales growth as a dependent variable. Theoretically, high depth of control may allow ECFs to exploit opportunities for higher sales within countries and thus foreign sales growth. Likewise, high breadth of control may enable ECFs to reduce uncertainties of distribution and increase foreign sales growth by exploiting opportunities for coordination across countries (e.g., Swoboda and Sinning 2022). The results underline the effects of both control measures on foreign sales growth.

Fourth, we tested for a possible nonlinear relationship between high breadth of control and foreign performance. Theoretically, ECFs may achieve synergies across their subsidiary network when their breadth of control is high but may face coordination and management challenges with too many WOS, which may decrease performance (Dimitrova, Kim and Smith 2019). The results show no indication of nonlinear effects, supporting our linear modeling.

Fifth, we tested ECFs' breadth of virtual presence (i.e., the number of markets in which an ECF operates, Schu, Morschett and Swoboda 2016). Theoretically, ECFs may achieve economies of scale digitally by serving multiple markets with a virtual presence, but we expect the effects to be less strong, as ECFs lack critical operational capabilities to improve distribution (Fleury et al. 2024). The results are nonsignificant, supporting our conceptualization.

Sixth, we tested ECFs' depth of control as a binary variable (i.e., WOS vs. other modes, which is often used as a mode measure, not as a control measure, but sometimes associated with different control levels, e.g., metanalysis by Wan et al. 2023). Theoretically, ECFs with subsidiaries have more control over operations than those with other modes (e.g., Fleury et al. 2024). The results support our conclusions in the main models and partly the moderation, which, however, could be due to a low variance of the binary variable in a complex multilevel model.

Seventh, we compare countries with high (vs. low) market size and growth to assess the stability of the continuous moderations (Goldman et al. 2021). Theoretically, the effect of higher depth of control may be significantly stronger in countries with low (vs. high) market growth, while the effects of breadth should be significantly stronger in countries with high (vs. low) market size. The results remained mostly stable and supported our conclusions.

Eight, the control marketplace may theoretically moderate the links studied (e.g., for ECFs with marketplaces (vs. online shops only), the association of depth and breadth with performance might be greater because of benefits for third-party sellers from ECFs' local and cross-national control or networks, e.g., Li and Li 2023). However, the results show a positive moderation only for depth (not breadth) of control.

4. Discussion

4.1. Theoretical Implications

Our study extends the limited but critical knowledge on ECFs' successful internationalization, especially the role of international control decisions, in response to many research calls (e.g., Ipsmiller, Dikova and Brouthers 2022; Batsakis et al. 2023). Considering ECFs' potential trade-off decisions and specific contexts of local e-commerce markets, we offer novel insights into integrating virtual and physical presence (Meyer et al. 2023) and provide theoretical and managerial implications.

With respect to our first research question, i.e., whether and how strongly ECFs' higher (vs. lower) international control in terms of depth vs. breadth drives ECFs' foreign sales performance, we initially show the importance of international control decisions for ECFs' performance. We provide evidence of previously unexplored mechanisms behind the discussed "space–place relationship" (e.g., Stallkamp, Chen and Li 2023). While research has focused on new theoretical mechanisms to explain digital firms' performance based on virtual expansion processes, online networks, and digital capabilities (Cumming et al. 2023), we show that also traditional mechanisms apply to explain ECFs' foreign performance. ECFs benefit from digital learning and market entry, online networks to expand the customer base, and digital capabilities based on real-time data. We conclude that applying a purely digital theory lens fails to explain the performance of ECFs and possibly platform firms, as it neglects onsite learning, local network relationships and key operational capabilities (Batsakis et al. 2023; Gong, He and Lengler 2024).

We strongly extend the literature that focuses on digital presence only and identify a trade-off, as depth of international control appears to drive ECFs' foreign sales performance significantly more than breadth does.

In terms of *depth*, ECFs can improve foreign sales performance through locally adapted offers, customer service, and supply chains. Digital *internationalization processes* reduce the need for physical control in a country, as ECFs interact with and sell offers to customers online (Monaghan, Tippmann and Coviello 2020). However, these ECFs risk falling into the "virtuality trap", i.e., relying on virtual presence too much (Sinkovics, Sinkovics and Jean 2013). Our findings support this notion, as ECFs improve their performance abroad through high physical control within countries. While scholars argue that physical *networks* are likely less important for ECFs due to digital relationships (Cumming et al. 2023), we show that ECFs' local networks and embeddedness remain crucial for local supply chains (without missing local opportunities, Batsakis et al. 2023). While ECFs use unique digital *capabilities* to meet customers' needs online, we stress the need for physical capabilities (e.g., logistics, commerce skills, Janjevic and Winkenbach 2020). ECFs appear to be most successful when both are integrated (e.g., Batsakis, Konara and Theoharakis 2023).

In terms of *breadth*, ECFs can optimize their efficiency by scaling their purchasing, offers, services or general management across countries. Digitalization has transformed ECFs' *internationalization process* by making them agile and less spatially dependent (Monaghan, Tippmann and Coviello 2020). We additionally show that ECFs' business requires physical control across countries to be scalable (Hua and Wu 2024). This is supported by our nonsignificant stability checks for ECFs' breadth of virtual presence. Scaling only virtual presence across countries does not improve foreign sales performance. Scholars also argue that digital *networks* can be scaled easily, offering network advantages for customer acquisition (e.g., Cha, Kotabe and Wu 2023, and in this study, firms running a marketplace show a positive, full moderation for depth of control; the direct control effect for performance disappears). However, this cannot replace the synergies that ECFs' physical networks offer (Schu and Morschett 2017). Similarly, ECFs' unique digital *capabilities* can be leveraged to scale their virtual presence (Cumming et al. 2023). However, again, ECFs need operational capabilities to successfully transfer management across countries (e.g., Janjevic and Winkenbach 2020).

In summary, our insights contribute to the discussion on virtual presence (in "space") as an alternative to physical control (in "place", Monaghan, Tippmann and Coviello 2020; Ipsmiller, Dikova and Brouthers 2022; Sinkovics, Sinkovics and Jean 2013). They contribute to the priorities of local or central decision making (e.g., faced by commerce, Evans, Mavondo and Bridson 2008). As higher depth of control is a stronger lever for performance, leveraging local opportunities, network relationships, and capabilities to address customer needs through control in markets seems preferable, followed by broadening control and thus synergies across countries.

Moreover, our stability checks reveal that ECFs operating their own marketplace benefit even more from higher depth (but not breadth) of control than those that do not. Greater local control allows these firms to attract third-party sellers locally, who can use the fulfillment services provided by ECFs, for example, and stimulate foreign sales. In contrast, scale benefits of ECFs' WOS network may not be directly relevant to them. This implies varying degrees of control required by different types of digital businesses. For example, B2B firms such as Alibaba, or consumer-to-consumer (C2C) platforms such as eBay can benefit from local control and adding local services, while i-business platforms such as Uber or Shopify rely on digital services and networks. We conclude that ECFs that can balance local and central decision making will be most successful abroad, as they can leverage adapted offers and streamline physical operations. This is supported by e-commerce market contexts.

Regarding our second research question concerning how host countries' e-commerce market size and growth moderate the discussed effects, we offer new insights into the contextual differences of local e-commerce markets, which suggest a further trade-off in mature vs. growing markets.

Surprisingly, our results show that ECFs' control decisions do not depend on market size. An explanation may be that ECFs face intense competition in larger markets against offline commerce (Goldman et al. 2021), which offsets the expected benefits of high demand. It may also be that market knowledge is more difficult to protect (Kishore, Agrawal and Rao 2004) or that capabilities are less beneficial for sales. ECFs may be able to manage control across markets without compromising scale, as their physical network is typically smaller/less complex than in commerce (Batsakis, Konara and Theoharakis 2023).

Market growth represents an important context for both ECFs' control decisions but in opposite directions. ECFs' benefits of high control in a country are offset in markets with high e-commerce growth. Local control is affected by changing demands, an evolving competitive landscape, and an overall volatile online environment, making it difficult to leverage learning and networks for adapted offers and services and transfer capabilities effectively (e.g., Janjevic and Winkenbach 2020; Kishore, Agrawal and Rao 2004). ECFs benefit from such growth conditions when scaling across countries. They can leverage the growth momentum in a country, supported by government incentives or local investors, to make FDI that allows their international distribution to be streamlined and to create cross-country synergies (Agarwal and Wu 2015; Wang, Mao and Archer 2012). For example, ECFs may standardize internal processes and capabilities across countries in logistics, offers (e.g., assortments, pricing), or customer services to drive sales (similar to offline commerce, e.g., Swoboda and Elsner 2013). ECFs that choose high depth of control to improve performance are limited in growing markets, whereas ECFs that aim to scale their network across countries can do so best under growth conditions but may miss out on local opportunities for adapted offers.

4.2. Practical Implications

This study offers important insights for managers of ECFs and emerging digital firms who may struggle with foreign sales performance (Batsakis, Konara and Theoharakis 2023, Ipsmiller, Dikova and Brouthers 2022). Unnoticed roles and trade-offs from ECFs' control decisions and e-commerce market contexts may lead to ineffective investments or short conclusions on how managers can navigate dynamic e-commerce markets successfully (e.g., Meyer et al. 2023).

Practitioners can learn from this study that higher (vs. lower) international control increases even digital firms' foreign sales performance. Manufacturing firms that use ECFs' platforms may prefer those that are more internationally successful with greater international control. A nearly 50% stronger effect of depth over breadth of control is apparent. This suggests a clear recommendation regarding a trade-off decision for ECFs that aim to increase foreign sales (Batsakis et al. 2023). Managers responsible for ECFs' virtual and physical presence abroad should push control within countries to provide adapted offers. Activities can be developed to scale the presence of ECFs across countries around a network of WOS. However, scaling the virtual presence or a network of WOS alone does not optimally increase sales performance abroad. Both should be pursued together, which may increase foreign sales performance most strongly regardless of whether ECFs are born or going digital (Batsakis, Konara and Theoharakis 2023; Stallkamp, Chen and Li 2023). Both require a physical footprint in which ECFs need to invest while considering local e-commerce markets, which affects this decision.

Similar implications arise in distinct e-commerce country contexts where both physical footprints remain important for foreign performance but where the local e-commerce context matters (e.g., Kishore, Agrawal and Rao 2004). Managers should consider e-commerce market growth as a context in both decisions rather than the widespread and perhaps more easily grasped market size. However, another trade-off arises. ECFs that seek to improve the benefits of high control should focus on the depth of control in mature e-commerce markets (e.g., Janjevic and Winkenbach 2020) and invest in the subsidiary network across higher-growth countries. This may be counterintuitive to the more obvious initial investments of offline firms in growing markets followed by a later focus on efficient WOS networks. However, for ECFs, increasing foreign sales through adaptation with WOS is less critical in higher-growth countries but is strongly recommended in mature markets. Over time, subsidiary networks are a basis for such adaptations.

5. Limitations and Further Research

Our study has several limitations that offer further research opportunities.

We used unique longitudinal data that could be expanded in the future to include other continents or B2B and C2C ECFs like Alibaba or eBay. Analyzing the control decisions of i-business firms (which can internationalize purely digitally, such as Netflix) compared with ECFs would be interesting, as both types are often mixed in the literature. This is unwarranted because the internationalization processes, networks, and capabilities of both differ. Data on specific business types, such as omnichannel firms or specific niche ECFs, could become available in the future. Studying marketplaces and third parties' foreign performance or the impact of different platform models from an information systems perspective is also promising (e.g., Gong, He and Lengler 2024, and *marketplace* positively moderates the effect of depth of control).

With respect to these *measures*, we could not study ECFs' host country performance, which would provide further insights into control decisions (e.g., Swoboda and Elsner 2013). Future data on financial and nonfinancial performance (e.g., return on investment, Tolstoy, Nordman and Vu 2022; conversion rates, Goldman et al. 2021) will offer new insights. Capturing marketplace-specific measures such as the gross merchandise value will allow further comparisons among ECFs. We measured ECFs' depth of control as operation modes but could not capture different forms of cooperation (e.g., Hua and Wu 2024) or dynamic changes in control over time (e.g., Putzhammer, Puck and Lindner 2020). We also captured the breadth of control across countries entered virtually, although few ECFs operate WOS in other countries (e.g., serving as regional hubs, Schu, Morschett and Swoboda 2016). Interesting further e-commerce market data could be available in the future (e.g., on consumer segments, ECDB 2024b).

Our *framework* refers to ECFs' international control, although control may also decrease over time (e.g., due to failures or strategic decisions, Brouthers et al. 2022), which may affect ECFs' local and possibly foreign sales performance (e.g., Wan et al. 2023). The current success of aggressively exporting ECFs such as Shein and insights into further e-commerce-specific contexts (e.g., regulations) are interesting. Contingency patterns beyond a contextual view (e.g., Wang et al. 2024) might be worth studying. Studying the performance effects of further decisions, such as simultaneous entry and standardization of offers, would provide further insights into international ECFs' expansion (Meyer et al. 2023; Mohr and Batsakis 2018).

E. Final Remarks

1. Discussion and Conclusions

1.1. Core Results

As digitalization reshapes global commerce, ECFs face the critical challenge of striking the right balance between virtual and physical presence across diverse host countries (Yang et al. 2025). These decisions are determined by ECFs' ability to leverage their unique online resources or capabilities abroad and are crucial for achieving competitive advantages in foreign markets. However, ECFs must navigate specific infrastructural and regulatory country environments that significantly affect their business model abroad (e.g., Meyer et al. 2023). This dissertation delves into ECFs' specific internationalization processes, offering actionable insights and implications to thrive in a dynamic global marketplace.

Section A.2.2. highlights that while various antecedents of manufacturers' geographic scope have been studied (e.g., Kirca et al. 2011; 2012a), only one study in commerce has focused on this topic (Batsakis and Mohr 2017). Prior studies have predominantly stressed the role of firms' resources and knowledge in geographic scope decisions. One study on early digital firms has analyzed antecedents of geographic scope online (e.g., intangible resources, Kotha, Rindova and Rothaermel 2001). However, ECFs' virtual presence has given rise to novel antecedents that have not been examined so far (Chabowski and Samiee 2020). Whether and how ECFs' specific online resources can be leveraged for their geographic scope online remained largely unknown (e.g., Jean and Kim 2020). Likewise, the impact of different host country contexts has rarely been considered even for offline firms (e.g., Jiménez 2010; Mansion and Bausch 2020). For ECFs' internationalization, the relevance of country context has recently been questioned, as they may benefit from reduced online entry barriers (e.g., Chen et al. 2019, debated by Schu and Morschett 2017; Swoboda and Sinning 2022).

As shown in Section A.2.3., research on manufacturing or service firms' operation mode choice and FDI has studied numerous firm- and country-level antecedents (e.g., Cuervo-Cazurra et al. 2023; Wan et al. 2023). In contrast, studies on commerce firms' operation mode choice are scarce (Evans, Mavondo and Bridson 2008; Picot-Coupey, Burt and Cliquet 2014; conceptually, Huang and Sternquist 2007). The only study on born digital firms' FDI has explored distance-related antecedents (Stallkamp, Chen and Li 2023). However, scholars have called for studying new (virtual) presence modes specific to digital firms like ECFs (Brouthers et al. 2022; Ipsmiller, Dikova and Brouthers 2022, debated by Hennart 2022) as well as their physical presences (e.g., Swoboda and Sinning 2022). Moreover, the role of (online) experience as a traditional antecedent

M. Müller, *Strategic Management of International E-Commerce Firms*,
Handel und Internationales Marketing Retailing and International Marketing,
https://doi.org/10.1007/978-3-658-49680-7_5

has been questioned (e.g., Pezderka and Sinkovics 2011), while specific country factors critical to ECFs' business model have been overlooked as well (e.g., Meyer et al. 2023). In summary, no study has jointly theorized the effects of firm- and country-level factors in ECFs' FDI decisions.

Section A.2.4. draws on two research streams. The first examines performance outcomes of international control decisions, with separate studies on effects of depth and breadth of international control focusing mainly on manufacturing firms (e.g., Kirca et al. 2011; Wan et al. 2023). Research on commerce firms is scarce and yields inconsistent results (e.g., positive or negative effects of depth of control, Evans, Mavondo and Bridson 2008; Gielens and Dekimpe 2001; or breadth of control, Chan, Finnegan and Sternquist 2011; Dimitrova, Kim and Smith 2019). No studies have addressed outcomes of control decisions in digital firms. The second stream explores effects of ECFs' internationalization on their performance, revealing that very few studies have addressed their international performance (only based on specific capabilities, Goldman et al. 2021; Tolstoy, Hånell and Özbek 2023; Tolstoy, Nordman and Vu 2022). Moreover, only one study has analyzed specific e-commerce market contexts as moderators (Eduardsen et al. 2023). Overall, knowledge of ECFs' successful international decision-making remains limited, including whether international control is beneficial for ECFs despite their digital nature (Swoboda and Sinning 2022).

In summary, substantial research gaps persist in the literature regarding ECFs' internationalization decisions across different country contexts, leaving key research questions unresolved. With the aim of closing these research gaps, the following research questions were answered in this dissertation:

(1) Whether and how (strongly) do intangible resources affect the geographic scope of ECFs and how do host country factors, i.e., ROL, country development, and logistics performance, moderate these effects?
(2) Whether and how (strongly) do specific firm- and host country-level factors drive ECFs' choice of wholly owned FDI?
(3) Whether and how (strongly) does ECFs' international control in terms of depth versus breadth drive ECFs' foreign sales performance and how do host countries' e-commerce market size and growth moderate these effects?

Three individual studies were conducted to explore each of these research objectives in greater detail. Each of these studies is based on a hierarchical assessment of the internationalization decisions of leading ECFs across different host countries, including cross-level interactions in Study 1 and Study 3. The findings yield important and novel implications for IB research and are summarized below.

Addressing the *first research question*, Study 1 analyzed the effects of ECFs' intangible resources on their geographic scope online across different country contexts. The findings reveal that ECFs leverage their international online experience as a critical new resource to increase their geographic scope (e.g., Chabowski and Samiee 2020). Knowledge acquired over time via experience in foreign online markets is still an important foundation for ECFs' subsequent virtual expansion (Pezderka and Sinkovics 2011; Schu, Morschett and Swoboda 2016). Unlike offline experience, international online experience can be transferred as a specific and valuable resource across online markets based on real-time data. Website traffic is another consumer-related online resource, affecting geographic scope positively. It allows ECFs to leverage their analytical tools across foreign markets, transfer their customer reputation, or benefit from advertising partnerships (e.g., Molla-Descals et al. 2014). Most importantly, social media use has the strongest positive effect on ECFs' geographic scope as a critical new online resource (e.g., Knösel, Cheng and Shiu 2025). The latter enables ECFs to transfer and exploit their communications and promoted services virtually across countries (Li, Larimo and Leonidou 2021). Social media interactions may even induce cross-border domino effects as ECFs' followers share their experiences (Dolega, Rowe and Branagan 2021; Gao et al. 2018).

Regarding the impact of local host country contexts, Study 1 reveals that ECFs' transfer of specific intangible resources is reinforced by several important factors. Increasing ROL enhances ECFs' transfer of international online experience and social media activities through higher transparency and transactional integrity to operate in additional foreign markets (e.g., Oxley and Yeung 2001). Instead of having to deal with legal issues due to weak ROL, they can transfer their previous knowledge and focus on opportunity exploitation (e.g., customer loyalty, Ramanathan 2010). Protected proprietary rights further allow ECFs to leverage social media for communication abroad, building online communities, and achieving cross-border domino effects (Dolega, Rowe and Branagan 2021; Katsikeas, Leonidou and Zeriti 2020). Similarly, the degree of host country development positively moderates the effects of international online experience and social media use. As developed countries are typically stable and predictable, international experience is more valuable and relying on previous knowledge is less risky. Promising opportunities can be identified and exploited more effectively, as consumer needs rarely fluctuate (e.g., Nuhu, Owens and McQuillan 2021). Moreover, due to widespread internet access and popular social media platforms in such countries, ECFs may reach consumers better and analyze their needs on social media (e.g., Vieira et al. 2019). Finally, logistics performance has a particularly strong reinforcing impact on ECFs' resource transfer. Sufficient logistics performance is a necessary condition for firms' ability to transfer previous knowledge to foreign markets and exploit opportunities.

Instead of evaluating on an own physical presence, ECFs may cooperate with local logistics partners (Douglas and Craig 2011). Likewise, the value of social media as a communication tool for firms' services is higher. The risks of detrimental domino effects and reputational damage are likely decreased, enabling ECFs to take full advantage of their social media resources (Zhang et al. 2019). Surprisingly, the value of website traffic as an intangible resources is not affected by any factor studied, possibly due to it being unobservable and not requiring adaptation to different countries in terms of different regulations, country development, or logistics (Kotha, Rindova and Rothaermel 2001).

The *second research question* was answered in Study 2, exploring the joint impact of firm- and country-level antecedents in ECFs' wholly owned FDI decisions. At the firm level, important novel types of online experience are shown to still be relevant in ECFs' physical presence decisions (e.g., Pezderka and Sinkovics 2011; Sinkovics, Sinkovics and Jean 2013). International online experience has a positive effect on ECFs' propensity to choose wholly owned FDI in foreign markets. The more experienced ECFs' are in general in foreign online markets, the better they can recognize market opportunities for FDI (e.g., Swoboda and Sinning 2022). They can accumulate critical knowledge and transfer successful digital offers or services such as products or promotions and relations to foreign authorities (e.g., Schu, Morschett and Swoboda 2016; Vahlne and Johanson 2017). More importantly, host country online experience emerges as the major lever for FDI in certain countries, with a particularly strong positive effect. This experience provides ECFs with unique knowledge from online interactions in a specific online market over time (e.g., Schu and Morschett 2017). Familiarity with local customer needs and preferences as well as local business practices or competitors allows them to recognize local opportunities and effectively exploit them with wholly owned FDI in a country (e.g., Ipsmiller, Dikova and Brouthers 2022; Pla-Barber, Villar and León-Darder 2014). Notably, and in contrast to manufacturing firms (e.g., Schwens et al. 2018b), ECFs do not use prior FDI online experience for their subsequent FDI. This hybrid experience type has no effect once general and host country experience are considered, suggesting a low relevance of offline experience for ECFs.

At the country level, several specific host country factors are identified as crucial for ECFs' ability to transfer their business models through wholly owned FDI. One key factor is logistics performance, referring to a host country's logistics infrastructure, which has a positive effect on ECFs' propensity to choose wholly owned FDI (e.g., Halaszovich and Kinra 2020). Strong logistics performance is the foundation for ECFs' ability to achieve competitive advantages based on efficient delivery, for example (e.g., Janjevic and Winkenbach 2020; Schu and Morschett 2017). Efficient storage and warehousing, order fulfillment, last-mile delivery, or return management are essential to support ECFs' supply chain operations, especially given that logistics costs account for over 25% of total costs (e.g., Hua and Wu 2024; Reuters 2023; Zalando 2023). Another important factor is the internet user population within a host country, which positively affects ECFs' propensity to choose FDI. A large internet user population reduces ECFs' barriers to implement digital activities based on real-time collection of customer data and allows them to reach a large potential customer base (e.g., Wang, Jiang and Zhang 2024). Such data enable ECFs to tailor their products or prices to individual needs via their unique one-to-one marketing, which they can best control and leverage via wholly owned FDI (Janjevic and Winkenbach 2020). Finally, the host country's ROL has a positive effect on ECFs' FDI decisions as well. Stronger ROL can create barriers for export-based ECFs (e.g., Luo, Zhao and Du 2005), while offering location advantages to those establishing a physical presence in a country. Due to specific and dynamic regulations on online contracts, competition, prices, transparent supply chains, or the protection of customer and property rights, ECFs are incentivized to pursue FDI abroad (e.g., Meyer et al. 2023; Oxley and Yeung 2001).

Addressing the *third research question*, Study 3 clarified the role of international control in ECFs' foreign sales performance and how it is shaped by local e-commerce market contexts. The results reveal that ECFs' depth of international control positively affects their foreign sales performance. Increasing depth of control enhances sales by enabling ECFs to adapt offerings and services to local customer needs through hands-on market knowledge and local subsidiaries (e.g., Swoboda and Sinning 2022). This may entail the opening of local subsidiaries for local assortments, faster delivery, or a better customer experience compared to using partners (e.g., Hua and Wu 2024; Tolstoy, Nordman and Vu 2022). Increasing breadth of control allows ECFs to leverage their network of WOS across countries to enhance foreign sales through economies of scale, cross-country synergies, and centralized management (e.g., Dimitrova, Kim and Smith 2019). Expanding the network of WOS across countries enables synergies in ECFs' own supply chains and with cross-country business networks (e.g., Johanson and Vahlne 2009). Centralized coordination across WOS further streamlines assortments, promotions, CRM, and logistics, driving foreign sales performance (Nath, Nachiappan and Ramanathan 2010). Notably, the effect of depth of control on performance is significantly stronger than that of breadth of control, confirming important trade-offs between local and central decision making (e.g., Swoboda and Elsner 2013). The former enables ECFs to adapt offers and services to local needs by leveraging market knowledge, local networks, and integrated capabilities, resulting in superior customer satisfaction (Janjevic and Winkenbach 2020; Meyer et al. 2023). In contrast, while breadth of control facilitates cross-country synergies and economies of scale, it often limits the ability to meet specific customer needs and establish local supply, which is critical to sales (e.g., Hua and Wu 2024).

Concerning the role of local e-commerce market contexts, Study 3 reveals different impacts on both depth and breadth of control effects. Surprisingly, the results suggest that ECFs' control decisions do not depend on the often-focused market size (e.g., in contrast to the findings of Schu and Morschett 2017). Intense competition in larger markets and challenges in protecting market knowledge may offset the expected advantages of high demand (Goldman et al. 2021; Kishore, Agrawal and Rao 2004). In contrast, market growth represents an important context for both control decisions but in opposite directions. ECFs' benefits of high control in a country are offset in markets with high e-commerce growth as they are affected by changing demands, an evolving competitive landscape, and an overall more volatile online environment (e.g., Janjevic and Winkenbach 2020; Kishore, Agrawal and Rao 2004). However, ECFs may benefit from such growth conditions when scaling across countries by leveraging the growth momentum in a country. They may be supported by governments or local investors to make FDI that allows for streamlined distribution and cross-country synergies (e.g., Agarwal and Wu 2015; Wang, Mao and Archer 2012). Thus, ECFs face another trade-off. For one, increasing depth of control can enhance performance, but is constrained by market growth. For another, scaling a WOS network across countries enables ECFs to leverage growth conditions, but may lead to missed opportunities for local adaptation.

In conclusion, this dissertation provides important new insights into ECFs' unique internationalization processes and digital capabilities. It sheds light on the antecedents of their virtual expansion (i.e., geographic scope), their selected physical presence (i.e., wholly owned FDI), and the role of international control in their foreign performance. Notably, it stresses how often-overlooked host country factors shape these outcomes to different degrees.

1.2. Theoretical Implications

The novel insights from this doctoral thesis offer valuable contributions to literature and important theoretical implications, which are outlined subsequently.

Study 1 extends our understanding of ECFs' virtual expansion by applying the RBV in a digital context (e.g., Yang et al. 2025). Research has emphasized new digital resources (e.g., Bhandari et al. 2023), but theoretical insights into their value for virtual expansion are limited. Although resources are critical for manufacturing firms' geographic scope (Kirca et al. 2011), only one study has applied this to online firms (Kotha, Rindova and Rothaermel 2001). Study 1 identifies international online experience, website traffic, and social media use as valuable digital resources facilitating ECFs' geographic scope to a different extent. International online experience, akin to traditional offline experience, is crucial for ECFs' knowledge transfer to further online markets (Schu and Morschett 2017; challenging skeptics, Pezderka and Sinkovics 2011). Notably, new consumer-related digital resources gain relevance. Website traffic as ECFs' customer relations and online shop popularity is a valuable resource to enter further markets (Kotha, Rindova and Rothaermel 2001; Molla-Descals et al. 2014). However, its relative value is lower, as international online experience is a more important (traditional) resource. In contrast, ECFs' social media use is the strongest digital resource and more valuable than online experience (Knösel, Cheng and Shiu 2025). Based on social media interactions, ECFs gain deep insights into consumers' needs, which are particularly rare and difficult to copy or substitute (e.g., Gao et al. 2018; Katsikeas, Leonidou and Zeriti 2020). These insights stress the need for resource-based reasonings that must be adapted to digital firms (referring to respective calls, Chabowski and Samiee 2020; Jean and Kim 2020).

Study 1 also enhances our understanding of how contextual factors affect digital resources abroad (Priem and Butler 2001; Wan 2005). It sheds light on the role of country context in ECFs' internationalization beyond that known of distances (Brouthers et al. 2022; Swoboda and Sinning 2022). One important factor is ROL, for example (He, Brouthers and Filatotchev 2013). In countries with transparent rules and regulations, ECFs' rights are protected, making their knowledge more valuable and difficult to imitate (Schu and Morschett 2017). Likewise, consumers' access to social media is facilitated, enabling ECFs to effectively transfer their communications to such markets (e.g., Katsikeas, Leonidou and Zeriti 2020). Moreover, countries' degree of development increases the value of prior experience as ECFs' knowledge can be better applied in predictable environments (Kirca et al. 2012b). As social media platforms are widely accessible, the value of ECFs' social media is increased as they can analyze consumers' needs and behavior more efficiently (e.g., Vieira et al. 2019). Notably, logistics performance emerges as a critical factor for increasing the value of ECFs' resources. It is a necessary condition for ECFs' ability to benefit from valuable international experience in foreign markets and exploit opportunities. Moreover, it enables ECFs to deliver service quality as promised on social media (e.g., Zhang et al. 2019). This is crucial, as logistics performance emerges as the most influential country context not previously addressed in the RBV. Finally, this study contributes to the investigation of specific context factors affecting digital firm expansion (e.g., Liu, Zhang-Zhang and Ghauri 2020; Tolstoy et al. 2021).

Building on this, Study 2 extends literature by exploring antecedents of ECFs' selected physical presence abroad. Theoretically, this study moves beyond the

RBV, extending insights from capability and adapted internationalization process theory (Cahen et al. 2025; Vahlne and Johanson 2017; Yang et al. 2025). In contrast to manufacturing firms, ECFs are found to leverage distinct online experience capabilities for FDI that they build, scale, and transfer virtually (Schu and Morschett 2017; beyond effects of distance, Stallkamp, Chen and Li 2023). They do so by operating in and learning from foreign markets in general (which was questioned, e.g., Coviello, Kano and Liesch 2017), but especially from specific markets over time. Such experience is gained from successful online offers, promotions, or local interactions that allow for exploiting FDI opportunities. Thus, ECFs no longer require sequential physical market entry, but their FDI decisions also remain path-dependent (e.g., Swoboda and Sinning 2022), unlike previously theorized for digital firms. This confirms that ECFs' focus shifts from recognizing opportunities abroad to actively exploiting them via selected FDI (Vahlne and Johanson 2017). The study goes beyond linking ECFs' rapid online internationalization to virtual presence only (e.g., Schu, Morschett and Swoboda 2016), showing that online experience is crucial for physical presence as well. Unlike for manufacturers (Schwens et al. 2018b), hybrid FDI experience is less relevant for ECFs' FDI exploitation. These findings contribute to recent debates on newly theorizing ECFs' modes (Brouthers et al. 2022; Hennart 2022) and to calls for empirical analyses (Gong, He and Lengler 2024; Yang et al. 2025).

Importantly, Study 2 extends these rationales by jointly theorizing the impact of specific country factors critical to ECFs' business model and FDI. In contrast to institution-based rationales (e.g., Özbek et al. 2024), the study is the first to explain how specific infrastructural factors such as logistics and internet use act as barriers or location advantages (Agarwal and Wu 2015; Benmamoun et al. 2019). The latter have only been considered in macroeconomic studies with inconsistent results (e.g., Halaszovich and Kinra 2020; Latif et al. 2018). However, these factors complement ECFs' ability to leverage online experience by providing specific advantages supporting their business model through FDI (vs. traditional production advantages, Yang et al. 2025). ECFs prefer markets with low barriers to replicate the business model in terms of seamless supply chains, digital infrastructure, or protection of local assets (Gong, He and Lengler 2024). These insights contribute to theorizing new location advantages that are discussed for digital firms but rarely studied (Dunning and Wymbs 2001; responding to calls, e.g., Gong, He and Lengler 2024). While some scholars have redefined advantages of digital firms (e.g., location vs. linkage advantages, Luo 2021; Surana et al. 2024), the study shows that adapted location advantages are still crucial to ECFs (Wang, Jiang and Zhang 2024). In this context, ECFs' online capabilities may be considered novel ownership advantages, whereas ROL reflects internalization advantages (e.g., Pezderka and Sinkovics 2011).

Finally, this study contributes to calls for clarifying the role of new host country barriers in ECFs' FDI decisions (Brouthers et al. 2022; Meyer et al. 2023).

Based on the above findings on ECFs' virtual and physical presence decisions, Study 3 advances research on the foreign performance implications of international control across countries. It revisits three theoretical perspectives recently questioning the role of control in digital firms' success (e.g., Birkinshaw 2022; Monaghan, Tippmann and Coviello 2020). Scholars have defined new virtual expansion processes, online networks, and digital capabilities to explain digital firms' performance (e.g., Yang et al. 2025). However, this study highlights the continued value of traditional mechanisms that must be applied to explain ECFs' success as well. Although ECFs benefit from online learning, networks, and capabilities, this digital lens neglects onsite learning, local business ties, and key operational capabilities (e.g., Batsakis et al. 2023; Gong, He and Lengler 2024). The latter are critical for ECFs' business model and leveraging control for performance abroad. Notably, ECFs' breadth of virtual presence alone has no effect on performance, confirming the risk of a "virtuality trap" (Sinkovics, Sinkovics and Jean 2013). Thus, these findings add to the theoretical discussion on virtual presence (in "space") as an alternative to physical control (in "place", Monaghan, Tippmann and Coviello 2020; Ipsmiller, Dikova and Brouthers 2022; Stallkamp, Chen and Li 2023). Moreover, ECFs' local vs. central decision making is clarified (e.g., Evans, Mavondo and Bridson 2008). Prioritizing depth of control enables ECFs to address critical customer needs, whereas breadth of control allows for operational synergies. Finally, answering calls, the study identifies key drivers of ECFs' success abroad (e.g., Dong, He and Blut 2024; Yang et al. 2025).

Moreover, Study 3 enriches our theoretical understanding of important local e-commerce market contexts in shaping ECFs' successful expansion (Yang et al. 2025). In fact, only one prior study has taken country context into account at all (Eduardsen et al. 2023). The study emphasizes the need to align foreign market learning, local network relationships, and capability transfer with different local market dynamics (e.g., Meyer et al. 2023; Swoboda and Sinning 2022). However, not all local contexts equally affect these mechanisms. Local market size does not affect ECFs' learning, networks, or capabilities through control within or across countries (unlike their market selection, Schu and Morschett 2017). Instead, the (dis)advantages in terms of control may be counterbalanced by high demand or intense competition (Goldman et al. 2021; Kishore, Agrawal and Rao 2004). In contrast, high market growth has a significant impact on ECFs' learning, network advantages, and capability transfer, suggesting a previously unknown trade-off. On the one hand, ECFs' ability to leverage market knowledge, local business networks, or operational capabilities is weakened due to volatile and shifting demands (e.g., Morschett, Schramm-Klein and Swoboda 2010). On the other hand, ECFs may standardize processes across such markets using new learning opportunities, partnerships, or refined operational capabilities (e.g., Agarwal and Wu 2015; Janjevic and Winkenbach 2020). Yet, the latter may limit performance due to missing local adaptation. Such nuanced theoretical insights emphasize the selective role of local contexts in driving ECFs' success (responding to calls, Eduardsen et al. 2023; Meyer et al. 2023).

In conclusion, this dissertation addressed critical research gaps and responded to numerous calls for research on digital firms' unique internationalization. By adopting novel perspectives on ECFs' specific resources, capabilities, and internationalization processes, it contributes to our understanding of how ECFs successfully expand globally. Importantly, these theories are enhanced by highlighting the role of host country contexts in shaping ECFs' transfer of resources and capabilities as well as their virtual and physical internationalization.

1.3. Managerial and Practical Implications

Effectively making use of ECFs' unique online capabilities across countries is vital for managers to balance virtual and physical presence effectively. This dissertation offers important implications for ECFs' managers, manufacturers using ECFs to reach international customers, or policy makers promoting local e-commerce. Detailed implications for these different stakeholders are outlined below.

Study 1 shows that managers require a deep understanding of ECFs' available intangible online resources to expand their virtual presence. They need to be aware that the value of these resources differs considerably across markets. As a traditional intangible resource, international experience is crucial for managers to recognize expansion opportunities (Hånell et al. 2020). Yet, they must realize that the required experience should be gained online to apply their knowledge across further online markets (Schu and Morschett 2017). However, managers are also advised to invest in digital consumer-related resources such as their website traffic, and especially social media use (Gao et al. 2018). By increasing website traffic, for example, ECFs can enhance the popularity of their online shop or their reputation across countries (e.g., Kotha, Rindova and Rothaermel 2001). More importantly, strengthening social media presence should be a top priority. Social media platforms enable global communication with consumers, fostering interaction and leveraging network effects to build a strong online community (e.g., Knösel, Cheng and Shiu 2025). These insights align with real-world examples like Zalando (2024), which have built large social media communities sharing their experiences across countries. Additionally, managers are advised to consider different host country contexts affecting the value of their international experience and social media for increased scope. Resources can be most effectively used in countries with a strong ROL, high levels of development, and robust logistics performance. The latter is the strongest lever as quick delivery is crucial for ECFs' performance and regional expansion (Ramanathan 2010).

Study 2 has important implications for managers considering a physical footprint in specific markets in addition to their virtual presence (Stallkamp, Chen and Li 2023). Based on decisions of leading ECFs such as Amazon, the study reveals that managers may take advantage of unique international and host country online experience capabilities. These can be gained online and used to inform physical presence decisions (e.g., Swoboda and Sinning 2022). Managers should primarily focus on gaining country-specific online experience to transfer their business models and adapt offers via FDI. ECFs lacking such experience may try to compensate for it using analytics in local online markets, partnering with local professionals, or learning from local stakeholders (e.g., Brouthers et al. 2022; Luo, Zhao and Du 2005). However, managers must also recognize the additional importance of specific host country factors such as logistics performance, internet users, and the ROL. These factors complement ECFs' ability to leverage their online capabilities and may turn into FDI barriers when ignored (e.g., Pezderka and Sinkovics 2011). Instead, managers aware of this may derive critical location advantages for their FDI. These insights are not only relevant to ECFs' manager but also to those of manufacturing firms starting their own virtual presence abroad (e.g., Ipsmiller, Dikova and Brouthers 2022). To them, respective insights into antecedents of ECFs' FDI are also valuable, as they increasingly turn to leading ECFs' marketplaces to benefit from their capabilities and foreign presence (Li et al. 2025). This may enable manufacturers to tailor their offers more closely to customer needs as well.

Finally, Study 3 offers guidance to managers of ECFs possibly struggling with increasing their foreign sales performance (e.g., Batsakis, Konara and Theoharakis 2023, Ipsmiller, Dikova and Brouthers 2022). Failing to recognize the benefits of international control through physical presence can result in unsustainable investments or missed opportunities to achieve advantages abroad (e.g., Meyer et al. 2023). Despite their digital nature, ECFs are advised to increase the depth and breadth of international control, as both drive foreign sales performance. This equally applies to ECF that are born or going digital (e.g., Stallkamp, Chen and Li 2023). In contrast, scaling only their virtual presence is not associated with better performance (Sinkovics, Sinkovics and Jean 2013). However, managers must be aware of possibly unknown trade-offs when having to prioritize either the depth or the breadth of control abroad. Focusing on local adaptation enables ECFs to implement offers tailored to customer needs, which is most important for foreign sales (Eduardsen et al. 2023). In contrast, scaling offers or management across countries via WOS may benefit sales through operational synergies, but risks overlooking critical customer needs (e.g., Batsakis et al. 2023). Moreover, the findings suggest that the local e-commerce market context matters in ECFs' benefits of control (Kishore, Agrawal and Rao 2004). Managers should be aware of the local market growth, which leads to another trade-off. ECFs can optimize foreign sales through local control in mature (vs. growing) e-commerce markets, but should expand their subsidiary network across growing (vs. mature) markets (e.g., Janjevic and Winkenbach 2020).

While these studies offer important insights for managers, the implications extend beyond ECFs and are relevant to digital firms and policy makers as well. Understanding online learning in both virtual and physical presence is essential for managers of i-business firms, for example. Similar to ECFs, firms like Uber or Airbnb must leverage their online presence to gain insights into consumer needs by operating platforms in different countries (Cumming et al. 2023). For them, leveraging social media as a critical digital resource is crucial as well (e.g., for visibility, credibility, and trust; Knösel, Cheng and Shiu 2025). However, managers must be aware of different competitive or demand dynamics, while platforms require additional IT or ecosystem capabilities (Gong, He and Lengler 2024; Mithani 2023). Moreover, ECFs operating marketplaces benefit more from local control, as third-party sellers can leverage ECFs' operational capabilities (Li et al. 2025). Thus, managers of digital B2B or C2C platforms may (re)consider FDI in specific markets and offer local fulfillment to enhance the platform's appeal to buyers and sellers (e.g., Stallkamp, Chen and Li 2023). Managers of digital firms may also recognize the benefits associated with specific host country factors shown in all three studies. For example, ROL plays a crucial role in virtual and physical expansion decisions due to dynamic regulations (e.g., data protection, taxation, and compliance, Ahi, Sinkovics and Sinkovics 2023). Such insights are equally valuable for policymakers aiming to promote investments into local e-commerce markets. Policymakers can support the internationalization of digital firms by enhancing local IT infrastructure for virtual presence (e.g., Eduardsen et al. 2023). Additionally, a strong logistics infrastructure and a transparent legal framework can attract ECFs' FDI (Meyer et al. 2023). However, they must consider possible challenges such as increased competition for local firms.

2. Limitations and Further Research

While contributing valuable new findings, this dissertation inherently carries certain limitations. These constraints, however, reveal promising opportunities for further research. Based on the individual studies, the following section considers limitations in the context of the overall thesis. It subsequently refers to the database, measurements, conceptual frameworks, theories, and methodology.

First, while the studies all refer to unique and carefully selected databases, incorporating additional data could enhance their generalizability. All three studies focused on leading ECFs in Europe that could, however, operate globally. Extending this data to include leading ECFs in other regions or worldwide would allow more robust analyses (e.g., Schu and Morschett 2017). However, focusing solely on leading ECFs carries the risk of selection bias, as these are mostly large ECFs from developed countries. Thus, SMEs may be overlooked, which often adopt different market entry strategies (Tolstoy, Nordman and Vu 2022). Study 1 relied on a cross-sectional sample selection of ECFs in 2018, whereas Study 2 and Study 3 referred to longitudinal samples that could be enriched with data from additional years (Swoboda and Sinning 2022). For example, longitudinal data on firms' social media use or website traffic could reveal causal relationships over time and add value to Study 1 or possibly extend Study 2. Study 3 revealed that ECFs' marketplace affects their performance but lacked sufficient insights into platform characteristics (Surana et al. 2024). Future studies may gather data on ECFs' marketplaces in different countries, as these are likely to shape their local decisions (e.g., Gong, He and Lengler 2024). Moreover, all three studies focused on B2C ECFs exclusively. Expanding the data to cover leading B2B ECFs, such as Alibaba, or C2C platforms, such as eBay, might reveal critical differences not covered here (Gabriel 2023, p. 90). Adding data on different industries in Study 1 and 2 (see Study 3, e.g., fashion vs. electronics, Batsakis et al. 2023) or regional strategies (e.g., regional concentration, Benmamoun et al. 2019) could reveal specific dynamics. Another factor possibly affecting results is the distinction of born vs. going digital ECFs; while structural differences are evident (Stallkamp, Chen and Li 2023), additional data is needed for nuanced analyses. Finally, future research may attempt to gather primary data by surveying decision-makers in ECFs to explore their motivations and perceptions. Although certainly challenging due to a lack of prior studies, this could yield new insights into managerial decision processes (e.g., Dong, He and Blut 2024).

Second, in each study specific challenges regarding measurement approaches arose that further research may try to overcome. In Study 1, geographic scope was measured by the number of foreign online markets entered as only one aspect of broader geographic diversification (Batsakis and Mohr 2017). Future studies could adopt multiple indicators or established indices, such as entropy measures (e.g., including sales per country, Bauweraerts et al. 2019), to provide a more nuanced understanding of ECFs' geographic scope. Alternatively, the number of subsidiaries (i.e., ECFs' physical presence) could be incorporated (e.g., Nath, Nachiappan and Ramanathan 2010), which was not possible prior to

Study 3 due to a lack of data. Similar issues arise when measuring ECFs' operation modes as the base of Study 2. Identifying ECFs' cooperative modes is highly challenging, which is why a binary dependent variable was chosen. Capturing the degree of control in Study 2, as was realized in Study 3, but which can be further developed, would also enrich future research. Likewise operation mode changes or market exits over time will reveal further dynamics (Evans, Mavondo and Bridson 2008; Swoboda, Elsner and Olejnik 2015). These dynamics could also enhance the depth of control measure applied in Study 3 by revealing temporal patterns in foreign performance effects (Hua and Wu 2024; Putzhammer, Puck and Lindner 2020). Unlike the overall foreign sales measure in Study 3, tracking ECFs' local performance over time in specific host countries will allow inferences about their success in individual markets (e.g., Swoboda and Elsner 2013). Importantly, further financial and nonfinancial performance measures will allow insights into ECFs' profitability and specific online performance (e.g., return on investment, Tolstoy, Nordman and Vu 2022; conversion rates, Goldman et al. 2021).

Third, there are ample opportunities for expanding the conceptual frameworks. One potential avenue is exploring antecedents highlighted in the literature in addition to those in Study 1 or Study 2, such as organizational resources, digital or entrepreneurial capabilities, or institutional distances (e.g., Cahen et al. 2025; Lee, Pattnaik and Gaur 2023; Stallkamp, Chen and Li 2023). Likewise, antecedents of further critical decisions in commerce like the degree of ECFs' standardization of offers or simultaneous entry warrant further investigation (e.g., Gong, He and Lengler 2024; Mohr and Batsakis 2018). For instance, comparing the effects of control on foreign performance with these or other internationalization decisions such as internationalization speed or rhythm could provide valuable extensions to Study 3 (Swoboda and Sinning 2022). This would provide deeper insights into the relative importance of control in successful internationalization. Another promising direction involves mediation models linking ECFs' capabilities for virtual and physical presence decisions (Study 1 and 2) with foreign performance (Study 3). Such models could help validate the findings across all three studies. Beyond foreign performance, other outcomes like ECFs' foreign divestments, survival rates, or market exits also merit attention (e.g., Schmid and Morschett 2023; Wan et al. 2023). Taking account of moderators at the firm level, such as various strategic orientations (e.g., focus on niche markets, product diversification, Gong, He and Lengler 2024; Özbek et al. 2024), could yield major new insights. Moreover, further exploration of the moderating role of country contexts is essential, particularly those unique to digital firms, such as online media risks or specific regulations (Pezderka and Sinkovics 2011). Consideration should also be given to the future impact of trends towards de-globalization or rising trade protectionism, inducing reconfigurations of global value chains in e-commerce (e.g., Zahoor et al. 2023). Finally, competitive dynamics in diverse e-commerce markets remain underexplored. These likely play a crucial role in shaping ECFs' local decisions, as suggested by Study 3. For example, factors like first-mover advantages may play a moderating role (Yang et al. 2025).

Fourth, this dissertation draws on several complementary theories focused on the transfer and exploitation of digital resources, capabilities, and knowledge in ECFs' internationalization (e.g., following Brouthers et al. 2022; Cahen et al. 2025). However, some prominent alternative rationales related to internalization or the exchange of assets in specific transactions are not considered (e.g., Hennart 2022). Study 1 and especially Study 2, base their hypotheses on ECFs' use of unique online resources and capabilities, including their learning processes. While this is grounded in literature, transaction cost-specific arguments commonly used in IB to explain mode or FDI choices may still hold relevance for digital firms (e.g., Yang et al. 2025). For example, ECFs' local control decisions might depend on the specific costs and risks of opportunistic behavior in online transactions or ability of monitoring delivery partners (e.g., Argilés-Bosch, Garcia-Blandón and Ravenda 2023; Cha, Kotabe and Wu 2023). This lens emphasizes efficiency in ECFs' operations, possibly a useful extension of Study 2 and 3. However, such an approach requires appropriate data (e.g., on asset specificity, Brouthers 2013; Lee, Pattnaik and Gaur 2023), which are currently unavailable (Drori et al. 2024). Moreover, it is constrained by its static nature (vs. dynamic process rationales), narrow behavioral assumptions (e.g., bounded rationality), and limited consideration of different country contexts (e.g., Narula et al. 2019). While plenty of theories exist to explain the international behavior of firms, explanations for the influence of country factors are much more limited. Study 2 adopts an eclectic approach, by considering the joint role of country factors as location advantages to explain ECFs' FDI in addition to their specific learning capabilities that can be ownership advantages (e.g., Benmamoun et al. 2019; Dunning and Wymbs 2001). This eclectic paradigm also offers further development options with regard to new types of location advantages relevant for digital companies (e.g., Wang, Jiang and Zhang 2024). Alternatively, country influences could be theorized based on the popular institutional economics approach (e.g., Kostova et al. 2020), which, however, is less intuitive for certain ECF-specific infrastructural factors (e.g., logistics performance or internet use).

Fifth, while the methodological multilevel approach across all three studies is considered advanced within literature, there are opportunities for methodological refinement. For example, the hierarchical structure of cross-national data, as used in the three studies, often extends beyond two levels (Hox, Moerbeek and Van de Schoot 2018, pp. 19-21). Additional levels could include time points (e.g., in longitudinal analyses like Study 2 and 3), as well as business groups, parent firms, subsidiaries, or home countries (e.g., Gaur et al. 2019; Hernández and Nieto 2015). However, implementing such approaches requires careful theoretical consideration and a sufficient number of clusters to maintain methodological rigor. Cross-classified modeling could be a valuable extension when units of analysis belong to multiple independent groups rather than fitting into a clear hierarchical structure (e.g., Hox, Moerbeek and Van de Schoot 2018, pp. 161-163). For example, ECFs' entry or mode decisions can be grouped by firms, host countries, or years at the same time. This method allows for precise variance estimation while accounting for the effects of two groupings (Putzhammer, Puck and Lindner 2020). Another methodological challenge lies in addressing collinearity issues when analyzing multiple host country variables jointly, as seen in Study 2. While such issues are often briefly assessed referring to VIF values, this alone is insufficient to rule out biases (e.g., Backhaus et al. 2023, pp. 111-113). Systematically addressing these concerns via relevant controls, robustness checks, and theoretical justification (Kalnins 2022; Lindner, Puck and Verbeke 2022) is vital for meaningful insights into international phenomena.

F. References

About You (2021). ABOUT YOU expands warehouse network with location in Slovakia https://corporate.aboutyou.de/en/presse/about-you-erweitert-lager-netzwerk-um-standort-in-der-slowakei. Accessed 20.06.2023.

Adomako, S., Frimpong, K., Mohammed, R. A., Opoku, R. A., & Hussain, R. (2021). Chief executive officers' dispositional optimism, host country's rule of law, and foreign market equity mode choice of Ghanaian small and medium-sized enterprises. *Thunderbird International Business Review*, 63(1), 63-75.

Agarwal, J., & Wu, T. (2015). Factors influencing growth potential of e-commerce in emerging economies: An institution-based N-OLI framework and research propositions. *Thunderbird International Business Review*, 57(3), 197-215.

Aguinis, H., Gottfredson, R. K., & Culpepper, S. A. (2013). Best-practice recommendations for estimating cross-level interaction effects using multilevel modeling. *Journal of Management*, 39(6), 1490-1528.

Ahi, A. A., Sinkovics, N., & Sinkovics, R. R. (2023). E-commerce policy and the global economy: A path to more inclusive development? *Management International Review*, 63(1), 27-56.

Alibaba (2024). Global Location. https://www.alibabagroup.com/en-US/global-location. Accessed 20.12.2024.

Amankwah-Amoah, J., Adomako, S., Danquah, J. K., Opoku, R. A., & Zahoor, N. (2022). Foreign market knowledge, entry mode choice and SME international performance in an emerging market. *Journal of International Management*, 28(4), 100955.

Amazon (1998). Amazon.com Enters European Book Market https://press.aboutamazon.com/1998/10/amazon-com-enters-european-book-market. Accessed 20.06.2023.

Amazon (2025). Amazon Global Export Countries and Regions. https://www.amazon.com/gp/help/customer/display.html?nodeId=GCBBSZMUXA6U2P8R. Accessed 15.01.2025.

Ang, S. H., Benischke, M. H., & Doh, J. P. (2015). The interactions of institutions on foreign market entry mode. *Strategic Management Journal*, 36(10), 1536-1553.

Antonakis, J., Bendahan, S., Jacquart, P., & Lalive, R. (2014). Causality and endogeneity: Problems and solutions, 93-117. In *The Oxford Handbook of Leadership and Organizations*. Ed. D. Day. New York: Oxford University Press.

Argilés-Bosch, J. M., Garcia-Blandón, J., & Ravenda, D. (2023). Cost behavior in e-commerce firms. *Electronic Commerce Research*, 23(4), 2101-2134.

M. Müller, *Strategic Management of International E-Commerce Firms*, Handel und Internationales Marketing Retailing and International Marketing, https://doi.org/10.1007/978-3-658-49680-7

Arte, P., & Larimo, J. (2022). Moderating influence of product diversification on the international diversification-performance relationship: A meta-analysis. *Journal of Business Research*, 139, 1408-1423.

Arvin, M. B., Pradhan, R. P., & Nair, M. (2021). Uncovering interlinks among ICT connectivity and penetration, trade openness, foreign direct investment, and economic growth: The case of the G-20 countries. *Telematics and Informatics*, 60, 101567.

Arvis, J.-F., Ojala, L., Wiederer, C., Shepherd, B., Raj, A., Dairabayeva, K., & Kiiski, T. (2018). *Connecting to compete 2018: Trade logistics in the global economy - The logistics performance index and its indicators*. Washington, DC: The World Bank Group.

Backhaus, K., Erichson, B., Gensler, S., Weiber, R., & Weiber, T. (2023). *Multivariate Analysis: An Application-Oriented Introduction*. Wiesbaden: Springer.

Bailey, N. (2018). Exploring the relationship between institutional factors and FDI attractiveness: A meta-analytic review. *International Business Review*, 27(1), 139-148.

Barkema, H. G., & Drogendijk, R. (2007). Internationalising in small, incremental or larger steps? *Journal of International Business Studies*, 38(7), 1132-1148.

Barney, J. (1991). Firm resources and sustained competitive advantage. *Journal of Management*, 17(1), 99-120.

Basu, D., Mitra, S., & Purohit, A. (2023). Does effective democracy explain MNE location choice?: Attractiveness to FDI and cross-border M&As. *Journal of Business Research*, 167, 114188.

Batsakis, G., Konara, P., & Theoharakis, V. (2023). Digital sales channels and the relationship between product and international diversification: Evidence from going digital retail MNEs. *Global Strategy Journal*, 13(4), 830-856.

Batsakis, G., & Mohr, A. T. (2017). Revisiting the relationship between product diversification and internationalization process in the context of emerging market MNEs. *Journal of World Business*, 52(4), 564-577.

Batsakis, G., & Singh, S. (2019). Added distance, entry mode choice, and the moderating effect of experience: The case of British MNEs in emerging markets. *Thunderbird International Business Review*, 61(4), 581-594.

Batsakis, G., Theoharakis, V., Li, C., & Konara, P. (2023). Internationalization and digitalization: Their differing role on grocer and non-grocer retailer performance. *Journal of Retailing*, 99(3), 400-419.

Bauweraerts, J., Sciascia, S., Naldi, L., & Mazzola, P. (2019). Family CEO and board service: Turning the tide for export scope in family SMEs. *International Business Review*, 28(5), 101583.

Beleska-Spasova, E., Glaister, K. W., & Stride, C. (2012). Resource determinants of strategy and performance: The case of British exporters. *Journal of World Business*, 47(4), 635-647.

Benmamoun, M., Singh, N., Lehnert, K., & Lee, S. B. (2019). Internationalization of e-commerce corporations (ECCs): Advanced vs emerging markets. *Multinational Business Review*, 27(4), 317-338.

Berry, H., Guillén, M. F., & Zhou, N. (2010). An institutional approach to cross-national distance. *Journal of International Business Studies*, 41(9), 1460-1480.

Berthon, P., Pitt, L., Cyr, D., & Campbell, C. (2008). E-readiness and trust: macro and micro dualities for e-commerce in a global environment. *International Marketing Review*, 25(6), 700-714.

Beugelsdijk, S., Kostova, T., Kunst, V. E., Spadafora, E., & Van Essen, M. (2018). Cultural distance and firm internationalization: A meta-analytical review and theoretical implications. *Journal of Management*, 44(1), 89-130.

Bhandari, K. R., Zámborský, P., Ranta, M., & Salo, J. (2023). Digitalization, internationalization, and firm performance: A resource-orchestration perspective on new OLI advantages. *International Business Review*, 32(4), 102135.

Birkinshaw, J. (2022). Move fast and break things: Reassessing IB research in the light of the digital revolution. *Global Strategy Journal*, 12(4), 619-631.

Blesa, A., & Ripolles, M. (2008). The influence of marketing capabilities on economic international performance. *International Marketing Review*, 25(6), 651-673.

Blomkvist, K., & Drogendijk, R. (2016). Chinese outward foreign direct investments in Europe. *European Journal of International Management*, 10(3), 343-358.

Blyde, J., & Molina, D. (2015). Logistic infrastructure and the international location of fragmented production. *Journal of International Economics*, 95(2), 319-332.

Brouthers, K. D. (2013). Institutional, cultural and transaction cost influences on entry mode choice and performance. *Journal of International Business Studies*, 44(1), 1-13.

Brouthers, K. D., Brouthers, L. E., & Werner, S. (2008). Real options, international entry mode choice and performance. *Journal of Management Studies*, 45(5), 936-960.

Brouthers, K. D., Chen, L., Li, S., & Shaheer, N. (2022). Charting new courses to enter foreign markets: Conceptualization, theoretical framework, and research directions on non-traditional entry modes. *Journal of International Business Studies*, 53(9), 2088-2115.

Brouthers, K. D., Geisser, K. D., & Rothlauf, F. (2016). Explaining the internationalization of ibusiness firms. *Journal of International Business Studies*, 47(5), 513-534.

Brouthers, K. D., & Hennart, J.-F. (2007). Boundaries of the firm: Insights from international entry mode research. *Journal of Management*, 33(3), 395-425.

Brouthers, K. D., & Nakos, G. (2004). SME entry mode choice and performance: A transaction cost perspective. *Entrepreneurship Theory and Practice*, 28(3), 229-247.

Cahen, F., & Borini, F. M. (2020). International digital competence. *Journal of International Management*, 26(1), 100691.

Cahen, F., Borini, F. M., Dhanaraj, C., & Morais, R. (2025). Unpacking global digital competence in the contemporary international venture. *International Business Review*, In press, 102414.

Cannizzaro, A. P., & Weiner, R. J. (2018). State ownership and transparency in foreign direct investment. *Journal of International Business Studies*, 49(2), 172-195.

Casillas, J. C., Barbero, J. L., & Sapienza, H. J. (2015). Knowledge acquisition, learning, and the initial pace of internationalization. *International Business Review*, 24(1), 102-114.

Centre for Retail Research (2023). Value of online retail sales in the United Kingdom (UK) from 2012 to 2022. https://www.statista.com/statistics/315506/online-retail-sales-in-the-united-kingdom/. Accessed 20.01.2025.

Cha, H., Kotabe, M., & Wu, J. (2023). Reshaping Internationalization Strategy and Control for Global E-Commerce and Digital Transactions: A Hayekian Perspective. *Management International Review*, 63(1), 161-192.

Chabowski, B. R., & Samiee, S. (2020). The internet and the international management literature: Its development and intellectual foundation. *Journal of International Management*, 26(1), 100741.

Chan, P., Finnegan, C., & Sternquist, B. (2011). Country and firm level factors in international retail expansion. *European Journal of Marketing*, 45(6), 1005-1022.

Chang, S. J., Chung, J., & Moon, J. J. (2013). When do wholly owned subsidiaries perform better than joint ventures? *Strategic Management Journal*, 34(3), 317-337.

Chen, H., & Hu, M. Y. (2002). An analysis of determinants of entry mode and its impact on performance. *International Business Review*, 11(2), 193-210.

Chen, L., Shaheer, N., Yi, J., & Li, S. (2019). The international penetration of ibusiness firms: Network effects, liabilities of outsidership and country clout. *Journal of International Business Studies*, 50(2), 172-192.

Chung, H. F., & Enderwick, P. (2001). An investigation of market entry strategy selection: Exporting vs foreign direct investment modes—a home-host country scenario. *Asia Pacific Journal of Management*, 18(4), 443-460.

Çilingirtürk, A. M., & Koçak, H. (2018). Human Development Index (HDI) rank-order variability. *Social Indicators Research*, 137(2), 481-504.

Clarke, J. E., Tamaschke, R., & Liesch, P. W. (2013). International experience in international business research: A conceptualization and exploration of key themes. *International Journal of Management Reviews*, 15(3), 265-279.

Colton, D. A., Roth, M. S., & Bearden, W. O. (2010). Drivers of international e-tail performance: the complexities of orientations and resources. *Journal of International Marketing*, 18(1), 1-22.

Contractor, F. J., Dangol, R., Nuruzzaman, N., & Raghunath, S. (2020). How do country regulations and business environment impact foreign direct investment (FDI) inflows? *International Business Review*, 29(2), 101640.

Contractor, F. J., Nuruzzaman, N., Dangol, R., & Raghunath, S. (2021). How FDI inflows to emerging markets are influenced by country regulatory factors: An exploratory study. *Journal of International Management*, 27(1), 100834.

Coviello, N., Kano, L., & Liesch, P. W. (2017). Adapting the Uppsala model to a modern world: Macro-context and microfoundations. *Journal of International Business Studies*, 48(9), 1151-1164.

Cuervo-Cazurra, A., Duran, P., Arregle, J. L., & van Essen, M. (2023). Host country politics and internationalization: a meta-analytic review. *Journal of Management Studies*, 60(1), 204-241.

Cui, L., & Jiang, F. (2009). FDI entry mode choice of Chinese firms: A strategic behavior perspective. *Journal of World Business*, 44(4), 434-444.

Cui, L., Li, Y., & Li, Z. (2013). Experiential drivers of foreign direct investment by late-comer Asian firms: The Chinese evidence. *Journal of Business Research*, 66(12), 2451-2459.

Cui, L., & Xu, Y. (2019). Outward FDI and profitability of emerging economy firms: Diversifying from home resource dependence in early stage internationalization. *Journal of World Business*, 54(4), 372-386.

Cumming, D., Johan, S., Khan, Z., & Meyer, M. (2023). E-Commerce Policy and International Business. *Management International Review*, 63(1), 3-25.

Czinkota, M. R., Grossman, D. A., Javalgi, R. R. G., & Nugent, N. (2009). Foreign market entry mode of service firms: The case of US MBA programs. *Journal of World Business*, 44(3), 274-286.

Del Bosco, B., & Bettinelli, C. (2020). How do family SMEs control their investments abroad? The role of distance and family control. *Management International Review*, 60(1), 1-35.

Del Giudice, M., Arslan, A., Scuotto, V., & Caputo, F. (2017). Influences of cognitive dimensions on the collaborative entry mode choice of small-and medium-sized enterprises. *International Marketing Review*, 34(5), 652-673.

Delgado-Gómez, J. M., Ramírez-Alesón, M., & Espitia-Escuer, M. A. (2004). Intangible resources as a key factor in the internationalisation of Spanish firms. *Journal of Economic Behavior & Organization*, 53(4), 477-494.

Delios, A., & Beamish, P. W. (1999). Geographic scope, product diversification, and the corporate performance of Japanese firms. *Strategic Management Journal*, 20(8), 711-727.

Demirbag, M., Tatoglu, E., & Glaister, K. W. (2008). Factors affecting perceptions of the choice between acquisition and greenfield entry: The case of Western FDI in an emerging market. *Management International Review*, 48(1), 5-38.

Digital Commerce 360 (2018). 2018 Digital Commerce 360 Europe 500 Database. https://www.digitalcommerce360.com/product/europe-500-database/?utm_source=Web&utm_campaign=2020-Article&cmp=1&utm_medium=Article. Accessed 21.06.2021.

Digital Commerce 360 (2021). Digital Commerce 360 Research & Data. https://www.digitalcommerce360.com/about-our-research/. Accessed 20.06.2023.

Dikova, D., & Van Witteloostuijn, A. (2007). Foreign direct investment mode choice: entry and establishment modes in transition economies. *Journal of International Business Studies*, 38(6), 1013-1033.

Dimitrova, B. V., Kim, S., & Smith, B. (2019). Performance of International Retailers: Empirical Evidence of an S-Curve Relationship. *Journal of Global Marketing*, 32(3), 154-176.

Dimitrova, B. V., Rosenbloom, B., & Andras, T. L. (2014). Does the degree of retailer international involvement affect retailer performance? *The International Review of Retail, Distribution and Consumer Research*, 24(3), 243-277.

Dolega, L., Rowe, F., & Branagan, E. (2021). Going digital? The impact of social media marketing on retail website traffic, orders and sales. *Journal of Retailing and Consumer Services*, 60, 102501.

Dong, Y., He, X., & Blut, M. (2024). How and when does digitalization influence export performance? A meta-analysis of its consequences and contingencies. *International Marketing Review*, 41(6), 1388-1413.

Douglas, S. P., & Craig, C. S. (2011). Convergence and divergence: Developing a semiglobal marketing strategy. *Journal of International Marketing*, 19(1), 82-101.

Dow, D., & Ferencikova, S. (2010). More than just national cultural distance: Testing new distance scales on FDI in Slovakia. *International Business Review*, 19(1), 46-58.

Dow, D., & Larimo, J. (2009). Challenging the conceptualization and measurement of distance and international experience in entry mode choice research. *Journal of International Marketing*, 17(2), 74-98.

Drori, N., Alessandri, T., Bart, Y., & Herstein, R. (2024). The impact of digitalization on internationalization from an internalization theory lens. *Long Range Planning*, 57(1), 102395.

Du, J., Lu, Y., & Tao, Z. (2008). FDI location choice: Agglomeration vs institutions. *International Journal of Finance & Economics*, 13(1), 92-107.

Dunning, J. H., & Wymbs, C. (2001). The challenge of electronic markets for international business theory. *International Journal of the Economics of Business*, 8(2), 273-301.

ECDB (2024a). Global eCommerce Retailer 2024. https://ecommercedb.com/whitepaper/ecommerce-retailer-2024. Accessed 20.12.2024.

ECDB (2024b). Largest eCommerce countries worldwide. https://ecommerce-db.com/ranking/markets/country/all. Accessed 01.02.2024.

ECDB (2024c). Store Ranking. https://ecommercedb.com/ranking/stores/ww/all. Accessed 01.02.2024.

ECDB (2024d). Why Did Amazon Fail in China: Local Competition Defeats the Retail Giant. https://ecommercedb.com/insights/why-amazon-failed-in-china-market-dynamics-strong-competition/4670. Accessed 10.11.2024.

Eduardsen, J., Marinova, S., Leonidou, L. C., & Christodoulides, P. (2023). Organizational Influences and Performance Impact of Cross-Border E-Commerce Barriers: The Moderating Role of Home Country Digital Infrastructure and Foreign Market Internet Penetration. *Management International Review*, 63(3), 433-467.

Efrat, K., & Shoham, A. (2013). The interaction between environment and strategic orientation in born globals' choice of entry mode. *International Marketing Review*, 30(6), 536-558.

Ekeledo, I., & Sivakumar, K. (2004a). International market entry mode strategies of manufacturing firms and service firms: A resource-based perspective. *International Marketing Review*, 21(1), 68-101.

Ekeledo, I., & Sivakumar, K. (2004b). The impact of e-commerce on entry-mode strategies of service firms: A conceptual framework and research propositions. *Journal of International Marketing*, 12(4), 46-70.

Elbanna, S., Hsieh, L., Child, J., Narooz, R., Marinova, S., Puthusserry, P., Karmowska, J., Tsai, T., & Zhang, Y. (2024). Foreign market involvement, entry-mode learning potential and SME internationalization outcomes. *Management Decision*, 62(1), 301-325.

Elia, S., Giuffrida, M., Mariani, M. M., & Bresciani, S. (2021). Resources and digital export: An RBV perspective on the role of digital technologies and capabilities in cross-border e-commerce. *Journal of Business Research*, 132, 158-169.

Erramilli, M. K. (1991). The experience factor in foreign market entry behavior of service firms. *Journal of International Business Studies*, 22(3), 479-501.

Esdemarca (2021). About Us. https://www.esdemarca.com/es/. Accessed 15.06.2021.

Evans, J., Mavondo, F. T., & Bridson, K. (2008). Psychic distance: antecedents, retail strategy implications, and performance outcomes. *Journal of International Marketing*, 16(2), 32-63.

Felzensztein, C., Ciravegna, L., Robson, P., & Amorós, J. E. (2015). Networks, entrepreneurial orientation, and internationalization scope: Evidence from Chilean small and medium enterprises. *Journal of Small Business Management*, 53(S1), 145-160.

Filatotchev, I., Strange, R., Piesse, J., & Lien, Y.-C. (2007). FDI by firms from newly industrialised economies in emerging markets: corporate governance, entry mode and location. *Journal of International Business Studies*, 38(1), 556-572.

Financial Times (2024). Shein, Temu and the Parcel Wars. https://www.ft.com/content/67319cc8-1f0e-4155-8f5e-664fe8603d2d. Accessed 10.11.2024.

Finch, H., & Bolin, J. (2017). *Multilevel modeling using Mplus*. Boca Raton: CRC Press.

Fleury, A., Fleury, M. T. L., Oliveira, L., & Leao, P. (2024). Going digital EMNEs: The role of digital maturity capability. *International Business Review*, 33(4), 102271.

Gabriel, L. (2023). *Die Macht digitaler Plattformen: Möglichkeiten und Konsequenzen der Personalisierung*. Wiesbaden: Springer.

Gabrielsson, M., Raatikainen, M., & Julkunen, S. (2022). Accelerated internationalization among inexperienced digital entrepreneurs: Toward a holistic entrepreneurial decision-making model. *Management International Review*, 62(2), 137-168.

Gallego, Á., & Casillas, J. C. (2014). Choice of markets for initial export activities: Differences between early and late exporters. *International Business Review*, 23(5), 1021-1033.

Gao, H., Tate, M., Zhang, H., Chen, S., & Liang, B. (2018). Social media ties strategy in international branding: An application of resource-based theory. *Journal of International Marketing*, 26(3), 45-69.

Gaur, A., & Kumar, M. (2018). A systematic approach to conducting review studies: An assessment of content analysis in 25 years of IB research. *Journal of World Business*, 53(2), 280-289.

Gaur, A. S., Pattnaik, C., Singh, D., & Lee, J. Y. (2019). Internalization advantage and subsidiary performance: The role of business group affiliation and host country characteristics. *Journal of International Business Studies*, 50(8), 1253-1282.

George, G., Wiklund, J., & Zahra, S. A. (2005). Ownership and the internationalization of small firms. *Journal of Management*, 31(2), 210-233.

Giachetti, C., Manzi, G., & Colapinto, C. (2019). Entry mode degree of control, firm performance and host country institutional development: A meta-analysis. *Management International Review*, 59(1), 3-39.

Gielens, K., & Dekimpe, M. G. (2001). Do international entry decisions of retail chains matter in the long run? *International Journal of Research in Marketing*, 18(3), 235-259.

Goerzen, A., & Beamish, P. W. (2003). Geographic scope and multinational enterprise performance. *Strategic Management Journal*, 24(13), 1289-1306.

Goldman, S. P., van Herk, H., Verhagen, T., & Weltevreden, J. W. (2021). Strategic orientations and digital marketing tactics in cross-border e-commerce: Comparing developed and emerging markets. *International Small Business Journal*, 39(4), 350-371.

Gong, C., He, X., & Lengler, J. (2024). Internationalisation through digital platforms: a systematic review and future research agenda. *International Marketing Review*, 41(5), 938-980.

Goyens, M. (2020). Effective consumer protection frameworks in a global and digital world. *Journal of Consumer Policy*, 43(1), 195-207.

Gregory, G. D., Ngo, L. V., & Karavdic, M. (2019). Developing e-commerce marketing capabilities and efficiencies for enhanced performance in business-to-business export ventures. *Industrial Marketing Management*, 78, 146-157.

Gripsrud, G., & Benito, G. R. (2005). Internationalization in retailing: modeling the pattern of foreign market entry. *Journal of Business Research*, 58(12), 1672-1680.

Halaszovich, T. F., & Kinra, A. (2020). The impact of distance, national transportation systems and logistics performance on FDI and international trade patterns: Results from Asian global value chains. *Transport Policy*, 98, 35-47.

Hånell, S. M., Nordman, E. R., Tolstoy, D., & Özbek, N. (2020). "It's a new game out there": E-commerce in internationalising retail SMEs. *International Marketing Review*, 37(3), 515-531.

Harzing, A.-W. (2024). Journal Quality List. https://harzing.com/resources/journal-quality-list. Accessed 20.12.2024.

Harzing, A.-W., & Pudelko, M. (2016). Do we need to distance ourselves from the distance concept? Why home and host country context might matter more than (cultural) distance. *Management International Review*, 56(1), 1-34.

Hausman, J. A. (1978). Specification tests in econometrics. *Econometrica*, 46(6), 1251-1271.

HDE (2024). Online-Monitor 2024. https://www.statista.com/statistics/454371/e-commerce-revenue-germany/. Accessed 20.01.2025.

He, X., Brouthers, K. D., & Filatotchev, I. (2013). Resource-based and institutional perspectives on export channel selection and export performance. *Journal of Management*, 39(1), 27-47.

He, Y., Wu, R., & Choi, Y.-J. (2021). International logistics and cross-border E-commerce trade: who matters whom? *Sustainability*, 13(4), 1745-1765.

Hennart, J.-F. (2022). How much is new in Brouthers et al.'s new foreign entry modes, and do they challenge the transaction cost theory of entry mode choice? *Journal of International Business Studies*, 53(9), 2116-2132.

Hernández, V., & Nieto, M. J. (2015). The effect of the magnitude and direction of institutional distance on the choice of international entry modes. *Journal of World Business*, 50(1), 122-132.

Herrmann, P., & Datta, D. K. (2002). CEO successor characteristics and the choice of foreign market entry mode: An empirical study. *Journal of International Business Studies*, 33(3), 551-569.

Hitt, M. A., Bierman, L., Uhlenbruck, K., & Shimizu, K. (2006). The importance of resources in the internationalization of professional service firms: The good, the bad, and the ugly. *Academy of Management Journal*, 49(6), 1137-1157.

Ho, S.-C., Kauffman, R. J., & Liang, T.-P. (2007). A growth theory perspective on B2C e-commerce growth in Europe: An exploratory study. *Electronic Commerce Research and Applications*, 6(3), 237-259.

Hofstede, G. (1984). *Culture's consequences: International differences in work-related values*. Beverly Hills, CA: Sage.

Hollender, L., Zapkau, F. B., & Schwens, C. (2017). SME foreign market entry mode choice and foreign venture performance: The moderating effect of international experience and product adaptation. *International Business Review*, 26(2), 250-263.

Holtbrügge, D., & Berning, S. C. (2018). Market entry strategies and performance of Chinese firms in Germany: The moderating effect of home government support. *Management International Review*, 58(1), 147-170.

Hong, S. J., & Lee, S.-H. (2015). Reducing cultural uncertainty through experience gained in the domestic market. *Journal of World Business*, 50(3), 428-438.

Hox, J. J., Moerbeek, M., & Van de Schoot, R. (2018). *Multilevel analysis: Techniques and applications*. New York: Routledge.

Hua, L., & Wu, Y. (2024). Strategic analysis of vertical integration in cross-border e-commerce logistics service supply chains. *Transportation Research Part E: Logistics and Transportation Review*, 188, 103626.

Huang, Y., & Sternquist, B. (2007). Retailers' foreign market entry decisions: An institutional perspective. *International Business Review*, 16(5), 613-629.

Ipsmiller, E., Brouthers, K. D., & Dikova, D. (2021). Which export channels provide real options to SMEs? *Journal of World Business*, 56(6), 101245.

Ipsmiller, E., Dikova, D., & Brouthers, K. D. (2022). Digital Internationalization of Traditional Firms: Virtual Presence and Entrepreneurial Orientation. *Journal of International Management*, 28(4), 100940.

ITA (2024). 2024 eCommerce Size & Sales Forecast. https://www.trade.gov/ecommerce-sales-size-forecast. Accessed 20.12.2024.

Janjevic, M., & Winkenbach, M. (2020). Characterizing urban last-mile distribution strategies in mature and emerging e-commerce markets. *Transportation Research Part A: Policy and Practice*, 133, 164-196.

Jean, R.-J., & Kim, D. (2020). Internet and SMEs' internationalization: The role of platform and website. *Journal of International Management*, 26(1), 100690.

Jean, R.-J., Kim, D., & Cavusgil, E. (2020). Antecedents and outcomes of digital platform risk for international new ventures' internationalization. *Journal of World Business*, 55(1), 101021.

Jiang, F., Ananthram, S., & Li, J. (2018). Global mindset and entry mode decisions: Moderating roles of managers' decision-making style and managerial experience. *Management International Review*, 58(3), 413-447.

Jiménez, A. (2010). Does political risk affect the scope of the expansion abroad? Evidence from Spanish MNEs. *International Business Review*, 19(6), 619-633.

Johanson, J., & Vahlne, J.-E. (1977). The internationalization process of the firm—a model of knowledge development and increasing foreign market commitments. *Journal of International Business Studies*, 8(1), 23-32.

Johanson, J., & Vahlne, J.-E. (2009). The Uppsala internationalization process model revisited: From liability of foreignness to liability of outsidership. *Journal of International Business Studies*, 40(9), 1411-1431.

Joong-Kun Cho, J., Ozment, J., & Sink, H. (2008). Logistics capability, logistics outsourcing and firm performance in an e-commerce market. *International Journal of Physical Distribution & Logistics Management*, 38(5), 336-359.

Kalinic, I., & Brouthers, K. D. (2022). Entrepreneurial orientation, export channel selection, and export performance of SMEs. *International Business Review*, 31(1), 101901.

Kalnins, A. (2022). When does multicollinearity bias coefficients and cause type 1 errors? A reconciliation of Lindner, Puck, and Verbeke (2020) with Kalnins (2018). *Journal of International Business Studies*, 53(7), 1536-1548.

Kardes, I., Flynn, L. R., & Dugan, M. (2020). Online retailing: Determinants of competition between multinationals and local firms in emerging markets. *International Journal of Retail & Distribution Management*, 49(2), 263-280.

Katsikeas, C., Leonidou, L., & Zeriti, A. (2020). Revisiting international marketing strategy in a digital era: Opportunities, challenges, and research directions. *International Marketing Review*, 37(3), 405-424.

Kaufman, R. L. (1996). Comparing effects in dichotomous logistic regression: A variety of standardized coefficients. *Social Science Quarterly*, 77(1), 90-109.

Khavul, S., Pérez-Nordtvedt, L., & Wood, E. (2010). Organizational entrainment and international new ventures from emerging markets. *Journal of Business Venturing*, 25(1), 104-119.

Kim, Y., & Gray, S. J. (2008). The impact of entry mode choice on foreign affiliate performance: The case of foreign MNEs in South Korea. *Management International Review*, 48(2), 165-188.

Kirca, A. H., Hult, G. T. M., Deligonul, S., Perryy, M. Z., & Cavusgil, S. T. (2012a). A multilevel examination of the drivers of firm multinationality: A meta-analysis. *Journal of Management*, 38(2), 502-530.

Kirca, A. H., Hult, G. T. M., Roth, K., Cavusgil, S. T., Perryy, M. Z., Akdeniz, M. B., Deligonul, S. Z., Mena, J. A., Pollitte, W. A., & Hoppner, J. J. (2011). Firm-specific assets, multinationality, and financial performance: A meta-analytic review and theoretical integration. *Academy of Management Journal*, 54(1), 47-72.

Kirca, A. H., Roth, K., Hult, G. T. M., & Cavusgil, S. T. (2012b). The role of context in the multinationality-performance relationship: A meta-analytic review. *Global Strategy Journal*, 2(2), 108-121.

Kishore, R., Agrawal, M., & Rao, H. R. (2004). Determinants of sourcing during technology growth and maturity: An empirical study of e-commerce sourcing. *Journal of Management Information Systems*, 21(3), 47-82.

Klier, H., Schwens, C., Zapkau, F. B., & Dikova, D. (2017). Which resources matter how and where? A meta-analysis on firms' foreign establishment mode choice. *Journal of Management Studies*, 54(3), 304-339.

Kline, R. B. (2015). *Principles and practice of structural equation modeling*. New York. Guilford publications.

Knösel, C. T., Cheng, C. C., & Shiu, E. C. (2025). Exploring Social Media Use in Cross-Border E-Commerce and the Internationalization Process: A Comparative Study of Cross-Country and Firm Size. *Thunderbird International Business Review*, 67(2), 257–283.

Kostova, T., Beugelsdijk, S., Scott, W. R., Kunst, V. E., Chua, C. H., & van Essen, M. (2020). The construct of institutional distance through the lens of different institutional perspectives: Review, analysis, and recommendations. *Journal of International Business Studies*, 51(4), 467-497.

Kotha, S., Rindova, V. P., & Rothaermel, F. T. (2001). Assets and actions: Firm-specific factors in the internationalization of US internet firms. *Journal of International Business Studies*, 32(4), 769-791.

Kozlenkova, I. V., Samaha, S. A., & Palmatier, R. W. (2014). Resource-based theory in marketing. *Journal of the Academy of Marketing Science*, 42(1), 1-21.

Kromidha, E., & Robson, P. J. (2021). The role of digital presence and investment network signals on the internationalisation of small firms. *International Small Business Journal*, 39(2), 109-129.

Kuivalainen, O., Sundqvist, S., & Servais, P. (2007). Firms' degree of born-globalness, international entrepreneurial orientation and export performance. *Journal of World Business*, 42(3), 253-267.

Kwon, Y. C., & Konopa, L. J. (1993). Impact of Host Country Market Characteristics on the Choiceof Foreign Market Entry Mode. *International Marketing Review*, 10(2), 60-76.

Lalla, M. (2017). Fundamental characteristics and statistical analysis of ordinal variables: a review. *Quality & Quantity*, 51(1), 435-458.

Latif, Z., Latif, S., Ximei, L., Pathan, Z. H., Salam, S., & Jianqiu, Z. (2018). The dynamics of ICT, foreign direct investment, globalization and economic growth: Panel estimation robust to heterogeneity and cross-sectional dependence. *Telematics and Informatics*, 35(2), 318-328.

Laufs, K., Bembom, M., & Schwens, C. (2016). CEO characteristics and SME foreign market entry mode choice: The moderating effect of firm's geographic experience and host-country political risk. *International Marketing Review*, 33(2), 246-275.

Lee, H. S., Pattnaik, C., & Gaur, A. S. (2023). Internationalization of I-business Firms: The role of distance on location choice. *Journal of Business Research*, 164, 114010.

Li, F., Larimo, J., & Leonidou, L. C. (2021). Social media marketing strategy: Definition, conceptualization, taxonomy, validation, and future agenda. *Journal of the Academy of Marketing Science*, 49(1), 51-70.

Li, J., Chen, Z., Kwon, O., & Wang, J. (2025). Modes of control in international digital commerce: evidence from Amazon.com. *Journal of International Business Studies*, 56(3), 440–450.

Li, K.-S., & Xiong, Y.-Q. (2022). Host country's environmental uncertainty, technological capability, and foreign market entry mode: evidence from high-end equipment manufacturing MNEs in emerging markets. *International Business Review*, 31(1), 101900.

Li, L., & Li, G. (2023). Integrating logistics service or not? The role of platform entry strategy in an online marketplace. *Transportation Research Part E: Logistics and Transportation Review*, 170, 102991.

Li, M., He, X., & Sousa, C. M. (2023). Product development capabilities-based export channel selection and export performance. *International Marketing Review*, 40(2), 385-411.

Li, P.-Y., & Meyer, K. E. (2009). Contextualizing experience effects in international business: A study of ownership strategies. *Journal of World Business*, 44(4), 370-382.

Li, Y., Zhang, B., Fan, D., & Li, Z. (2021). Digital media, control of corruption, and emerging multinational enterprise's FDI entry mode choice. *Journal of Business Research*, 130, 247-259.

Lin, F. (2015). Estimating the effect of the Internet on international trade. *The Journal of International Trade & Economic Development*, 24(3), 409-428.

Lin, W.-T. (2012). Family ownership and internationalization processes: Internationalization pace, internationalization scope, and internationalization rhythm. *European Management Journal*, 30(1), 47-56.

Lin, W.-T. (2014). How do managers decide on internationalization processes? The role of organizational slack and performance feedback. *Journal of World Business*, 49(3), 396-408.

Lindner, T., Puck, J., & Verbeke, A. (2022). Beyond addressing multicollinearity: Robust quantitative analysis and machine learning in international business research. *Journal of International Business Studies*, 53(7), 1307-1314.

Liu, C.-L. E., Zhang-Zhang, Y., & Ghauri, P. N. (2020). The influence of internet marketing capabilities on international market performance. *International Marketing Review*, 37(3), 447-469.

Lo, F.-Y., Chiao, Y.-C., & Yu, C.-M. J. (2016). Network and institutional effects on SMEs' entry strategies. *Management International Review*, 56(4), 531-563.

Love, J. H., Roper, S., & Zhou, Y. (2016). Experience, age and exporting performance in UK SMEs. *International Business Review*, 25(4), 806-819.

Lu, J., Liu, X., Wright, M., & Filatotchev, I. (2014). International experience and FDI location choices of Chinese firms: The moderating effects of home country government support and host country institutions. *Journal of International Business Studies*, 45(4), 428-449.

Lu, J. W., & Beamish, P. W. (2004). International diversification and firm performance: The S-curve hypothesis. *Academy of Management Journal*, 47(4), 598-609.

Luo, Y. (2021). New OLI advantages in digital globalization. *International Business Review*, 30(2), 101797.

Luo, Y. (2022). A general framework of digitization risks in international business. *Journal of International Business Studies*, 53(2), 344-361.

Luo, Y., Zhao, J. H., & Du, J. (2005). The internationalization speed of e-commerce companies: an empirical analysis. *International Marketing Review*, 22(6), 693-709.

Magnusson, P., Baack, D. W., Zdravkovic, S., Staub, K. M., & Amine, L. S. (2008). Meta-analysis of cultural differences: Another slice at the apple. *International Business Review*, 17(5), 520-532.

Mahnke, V., & Venzin, M. (2003). The Internationalization Process of Digital Information Good Providers. *Management International Review*, 43(1), 115-142.

Mansion, S. E., & Bausch, A. (2020). Intangible assets and SMEs' export behavior: A meta-analytical perspective. *Small Business Economics*, 55(3), 727-760.

Marsh, H. W., Lüdtke, O., Robitzsch, A., Trautwein, U., Asparouhov, T., Muthén, B., & Nagengast, B. (2009). Doubly-latent models of school contextual effects: Integrating multilevel and structural equation approaches to control measurement and sampling error. *Multivariate Behavioral Research*, 44(6), 764-802.

Martinez, C. A., & Williams, C. (2010). National Institutions, Entrepreneurship and Global ICT Adoption: A Cross-Country Test of Competing Theories. *Journal of Electronic Commerce Research*, 11(1), 73-91.

Maydeu-Olivares, A. (2017). Maximum likelihood estimation of structural equation models for continuous data: Standard errors and goodness of fit. *Structural Equation Modeling: A Multidisciplinary Journal*, 24(3), 383-394.

Mello, G. (2019). Amazon.com starts direct sales of merchandise in Brazil after delays. https://www.reuters.com/article/us-amazon-com-brazil-idUSKCN1PG0AG. Accessed 20.06.2023.

Meyer, K. E., Li, J., Brouthers, K. D., & Jean, R.-J. B. (2023). International business in the digital age: Global strategies in a world of national institutions. *Journal of International Business Studies*, 54(4), 577-598.

Miller, S. R., Lavie, D., & Delios, A. (2016). International intensity, diversity, and distance: Unpacking the internationalization–performance relationship. *International Business Review*, 25(4), 907-920.

Mithani, M. A. (2023). Scaling digital and non-digital business models in foreign markets: The case of financial advice industry in the United States. *Journal of World Business*, 58(4), 101457.

Moalla, E., & Mayrhofer, U. (2020). How does distance affect market entry mode choice? Evidence from French companies. *European Management Journal*, 38(1), 135-145.

Mohr, A., & Batsakis, G. (2018). Firm resources, cultural distance and simultaneous international expansion in the retail sector. *International Business Review*, 27(1), 113-124.

Molla-Descals, A., Frasquet, M., Ruiz-Molina, M.-E., & Navarro-Sanchez, E. (2014). Determinants of website traffic: The case of European fashion apparel retailers. *The International Review of Retail, Distribution and Consumer Research*, 24(4), 411-430.

Molloy, J. C., Chadwick, C., Ployhart, R. E., & Golden, S. J. (2011). Making intangibles "tangible" in tests of resource-based theory: A multidisciplinary construct validation approach. *Journal of Management*, 37(5), 1496-1518.

Monaghan, S., Tippmann, E., & Coviello, N. (2020). Born digitals: Thoughts on their internationalization and a research agenda. *Journal of International Business Studies*, 51(1), 11-22.

Morschett, D., Schramm-Klein, H., & Swoboda, B. (2010). Decades of research on market entry modes: What do we really know about external antecedents of entry mode choice? *Journal of International Management*, 16(1), 60-77.

Mueller, M., & Swoboda, B. (2025). Effects of International E-Commerce Firms' Depth versus Breadth of Control on Foreign Sales Performance and the Role of Market Size and Growth as Context Factors. *Management International Review*, In Press.

MWPVL (2025). Amazon Global Supply Chain and Fulfillment Center Network. https://www.mwpvl.com/html/amazon_com.html. Accessed 15.01.2025.

Nambisan, S., & Luo, Y. (2022). *The digital multinational: Navigating the new normal in global business*. Cambridge: MIT Press.

Narula, R., Asmussen, C. G., Chi, T., & Kundu, S. K. (2019). Applying and advancing internalization theory: The multinational enterprise in the twenty-first century. *Journal of International Business Studies*, 50(8), 1231-1252.

Nath, P., Kirca, A. H., & Kim, S. (2021). A study of the internationalization–performance relationship in global retailing: the moderating role of brand standardization and cultural diversity. *Journal of International Marketing*, 29(1), 57-76.

Nath, P., Nachiappan, S., & Ramanathan, R. (2010). The impact of marketing capability, operations capability and diversification strategy on performance: A resource-based view. *Industrial Marketing Management*, 39(2), 317-329.

Navarro-García, A. (2016). Drivers of export entrepreneurship. *International Business Review*, 25(1), 244-254.

Nielsen, B. B., Asmussen, C. G., & Weatherall, C. D. (2017). The location choice of foreign direct investments: Empirical evidence and methodological challenges. *Journal of World Business*, 52(1), 62-82.

Nielsen, B. B., & Nielsen, S. (2011). The role of top management team international orientation in international strategic decision-making: The choice of foreign entry mode. *Journal of World Business*, 46(2), 185-193.

Nuhu, N. S., Owens, M., & McQuillan, D. (2021). International entrepreneurship from emerging to developed markets: An institutional perspective. *International Marketing Review*, 38(3), 453-486.

O'Brien, R. M. (2007). A caution regarding rules of thumb for variance inflation factors. *Quality & Quantity*, 41(5), 673-690.

Oh, C. H., Sohl, T., & Rugman, A. M. (2015). Regional and product diversification and the performance of retail multinationals. *Journal of International Management*, 21(3), 220-234.

Oxley, J. E., & Yeung, B. (2001). E-commerce readiness: Institutional environment and international competitiveness. *Journal of International Business Studies*, 32(4), 705-723.

Özbek, N., Melén Hånell, S., Tolstoy, D., & Rovira Nordman, E. (2024). Exploring different responses to mimetic pressures: an institutional theory perspective on e-commerce adoption of an internationalizing retail SME. *The International Review of Retail, Distribution and Consumer Research*, 34(1), 14-32.

Pan, Y., & Tse, D. K. (2000). The hierarchical model of market entry modes. *Journal of International Business Studies*, 31(4), 535-554.

Paniagua, J., Korzynski, P., & Mas-Tur, A. (2017). Crossing borders with social media: Online social networks and FDI. *European Management Journal*, 35(3), 314-326.

Pash, C. (2017). Amazon is coming to Australia with 'low prices, vast selection, and fast delivery. https://www.smh.com.au/business/companies/amazon-is-coming-to-australia-with-low-prices-vast-selection-and-fast-delivery-20170420-gvo6lb.html. Accessed 20.06.2023.

Paul, J., & Gupta, P. (2014). Process and intensity of internationalization of IT firms–Evidence from India. *International Business Review*, 23(3), 594-603.

Pehrsson, A. (2008). Strategy antecedents of modes of entry into foreign markets. *Journal of Business Research*, 61(2), 132-140.

Pezderka, N., & Sinkovics, R. R. (2011). A conceptualization of e-risk perceptions and implications for small firm active online internationalization. *International Business Review*, 20(4), 409-422.

Picot-Coupey, K., Burt, S. L., & Cliquet, G. (2014). Retailers' expansion mode choice in foreign markets: Antecedents for expansion mode choice in the light of internationalization theories. *Journal of Retailing and Consumer Services*, 21(6), 976-991.

Pinho, J. C. (2007). The impact of ownership: Location-specific advantages and managerial characteristics on SME foreign entry mode choices. *International Marketing Review*, 24(6), 715-734.

Pla-Barber, J., Villar, C., & León-Darder, F. (2014). Augmenting versus exploiting entry modes in soft services: Reconsidering the role of experiential knowledge. *International Marketing Review*, 31(6), 621-636.

Priem, R. L., & Butler, J. E. (2001). Is the resource-based "view" a useful perspective for strategic management research? *Academy of Management Review*, 26(1), 22-40.

Putzhammer, M., Fainshmidt, S., Puck, J., & Slangen, A. (2018). To elevate or to duplicate? Experiential learning, host-country institutions, and MNE post-entry commitment increase. *Journal of World Business*, 53(4), 568-580.

Putzhammer, M., Puck, J., & Lindner, T. (2020). Changes in foreign operation modes: A review and research agenda. *International Business Review*, 29(1), 101619.

Rakuten (2024). Our Businesses. https://global.rakuten.com/corp/about/company/. Accessed 20.12.2024.

Ramanathan, R. (2010). The moderating roles of risk and efficiency on the relationship between logistics performance and customer loyalty in e-commerce. *Transportation Research Part E: Logistics and Transportation Review*, 46(6), 950-962.

Rasheed, H. S. (2005). Foreign entry mode and performance: The moderating effects of environment. *Journal of Small Business Management*, 43(1), 41-54.

Reuters (2023). Amazon, other retailers revamp 'free' shipping as costs soar. https://www.reuters.com/business/retail-consumer/amazon-other-retailers-revamp-free-shipping-costs-soar-2023-03-24/. Accessed 20.06.2023.

Rindfleisch, A., Malter, A. J., Ganesan, S., & Moorman, C. (2008). Cross-sectional versus longitudinal survey research: Concepts, findings, and guidelines. *Journal of Marketing Research*, 45(3), 261-279.

Ripollés, M., & Blesa, A. (2012). International new ventures as "small multinationals": The importance of marketing capabilities. *Journal of World Business*, 47(2), 277-287.

Ripollés, M., Blesa, A., & Monferrer, D. (2012). Factors enhancing the choice of higher resource commitment entry modes in international new ventures. *International Business Review*, 21(4), 648-666.

Rothaermel, F. T., Kotha, S., & Steensma, H. K. (2006). International market entry by US internet firms: An empirical analysis of country risk, national culture, and market size. *Journal of Management*, 32(1), 56-82.

Ruzo, E., Losada, F., Navarro, A., & Díez, J. A. (2011). Resources and international marketing strategy in export firms: Implications for export performance. *Management Research Review*, 34(5), 496-518.

Saini, A., & Johnson, J. L. (2005). Organizational capabilities in e-commerce: An empirical investigation of e-brokerage service providers. *Journal of the Academy of Marketing Science*, 33(3), 360-375.

Sambharya, R. B., & Lee, J. (2014). Renewing dynamic capabilities globally: An empirical study of the world's largest MNCs. *Management International Review*, 54(2), 137-169.

Samiee, S. (2020). International marketing and the internet: A research overview and the path forward. *International Marketing Review*, 37(3), 425-436.

Samiee, S., Katsikeas, C. S., & Hult, G. T. M. (2021). The overarching role of international marketing: Relevance and centrality in research and practice. *Journal of International Business Studies*, 52(8), 1429-1444.

Sánchez Peinado, E., & Pla Barber, J. (2006). Mode of entry in service firms: Strategic variables and characteristics of services influencing the internationalization process, 159-192. In *International Marketing Research*. Leeds: Emerald.

Scayle GmbH (2024). International eCommerce: How to Effectively Grow in Eastern Europe https://www.scayle.com/blog/international-ecommerce-eastern-europe/. Accessed 15.05.2024.

Schmid, D., & Morschett, D. (2023). Retailers' foreign market exits over time: A strategic management perspective. *International Business Review*, 32(5), 102164.

Schu, M., & Morschett, D. (2017). Foreign market selection of online retailers—A path-dependent perspective on influence factors. *International Business Review*, 26(4), 710-723.

Schu, M., Morschett, D., & Swoboda, B. (2016). Internationalization speed of online retailers: A resource-based perspective on the influence factors. *Management International Review*, 56(5), 733-757.

Schwartz, S. H. (1994). Are there universal aspects in the structure and contents of human values? *Journal of Social Issues*, 50(4), 19-45.

Schwens, C., Eiche, J., & Kabst, R. (2011). The moderating impact of informal institutional distance and formal institutional risk on SME entry mode choice. *Journal of Management Studies*, 48(2), 330-351.

Schwens, C., Zapkau, F. B., Bierwerth, M., Isidor, R., Knight, G., & Kabst, R. (2018a). International entrepreneurship: A meta–analysis on the internationalization and performance relationship. *Entrepreneurship Theory and Practice*, 42(5), 734-768.

Schwens, C., Zapkau, F. B., Brouthers, K. D., & Hollender, L. (2018b). Limits to international entry mode learning in SMEs. *Journal of International Business Studies*, 49(7), 809-831.

Scott, W. R. (2014). *Institutions and organizations: Ideas, Interests, and Identities*. Thousand Oaks, CA: Sage.

Shaheer, N. A., & Li, S. (2020). The CAGE around cyberspace? How digital innovations internationalize in a virtual world. *Journal of Business Venturing*, 35(1), 105892.

Shi, Y., Lim, J. M., Weitz, B. A., & France, S. L. (2018). The impact of retail format diversification on retailers' financial performance. *Journal of the Academy of Marketing Science*, 46(1), 147-167.

Shneor, R., & Flåten, B.-T. (2008). The internet-enabled internationalization process: A focus on stages and sequences. *Journal of e-Business*, 8(1), 45-52.

Sinkovics, N., Sinkovics, R. R., & Jean, R.-J. (2013). The internet as an alternative path to internationalization? *International Marketing Review*, 30(2), 130-155.

Slangen, A. H., & Van Tulder, R. J. (2009). Cultural distance, political risk, or governance quality? Towards a more accurate conceptualization and measurement of external uncertainty in foreign entry mode research. *International Business Review*, 18(3), 276-291.

Stallkamp, M., Chen, L., & Li, S. (2023). Boots on the ground: Foreign direct investment by born digital firms. *Global Strategy Journal*, 13(4), 805-829.

Stock, J. H., & Watson, M. W. (2020). *Introduction to Econometrics*. London: Pearson.

Stoian, C., & Filippaios, F. (2008). Dunning's eclectic paradigm: A holistic, yet context specific framework for analysing the determinants of outward FDI: Evidence from international Greek investments. *International Business Review*, 17(3), 349-367.

Sui, S., & Baum, M. (2014). Internationalization strategy, firm resources and the survival of SMEs in the export market. *Journal of International Business Studies*, 45(7), 821-841.

Surana, A., Chavan, M., Kumar, V., & Chirico, F. (2024). The internationalization process: A contextual analysis of Indian ibusiness firms. *International Business Review*, 33(4), 102255.

Swoboda, B., & Elsner, S. (2013). Transferring the retail format successfully into foreign countries. *Journal of International Marketing*, 21(1), 81-109.

Swoboda, B., Elsner, S., & Olejnik, E. (2015). How do past mode choices influence subsequent entry? A study on the boundary conditions of preferred entry modes of retail firms. *International Business Review*, 24(3), 506-517.

Swoboda, B., Schwarz, S., & Hälsig, F. (2007). Towards a conceptual model of country market selection: Selection processes of retailers and C&C wholesalers. *International Review of Retail, Distribution and Consumer Research*, 17(3), 253-282.

Swoboda, B., & Sinning, C. (2022). Effects of Internationalization Rhythm and Speed on E-Commerce Firms' Growth and the Role of Institutional Distances. *Management International Review*, 62(2), 169-201.

Tang, R. W., & Buckley, P. J. (2020). Host country risk and foreign ownership strategy: Meta-analysis and theory on the moderating role of home country institutions. *International Business Review*, 29(4), 101666.

Tang, R. W., & Gudergan, S. P. (2018). A Meta-analysis of the international experience–ownership strategy relationship: A dynamic capabilities view. *Management International Review*, 58(4), 541-570.

Tasheva, S., & Nielsen, B. B. (2022). The role of global dynamic managerial capability in the pursuit of international strategy and superior performance. *Journal of International Business Studies*, 53(4), 689-708.

Tihanyi, L., Griffith, D. A., & Russell, C. J. (2005). The effect of cultural distance on entry mode choice, international diversification, and MNE performance: A meta-analysis. *Journal of International Business Studies*, 36(1), 270-283.

Tolstoy, D., Hånell, S. M., & Özbek, N. (2023). Effectual market creation in the cross-border e-commerce of small-and medium-sized enterprises. *International Small Business Journal*, 41(1), 35-54.

Tolstoy, D., Jonsson, A., & Sharma, D. D. (2016). The influence of a retail firm's geographic scope of operations on its international online sales. *International Journal of Electronic Commerce*, 20(3), 293-318.

Tolstoy, D., Nordman, E. R., Hånell, S. M., & Özbek, N. (2021). The development of international e-commerce in retail SMEs: An effectuation perspective. *Journal of World Business*, 56(3), 101165.

Tolstoy, D., Nordman, E. R., & Vu, U. (2022). The indirect effect of online marketing capabilities on the international performance of e-commerce SMEs. *International Business Review*, 31(3), 101946.

Trąpczyński, P., Halaszovich, T. F., & Piaskowska, D. (2020). The role of perceived institutional distance in foreign ownership level decisions of new MNEs. *Journal of Business Research*, 108, 435-449.

Tsang, E. W. (2005). Influences on foreign ownership level and entry mode choice in Vietnam. *International Business Review*, 14(4), 441-463.

U.S. Census Bureau (2010). Quarterly Retail E-Commerce Sales. https://www2.census.gov/retail/releases/historical/ecomm/10q4.pdf. Accessed 05.11.2024.

U.S. Census Bureau (2022). Annual Retail Trade Survey. https://www.census.gov/data/tables/2022/econ/arts/supplemental-ecommerce.html. Accessed 05.11.2024.

UNCTAD (2024). UNCTAD B2C E-commerce Index. https://prosperitydata360.worldbank.org/en/dataset/UNCTAD+B2C. Accessed 15.06.2024.

United Nations Development Programme (2020). Human development reports. http://hdr.undp.org/en/data. Accessed 15.06.2021.

Vahlne, J.-E., & Johanson, J. (2017). From internationalization to evolution: The Uppsala model at 40 years. *Journal of International Business Studies*, 48(9), 1087-1102.

Verbeke, A., Coeurderoy, R., & Matt, T. (2018). The future of international business research on corporate globalization that never was.... *Journal of International Business Studies*, 49(9), 1101-1112.

VHB (2024). VHB Publication Media Rating 2024. https://www.vhbonline.org/en/services/vhb-rating-2024. Accessed 20.12.2024.

Vieira, V. A., de Almeida, M. I. S., Agnihotri, R., & Arunachalam, S. (2019). In pursuit of an effective B2B digital marketing strategy in an emerging market. *Journal of the Academy of Marketing Science*, 47(6), 1085-1108.

Visser, R. (2019). The effect of the internet on the margins of trade. *Information Economics and Policy*, 46, 41-54.

Wan, C., Sousa, C. M., Lengler, J., & Tan, Q. (2023). Entry Mode Choice: A Meta-Analysis of Antecedents and Outcomes. *Management International Review*, 63(2), 193-246.

Wan, W. P. (2005). Country resource environments, firm capabilities, and corporate diversification strategies. *Journal of Management Studies*, 42(1), 161-182.

Wang, Q., Liu, X., Hu, M., & Huo, B. (2024). A reductionistic or holistic approach? The impacts of fit patterns of supplier and customer integration on company and supply chain performance. *International Journal of Production Economics*, 273, 109265.

Wang, S., Mao, J.-Y., & Archer, N. (2012). On the performance of B2B e-markets: An analysis of organizational capabilities and market opportunities. *Electronic Commerce Research and Applications*, 11(1), 59-74.

Wang, Z., Jiang, D., & Zhang, M. (2024). Seeking new location advantages: Analysis of emerging digital cross-border M&As—Based on TIMG index. *International Business Review*, 33(2), 102243.

Watson, G. F., Weaven, S., Perkins, H., Sardana, D., & Palmatier, R. W. (2018). International market entry strategies: Relational, digital, and hybrid approaches. *Journal of International Marketing*, 26(1), 30-60.

Wei, Y., Zheng, N., Liu, X., & Lu, J. (2014). Expanding to outward foreign direct investment or not? A multi-dimensional analysis of entry mode transformation of Chinese private exporting firms. *International Business Review*, 23(2), 356-370.

Weiber, R., & Mohr, L. (2020). Dienstleistungen 4.0, 1091-1125. In *Handbuch Digitale Wirtschaft*. Ed. T. Kollmann. Wiesbaden: Springer.

Wentrup, R. (2016). The online–offline balance: internationalization for Swedish online service providers. *Journal of International Entrepreneurship*, 14(4), 562-594.

Wiersema, M. F., & Bowen, H. P. (2008). Corporate diversification: The impact of foreign competition, industry globalization, and product diversification. *Strategic Management Journal*, 29(2), 115-132.

Winship, C., & Mare, R. D. (1984). Regression models with ordinal variables. *American Sociological Review*, 49(4), 512-525.

World Bank (2022a). Logistics Performance Index. https://lpi.worldbank.org/international. Accessed 20.06.2023.

World Bank (2022b). Worldwide Governance Indicators. https://databank.worldbank.org/source/worldwide-governance-indicators. Accessed 20.06.2023.

World Bank (2023a). World Bank open data. https://data.worldbank.org/. Accessed 20.06.2023.

World Bank (2023b). World Development Indicators. https://databank.worldbank.org/source/world-development-indicators. Accessed 01.12.2023.

World Economic Forum (2019). The Global Competitiveness Report 2019. https://www.weforum.org/publications/how-to-end-a-decade-of-lost-productivity-growth/. Accessed 20.06.2023.

Wu, B., & Deng, P. (2020). Internationalization of SMEs from emerging markets: An institutional escape perspective. *Journal of Business Research*, 108, 337-350.

Xie, Q. (2017). Firm age, marketization, and entry mode choices of emerging economy firms: Evidence from listed firms in China. *Journal of World Business*, 52(3), 372-385.

Xue, R., Qian, G., Qian, Z., & Li, L. (2021). Entrepreneurs' implicit and explicit achievement motives and their early international commitment. *Management International Review*, 61(1), 91-121.

Yamanoi, J., & Asaba, S. (2018). The impact of family ownership on establishment and ownership modes in foreign direct investment: The moderating role of corruption in host countries. *Global Strategy Journal*, 8(1), 106-135.

Yang, B., Bai, W., Chen, Y., & Rong, K. (2025). Internationalization of digital firms: A systematic review and research agenda. *Journal of Business Research*, 189, 115124.

Yang, Y., Martins, P. S., & Driffield, N. (2013). Multinational performance and the geography of FDI: Evidence from 46 countries. *Management International Review*, 53(6), 763-794.

Young, J. (2021). Global online sales reach nearly $4.29 trillion in 2020. https://www.digitalcommerce360.com/article/global-ecommerce-sales/. Accessed 15.06.2021.

Yu, S., Beugelsdijk, S., & de Haan, J. (2015). Trade, trust and the rule of law. *European Journal of Political Economy*, 37, 102-115.

Zahoor, N., Wu, J., Khan, H., & Khan, Z. (2023). De-globalization, international trade protectionism, and the reconfigurations of global value chains. *Management International Review*, 63(5), 823-859.

Zalando (2015). Zalando to Start Operations in Its Italian Satellite Fulfillment Center. https://corporate.zalando.com/en/company/zalando-start-operations-its-italian-satellite-fulfillment-center. Accessed 20.02.2024.

Zalando (2021a). Annual report. https://corporate.zalando.com/en/investor-relations/annual-report-2020. Accessed 01.07.2021.

Zalando (2021b). Corporate strategy. https://corporate.zalando.com/de/unternehmen/unsere-geschaeftsfelder. Accessed 15.06.2021.

Zalando (2023). Annual Report 2022. https://corporate.zalando.com/en/investor-relations/annual-report-2022. Accessed 20.06.2023.

Zalando (2024). Annual Report. https://corporate.zalando.com/en/investor-relations/annual-report-2023. Accessed 28.11.2024.

Zhang, J., Onal, S., Das, R., Helminsky, A., & Das, S. (2019). Fulfilment time performance of online retailers–an empirical analysis. *International Journal of Retail & Distribution Management*, 47(5), 493-510.

Zhang, W., He, X., Wang, T., & Wang, K. (2023). Institutional distance and the international market entry mode: A meta-analysis. *Journal of International Management*, 29(1), 100990.

Zhao, H., Luo, Y., & Suh, T. (2004). Transaction cost determinants and ownership-based entry mode choice: A meta-analytical review. *Journal of International Business Studies*, 35(6), 524-544.

Zhao, H., Ma, J., & Yang, J. (2017). 30 years of research on entry mode and performance relationship: A meta-analytical review. *Management International Review*, 57(5), 653-682.

Zhu, L., & Thatcher, S. (2010). National information ecology: A new institutional economics perspective on global e-commerce adoption. *Journal of Electronic Commerce Research*, 11(1), 53-72.

MIX
Papier aus verantwortungsvollen Quellen
Paper from responsible sources
FSC® C105338
FSC
www.fsc.org

If you have any concerns about our products,
you can contact us on
ProductSafety@springernature.com

In case Publisher is established outside the EU,
the EU authorized representative is:
Springer Nature Customer Service Center GmbH
Europaplatz 3, 69115 Heidelberg, Germany

Printed by Libri Plureos GmbH
in Hamburg, Germany